NEOFUNCTIONALISM

KEY ISSUES IN SOCIOLOGICAL THEORY

Series Editors
JEFFREY C. ALEXANDER and JONATHAN TURNER

This series of annual publications is designed to crystallize key issues in contemporary theoretical debate. Each year, the chair of the Theory Section of the American Sociological Association has the authority to organize a "conference within a conference" at the annual meeting. The intention is to provide a forum for intensive public discussion of an issue that has assumed overriding theoretical importance. After the miniconference, the chair assumes the role of volume editor and, subject to final approval by the series editors, prepares a volume based on the reworked conference papers.

We hope that this periodic focusing of theoretical energy will strengthen the "disciplinary matrix" upon which theoretical progress in every science depends. Theoretical consensus may be impossible, but disciplinary integration is not. Only if a solid infrastructure is provided can communication between different orientations be carried out in the kind of ongoing, continuous way that is so necessary for mutual understanding and scientifically constructive criticism.

This is particularly important, in our view, because sociological theory is entering a new and important phase. In the postwar period, European theory was diminished and Parsons's structural-functional approach held the day. In the 1960s, there developed the challenges to Parsons's hegemony that became the major traditions in the second, post-Parsonian period: constructivist and logico-deductive trends; new waves of micro-theorizing; and the reemergence of macro-structuralist approaches. The polarization that defined these first two periods has come to an end. We are in the beginning of a third phase that has a much less clearly defined character. The post-Parsonian traditions continue to develop; European theories such as symbolic structuralism, Marxism, and critical theory have emerged as significant movements; classical traditions such as the Weberian, Durkheimian, and Utilitarian are being recast; functionalism itself is being rethought and brought forward once again.

What will emerge from this period of theoretical ferment remains to be seen. We are certain, however, that in this process of crystallization *Key Issues in Sociological Theory* will play a prominent role.

NEOFUNCTIONALISM

JEFFREY C. ALEXANDER
Editor

1

KEY ISSUES IN
SOCIOLOGICAL THEORY

Editors: **Jeffrey C. Alexander,**
University of California, Los Angeles
Jonathan Turner,
University of California, Riverside

 SAGE PUBLICATIONS Beverly Hills London New Delhi

For information address:

SAGE Publications, Inc.
275 South Beverly Drive
Beverly Hills, California 90212

SAGE Publications India Pvt. Ltd.
M-32 Market
Greater Kailash I
New Delhi 110 048 India

SAGE Publications Ltd
28 Banner Street
London EC1Y 8QE
England

Printed in the United States of America

Library of Congress Cataloging-in-Publication Data

Main entry under title:

Neofunctionalism.

   (Key issues in sociological theory ; v. 1)
   Bibliography: p.
   1. Sociology—United States—Addresses, essays,
lectures. 2. Parsons, Talcott, 1902-   —Criticism
and interpretation—Addresses, essays, lectures.
I. Alexander, Jeffrey C. II. Series.
HM22.U6P376 1985   301   85-8264
ISBN 0-8039-2496-8
ISBN 0-8039-2497-6 (pbk.)

FIRST PRINTING

CONTENTS

PART III: POLITICS AND RESPONSIBILITY

INTRODUCTION

JEFFREY C. ALEXANDER
University of California at Los Angeles

AT THE AMERICAN SOCIOLOGICAL ASSOCIATION'S
annual meeting in 1975 in San Francisco, Dennis Wrong chaired a session on the "state of contemporary theory" that drew hundreds of people. One of the panelists, Stephen Warner, drew a loud, appreciative laugh from the crowd when, playing on a slogan of the youth culture, he observed "there are no functionalists under thirty years old!" Warner actually went on to suggest that youthful critics might well want to rethink their position; but in the spirit of the time it was his ironic observation that seemed to his audience not only true, but just.

Little less than a decade later, an anonymous reviewer for the *American Journal of Sociology (AJS)* began his or her critique of an article I had submitted in the following way: "This is only one example of the revival of functionalist theorizing which has recently surfaced, a development of which I am fully aware even while I find it appalling"! Another *AJS* review of my work, a published one of my first volume, lamented, "the library of critiques" of functionalism "must be taken from the shelves again." In a similar vein but with opposite affect, a participant at a session on cultural sociology at the 1984 ASA meetings spoke in ringing tones about "the new Parsonian revolution" taking place in the discipline. These remarks were made in a very different time, but they were equally true and perhaps equally just.

It is history that Parsonian sociology, né "functionalism," crashed in the 1960s. The king fell; and for a long time it looked as if he would share Humpty Dumpty's fate; that is, nobody would be able to put him back together again. It has now become clear that this is not the case.

EDITOR'S NOTE: This introduction enlarges on my "Chair's Message" in *Perspectives,* 1983, 2(2), pp. 1-3. In a revised form it was first presented at the Sociology Colloquium at the University of Alberta in February 1984 and later at the Conference on Neofunctionalism sponsored by the Theory Section of the American Sociological Association in San Antonio, Texas, in September of that year. Most of the chapters that appear in this volume were initially presented for that conference as well.

The Parsonian legacy—if not Parson's original theory—has begun to be reconstructed.[1] We are witnessing today the emergence of neo-functionalism, not functionalism exactly, but a family relation.

"Functionalism" was never a particularly good word for Parsons's sociological theory. Its use was more the upshot of intuition and tradition than of theoretical logic. The term evidently emerged from the study group that L. J. Henderson conducted at Harvard in the 1930s. A physiologist deeply affected by biological functionalism and by Pareto (Barber, 1970), Henderson introduced Parsons, Homans, Merton, and other fledgling theorists at Harvard to Canon's powerful use of homeo-stasis in *The Wisdom of the Body*; he also evangelized for Pareto's general theory, in which systems and equilibrium concepts played prominent roles (Homans, 1984). Homans moved from here to the functionalist anthropology of Radcliffe-Brown. Parsons went on to Durkheim and Weber. He began using the term in the late 1930s, implying by it a vague notion of system and "interdependent parts," and he made it a central and elaborate feature of his Presidential Address to the ASA in 1945 (Parsons, 1945). Yet if we look at references to functionalism among the younger group of Harvard-trained theorists in the 1930s and 1940s—Homans, Parsons, Merton, Barber, and Davis among others—we see quite a bewildering variety of epistemological, ideological, empirical, and theoretical connotations.

Even as "functionalism" emerged as a major theoretical movement in the late 1940s, however, its ability for precise denotation was fiercely contested. Merton was regarded as one of its principal exponents; but in the late 1940s, he set out (Merton, 1967) to strip the term of its ideological implications, its status as an abstract model, and its sub-stantive empirical commitments. He sought to reduce it, via the an-thropology of Radcliffe-Brown, to a kind of supermethod. To be functionalist, Merton held, was quite simply to explain causes by effects. But although this response to critics was enormously successful in a diplomatic sense, it was not, it seems to me, particularly helpful theo-retically. It had much more to do with the anthropologists' critique of nineteenth-century evolutionary theory than with the actual practice of sociological functionalism in the twentieth century. It did not, in fact, actually describe what the foremost practitioners of functionalism, Merton himself very much included, actually did.[2]

Merton's students, themselves key figures in the first functionalist hey-day, provide further evidence for the ambiguity of the term. Coser (1956), Gouldner (e.g., Gouldner, 1960), and Goode (1960) developed a distinctively "left-functionalism," to use Gouldner's term. They stressed the theory's accessibility to critical and materialist thought and claimed that functionalism was a crucial element for explaining disintegration and social conflict. By the mid-1960s, Parsons—the arch "integrationist" of the tradition—himself denied the functionalist designation, suggesting that his cybernetic emphasis and interchange model made such a static label obsolete. Henceforth, his collaborators and students would refer to their work as "action theory."

Despite such contradictory usage and internal dissent, however, "functionalism" seems to be a name that has stuck. I want to take the bull by the horns and suggest that the term indicates nothing so precise as a set of concepts, a method, a model, or an ideology. It indicates, rather, a tradition. Qua tradition, certain distinctive characteristics can, indeed, be adduced fairly from the efforts that have been conducted and criticized in their names. Traditions, of course, are accessible only through interpretation. What follows indicates my own sense of the future direction of this tradition as much as a discovery of its past.

(1) Although not providing a model in an explanatory sense, functionalism does provide a general picture of the interrelation of social parts, a model in a more descriptive sense. Functionalism models society as an intelligible system. It views society as composed of elements whose interaction forms a pattern that can be clearly differentiated from some surrounding environment. These parts are symbiotically connected to one another and interact without a priori direction from a governing force. This understanding of system and/or "totality" must, as Althusser (1970) has forcefully argued, be sharply distinguished from the Hegelian, Marxist one. The Hegelian system resembles the functionalist, but it posits an "expressive totality" in which all of a society's or culture's parts are seen as representing variations on some "really" determining, fundamental system. Functionalism suggests, by contrast, open-ended and pluralistic rather than monocausal determinism.

(2) Functionalism concentrates on action as much as on structure. Its conception of action, moreover, focuses as much on expressive activity and the ends of action as on practicality and means. In particular, functionalism is concerned with the degree to which ends succeed in regulating and stipulating means. It seems quite mistaken, in this regard, to equate functionalism with the sociologism of Durkheim or the quasi-utilitarianism of Radcliffe-Brown.

(3) Functionalism is concerned with integration as a possibility and with deviance and processes of social control as facts. Equilibrium is taken as a reference point for functionalist systems analysis, though not for participants in actual social systems as such. It is used in several different ways, as a homeostatic, self-correcting equilibrium, as a moving equilibrium to describe developmental structures of growth and change,

and as a partial equilibrium model of the type that Keynes used to describe the systemic strains in a capitalist economy.[3]

(4) Functionalism posits the distinctions between personality, culture, and society as vital to social structure, and the tensions produced by their interpenetration as a continuous source of change and control. In addition to "social" or institutional analysis, then, functionalism focuses on a relatively autonomous culture and on the centrality of socialization.

(5) Functionalism implies a recognition of differentiation as a major mode of social change—whether cultural, social, or psychological—and of the individuation and institutional strains that this historical process creates.

(6) Functionalism implies the commitment to the independence of conceptualization and theorizing from other levels of sociological analysis. Each of these six theses can certainly be identified with other lines of work in the social sciences. No other tradition, however, can be identified with all of them.

It is true, of course, that these are certainly not the only, or even the principal, characteristics of functionalism that are lodged in the public mind of social science. Functionalism has been burdened with anti-individualism, with antagonism to change, with conservatism, with idealism, and with an antiempirical bias. Parsons's defenders have usually dismissed this baggage as ideological illusion. In my own work, by contrast, I have found Parsons's functionalist theory to be highly ambivalent and often contradictory (Alexander, 1983, pp. 151-276). Every element critics have polemicized against is there, though these elements by no means exhaust the meanings of his work. Parsons's functionalism gave sociologists a lot to choose from. Depending on their intellectual and historical circumstances, they took their choice.

Beginning in the early 1960s, historical and intellectual developments allowed the negative elements in this complex picture increasingly to dominate the collective consciousness of the discipline. By the mid-1970s they had crystallized into a conventional wisdom that froze the functionalist image in time. This was doubly unfortunate, for it was precisely at this time that the most sophisticated interpretations of Parsons's theorizing had begun to change dramatically.

This changing understanding has unfolded over the last 10 years. It has taken place for several reasons. One must look first, ironically, to the very success of the "vulgate." The critical vulgarization of Parsons succeeded in undermining his overwhelming authority. Once this hegemony had been destroyed, parts of his theoretical system could much more easily be appropriated in creative ways. One was no longer viewed as a "Parsonian" if one incorporated significant insights from

Parsons's work, despite the best efforts of recalcitrant "anti-Parsonian warriors" to make the anachronistic and polemical label stick. Second, the ideological climate had noticeably cooled. A younger generation of theorists emerged who did not experience the political need to attack the liberalism for which Parsons stood. In the present neoconservative climate, indeed, it is hard to remember how Parsons's social-democratic reformism could have inspired such political hatred and venality. Third, European social theory has begun to grow once again. Without the earlier, exaggerated American attachment to Parsons, these Europeans, especially Germans, have been able to appropriate Parsons in surprisingly positive ways. Fourth, functionalist theory was, quite simply, a very sophisticated theoretical scheme. Parsons had a genial intelligence matched by few of his peers, or ours. That is the necessary, if not the sufficient, reason why the functionalist tradition still has the makings of a successful sociological theory.

What has been emerging from this reconsideration is less a theory than a broad intellectual tendency. I call it neofunctionalist in conscious similitude to neo-Marxism. First, like neo-Marxism, this development has involved a determined critique of some of the basic tenets of the original theory. Second, like neo-Marxism, it has sought to incorporate elements of purportedly antagonistic theoretical traditions. Third, like neo-Marxism, this neofunctionalist tendency is manifest in a variety of often competing developments rather than in a single coherent form. Let me consider each of these parallels in turn.

Neo-Marxism began in the 1950s as a movement of critical reflection on what came to be called orthodox Marxism; it began, that is, as an interpretive genre. What happened was that a series of self-consciously revisionist interpretations "discovered"—in reality, produced—a different Marx. Neo-Marxist interpretation emphasized a radically different periodization of Marx's work, highlighting the significance of the early over the later writings. It found in Marx a very different epistemological framework, emphasizing idealism rather than materialism or Kantianism. It located new, significant intellectual precursors like Hegel, rather than thinkers like Saint-Simon and Ricardo. It claimed for Marx strikingly different ideological affinities, arguing for a democratic and humanistic Marx rather than a Leninist, authoritarian one.

Over the last decade a similar process of reinterpretation has ensued within, or on behalf of, the functionalist tradition. The ideological rereading has perhaps been the most dramatic. The argument for a non-conservative functionalism, a more conflict-oriented and critical reading, was begun by leftist theorists like Atkinson (1972) in the early 1970s, who claimed that Parsons's theory was not fundamentally different from

Marx's or even from that of Marcuse, which embodied the theory of New Left. Other critical theorists, like Taylor (1979) and Gintis (1969), who identified even more closely with Marxism, began also to stress the parallels between Parsons and Marx and the critical side of the functionalist approach. The latest development of this influential movement within critical theory is the interpretation that Habermas has developed in the *Theory of Communicative Action* (1984), which finds significant liberating elements in Parsons's thought even while it scores his conservatism. Liberal theorists have also contributed to this ideological reevaluation. Rocher's (1975) early interpretation, for example, stressed that Parsons's theory could rise above its American bias despite Parsons's own personnel commitments to it. Menzies (1976) documented some socialist implications in Parsons's stratification theory. In an extraordinarily revealing reversal of his earlier position, Gouldner (1980, pp. 355-373) described Parsonian sociology as contributing to a liberal theory of civil society that could provide a democratic and humanistic alternative to orthodox Marxism. My own work on Parsons's ideology (Alexander, 1978, pp. 61-72; 1983, pp. 128-150) has tried to bring out its critical potential, though I have pointed to the much more quiescent view of modern life that develops in his later work.

Most of these theorists have revised the epistemological understanding of Parsons as well, viewing him as much less idealistic than the earlier, established position had claimed. Taylor sees functionalism as giving significant weight to economic and political, not just cultural, factors; and Habermas goes to the extent of criticizing Parsons for an antinormative explanation of political and economic spheres. Menzies, too, sees the later Parsons as all too naturalistic. More recent works, like those of Bourricaud (1977) and Adriaansens (1980), provide detailed evidence for an antiidealist epistemology. Savage's (1981) Althusserian interpretation dismisses the idealist interpretation. Although I have found Parsons's idealism to be, on the contrary, quite debilitating, I have also found (Alexander, 1983, pp. 8-150) that there is a significant multidimensional theme as well. The most ambitious reconstruction of Parsons's epistemology, that conducted by Munch (1981-1982), argues that his Kantian framework allowed material factors free reign while preserving the freedom that comes with a normative bent.

These new epistemological and ideological interpretations clearly call for different precursors, though the construction of a new, intellectual lineage for Parsons has not yet proceeded as far. Whereas Mills linked Parsons to the conservative Hegel and Gouldner to the English and French antirevolutionary reaction, Bershady (1973) and Munch place him squarely in the democratic and humanistic tradition of Kant. I have linked Parsons to the social-democratic, welfare state tradition of T. H. Marshall and have suggested, in addition, that the more critical strain in his work has roots in the reformist "social control" tradition of American pragmatism (Alexander, 1983, pp. 385-387).

Finally, most of these new interpretations of the meaning of Parsons's work have generated new periodizations. The thrust has been to argue against the orthodox position that Parsons's work necessarily improved with age. Habermas and Menzies, for example, praise his earlier writings but see in the later work a systems bias that involves serious reification. Andriaansens attacks the middle-period work, especially *The Social System,* as a fundamental deviation from the synthetic thrust of the early and later work, a view that is shared by Sciulli and Gerstein (1985). Although I have argued for the analytical superiority of Parsons's later work (Alexander, 1983, pp. 61-73, 194-211, 259-272), I have also suggested that his essays of the late 1930s and 1940s, because they are more empirically concrete, more group-oriented, and more critical, provide a significant corrective to his later work on social change.

Neo-Marxist interpretation gradually paved the way for social scientific explanation that moved in the same direction. New substantive theory and new empirical work were produced by the older generation of scholars like Hobsbawm and Genovese—who sought to salvage the Marxian legacy—and eventually by a younger generation attracted to neo-Marxism for intellectual and political reasons. Once again, within functionalism the situation has been much the same. In the course of the turbulent period of the 1960s, an older generation of functionalists initiated subtle but often far-reaching changes in "orthodox" theory. Suggesting new twists on traditional ideas and incorporating what had usually been taken to be antagonistic theories, these sociologists drew upon Tocqueville, Weber, Marx, and Habermas in their efforts to attain new levels of empirical specificity, a fuller appreciation for power and conflict, and more probing kinds of ideological critiques. Following in their wake, theorists in the younger generation have taken up a variety of neofunctionalist paths. This recent movement, moreover, has not been confined to the United States. The extraordinary revival of Parsonianism in Germany (Alexander, 1984) has, in fact, been a reconstruction of Parsons's legacy in a neofunctionalist vein, providing new substantive theories and empirical explorations (e.g., Miebach, 1984) of diverse scope and outstanding quality.[4]

The articles that follow—all of which appear here for the first time—exemplify the tendencies I have described. All of them, for example, argue for a form of functionalism that is epistemologically multidimensional. A few are overtly critical of idealist tendencies in Parsons's original work, as when Barber argues against the Parsonians'—i.e., the ortho-dox—tendency to credit professional groups with purely normative, altruistic interest. Turning Parsons's professions theory against itself, Barber outlines a more synthetic functionalist approach to social control that can incorporate the insights of materialist critics like Friedson and Berlant. Other contributors eschew the critical mode. Whatever Parsons's own inclinations, they themselves start from the assumption that a materialist, or conditional, reference must always be there. Thus Colomy writes about the cultural and political-economic bases of party forma-tion; Eisenstadt and Smelser argue for the recognition of group self-interest and coalitions in explaining social change.

There is also the unmistakable strain in these chapters of ideological critique. Virtually every contributor pushes functionalism to the left. In several chapters this takes the form of a warning against Parsons's optimism about modernization. Lechner turns Parsons's change theory on its head by converting his focus on "the problem of order" into a theory of disorder. In this way he can use categories of Parsons's later change theory to investigate fundamentalist reactions to modernization rather than progressive realizations of it. In a similar vein, Colomy for-mulates an approach to differentiation that is as prepared to explain its failure as its success. But this leftward push also takes a specifically Marxian form. Gould argues that functionalist theory must be developmental as well. He uses Hegel, Marx, and Piaget to develop—within the functionalist vocabulary of Parsonian theory—an explanatory framework for the transitions between feudalism, capitalism, and socialism. Scuilli also elaborates a functionalist-Marxist integration. On the one hand, he suggests that Parsons's empirical generalization about growing collegiality is the necessary complement to Habermas's pro-posal for consensual and voluntary communication. On the other hand, he insists that functionalist theory is lacking just the kind of normative and critical dimension that a theory like Habermas's can provide.

We can also find in these contributions an argument for an explicit democratic thrust within functionalist analysis. Barber's demand for a commitment to informed consent in the theory of professions is one example; Sciulli's emphasis on the necessity for antiauthoritarian col-legiality is another. The most detailed elaboration of the democratic framework that is implied by Parsons's theory can be found in Prager's theory of the public. A differentiated societal community, Prager shows, involves the commitment to a vigorous and democratic public life.

Neofunctionalism, then, responds sharply to the ideological and epistemological attacks that were leveled at the orthodox tradition. The two other major substantive challenges to functionalism have emerged from conflict and interactionist approaches. If anything, neofunctionalist theorists have been even more concerned with responding to these. It is a remarkable fact—which Munch, in his commentary, has quite rightly underlined—that almost every contribution to this volume is a "conflict theory" of one sort or another. Gould argues for a third, structuralist dimension to sociological theory because he wants general functionalist reasoning to be specified by historically concrete predictions of strain and contradiction. Eisenstadt argues against a reified approach to system boundaries because he sees them as constructed through conflict and maneuver. Smelser rejects the notion of differentiation being decided by adaptive efficiency in favor of a criterion that resembles hegemonic group interest, defined in ideal and material ways. Colomy makes group conflict the central object of his analysis, insisting that differentiation and conflict are two sides of the same coin. Prager conceptualizes the public as an arena for democratic conflict; Barber inserts a conflict dimension into the professional/client relationship.

These references to conflict, moreover, are often accompanied by an emphasis on contingency and interactional creativity. Rossi finds a convergence between the indeterminacy of subsystem exchange and the dialectical tension between subjectivity and constraint that he himself stressed in his own revisions of structuralist theory. Eisenstadt insists on the openness of systemic tendencies to individual choice and group process. Colomy draws upon Eisenstadt's work on symbolic entrepreneurs to elaborate a systematic theory of how voluntary "strategic groups" modify and direct the more structural elements of social change.

What is truly important about these contributions, however, is not that they have "taken account" of contemporary theoretical developments. It is that they have done so from the point of view of a common tradition; it is this common tradition that allows the "whole" of each contribution to be more than the mere sum of its parts. The lessons of 20 years of theoretical debate become articulated in a functionalist way. The idea of a system with interrelated and relatively autonomous parts, the tension between ends and means, the reference to equilibrium, the distinction between personality, culture, and society, the sensitivity to differentiation as a master trend, and a commitment to independent theorizing—all of these basic fundamentals of "functional" thinking permeate the chapters included here. Ideological critique, materialist reference, conflict orientation, and interactional thrust can in this way emerge as relatively coherent variations on a theme rather than as a collection of eclectic, completely diverse essays in sociological theory. In the quest for scientific accumulation, the coherence that this kind of coordinated revision provides is a definite advantage. But there are more substantive advantages as well. Within a neofunctionalist frame-work, materialist reference is never separated from culture or personality systems; contingency is related to systemic process; ideological criticism of society occurs within a multifaced understanding of social differentia-tion; and thinking about conflict is intertwined with theories of integra-tion and societal solidarity.

This is not to say, of course, that the authors presented agree with one another in anything other than a broad, orienting way. For some there is such agreement; the chapters by Eisenstadt, Smelser, and Colomy form quite a close-knit group. These chapters, however, differ in quite striking ways from Lechner's more general and classificatory approach; Munch, for his part, finds all four lacking an explicit systems framework. Munch's view of theoretical autonomy is much more abstract and normative than the empirically concerned theory of Barber. Rossi interprets values in structuralist terms; Sciulli finds an antivalue, pro-cessual tendency in Parsons's later work. Colomy finds a substantive, developmental theory of change; Gould finds none. Sciulli calls for a theory of normative development; Prager finds much that is already there. These controversies occur within more generalized agreement. They illustrate my earlier point that neofunctionalism is a tendency rather than a developed theory.

The chapters presented here, moreover, by no means exhaust neofunctionalist work. Among the older generation of revisionists, the recent writings of Robert Bellah, Edward Tiryakian, Clifford Geertz, Alex Inkeles, Leon Mayhew, Dietrich Rueschemeyer, Roland Robertson, Rainer Baum, and Donald N. Levine come to mind. Among the younger generation, one would also cite the work of R. Stephen Warner, Dean Gerstein, Viviana Zelizer, Victor Lidz, Gerald Platt, Charles Bosk, Adrian Hayes, and Gary Rhoades. Within the current German revival, one would want to include, along with Munch, Luhmann, Schluchter, and even Habermas.

No one knows where such developments will lead, whether a neofunctionalist school actually will emerge, or whether, instead, neofunctionalism will shape contemporary sociology in less conspicuous ways. In the past, Parsons's controversial reputation meant that even some of the participants in this revival were loathe to acknowledge his influence. The appearance of this volume and other recent publications (e.g., Sciulli & Gerstein, 1985) seems to indicate that this period is over. The movement to reappropriate Parsons in a neofunctionalist way is gaining momentum. Whether it is simply old wine in new bottles, or a new brew, is something history will decide.

NOTES

1. This dramatic revival of functionalist interpretation, theory, and empirical work is documented by Sciulli and Gerstein (1985) in their recent article in the *Annual Review of Sociology.*

2. In an interesting and revealing echo of that early response to functionalist theorizing and its critique, Michael A. Faia (forthcoming) has written a major "defense" of functionalist sociology. In *The Strategy and Tactics of Dynamic Functionalism,* he responds to critics by defining functionalism as a logic of empirical analysis that studies causes through effects, suggests this is much more widely practiced than is usually thought, and argues that it should be taken as the best way to approach structural and dynamic explanations. Faia's impressive book very much reflects the revived interest in functionalism, but its "methodological" definition places it outside of what I call neofunctionalism.

3. See Bailey's (1984) recent efforts to differentiate the ways in which Parsons used equilibrium and to develop a more precise way of talking about systems integration.

4. This German work brings out clearly what is also a pronounced tendency in the American material: Neofunctionalism sets up "hyphenated" relationships with other traditions, including critical Marxist theory, Weberian thought, Durkheimianism, Freudianism, and so forth. In its orthodox Parsonian phase, functionalism tried to coopt these other classical theories; in the post-Parsonian phase, their differences with Parsons's thought seem, to the contrary, positive and fruitful, and functionalist theorists have taken them up once again. This, of course, has also been a striking characteristic of the neo-Marxist movement, which has produced psychoanalytic Marxism, structural Marxism, and existential Marxism, to name the best-known cases.

REFERENCES

Adriannsens, H.P.M. (1980). *Talcott Parsons and the conceptual dilemma.* London: Routledge & Kegan Paul.

Alexander, J. C. (1978). Formal and substantive voluntarism in the work of Talcott Parsons: A theoretical and ideological reinterpretation. *American Socioloical Review, 43,* 177-198.

Alexander, J. C. (1983). The modern reconstruction of classical thought: Talcott Parsons. In *Theoretical logic in sociology* (Vol. 4). Berkeley: University of California Press.

Alexander, J. C. (1984). The Parsons' revival in German sociology. *Sociological Theory, 2.*

Althusser, L. (1970). Marxism is not a historicism. In L. Althusser & E. Balibar (Eds.), *Reading capital* (pp. 119-144). London: New Left Review Books.

Atkinson, D. (1972). *Orthodox consensus and radical alternation.* New York: Basic Books.

Bailey, K. (1984). Beyond functionalism: Toward a non-equilibrium analysis of complex systems. *British Journal of Sociology, 35,* 1-18.

Barber, B. (Ed.). (1970). *L. J. Henderson on the social system.* Chicago: University of Chicago Press.

Bourricaud, F. (1977). *L'Individualisme institutionnel.* Paris: PUF.

Bershady, H. J. (1973). *Ideology and social knowledge.* New York: John Wiley.

Coser, L. A. (1956). *The functions of social conflict.* New York: Free Press.

Faia, M. A. (in press). *The strategy and tactics of dynamic functionalism.* New York: Cambridge University Press.

Gintis, H. (1969). *Alienation and power: Towards a radical critique of welfare economics.* Doctoral dissertation, Harvard University.

Goode, W. J. (1960). A theory of role strain. *American Sociological Review, 25,* 483-496.

Gouldner, A. W. (1960). The norm of reciprocity. *American Sociological Review, 25,* 161-178.

Gouldner, A. W. (1980). *The two Marxisms.* New York: Seabury.

Habermas, J. (1984). *Theory of communicative action* (Vol. 1). Boston: Beacon.

Homans, G. C. (1984). *Coming to my senses.* New Brunswick, NJ: Transaction.

Menzies, K. (1976). *Talcott Parsons and the social image of man.* London: Routledge & Kegan Paul.

Merton, R. K. (Ed.). (1967). Manifest and latent functions. Merton *On theoretical sociology.* New York: Free Press.

Miebach, B. (1984). *Strukturalistiche handlungstheorien: Zum verhaltnis zwischen soziologischer theorie und empirischer forschung in werk Talcott Parsons.* Opladen: Westdeutscher.

Münch, R. (1981-1982). Talcott Parsons and the theory of action, I and II. *American Journal of Sociology, 86,* 709-739; *87,* 771-826.

Parsons, T. (1945). The present position and prospects of systematic theory in sociology. In T. Parsons (Ed.), *Essays in sociological theory.* New York: Free Press.

Rocher, G. (1975). *Talcott Parsons and American sociology.* New York: Barnes & Noble.

Savage, S. (1981). *The theories of Talcott Parsons.* New York: St. Martin's.

Sciulli, D., & Gerstein, D. R. (1985). *Social theory and Talcott Parsons in the 1980s. Annual Review of Sociology, 11.*

Taylor, J. G. (1979). *From modernization to modes of production.* London: Humanities Press.

PART I

Interpretation and Theoretical Boundaries

Chapter 1

THE PRACTICAL GROUNDWORK OF CRITICAL THEORY

Bringing Parsons to Habermas (and vice versa)

DAVID SCIULLI

Georgetown University

DESPITE THE ADVANCES contributed to social theory by his concepts of communicative action and discourse, Jürgen Habermas has recapitulated the gap between theory and practice that marked Marx's critique of ideology and the Frankfurt School's critical theory of advanced capitalism. For nearly two decades Habermas has acknowledged that he is unable to bring his procedural but idealized (meta-empirical) standard of communicative reason to collective practice. His standard can be used to broadly criticize the "manipulative" or "strategic" aspects of empirical organizations and institutions (e.g., 1973a, 1974, 1981, Chap. 1). But it cannot suggest what possible empirical organizations and institutions could qualify, even in part, as reasoned or communicative (e.g., 1973a, pp. 130-143; 1974, pp. 186-188; 1981, p. 43; 1982, pp. 220, 232-233, 251-254, 261-263).

I discuss how the move from Habermas's communication theory to political practice can be accomplished. Habermas's idealized, procedural standard of reason must be linked to *empirical* procedures and a *form* of organization consistent with his standard. They mark irreducible threshold restraints on arbitrary collective power. Any possible social action that aspires to realize Habermas's idealized procedures of communicative action and discourse must already have institutionalized the empirical procedural restraints on arbitrary power. The restraints represent, therefore, an irreducible standard of progress toward or regress from communicative action.

This proposed linkage of theory and practice rests on a synthesis of unique concepts taken from the works of Habermas, Talcott Parsons, and Lon L. Fuller, the Harvard legal theorist. All of the concepts are

AUTHOR'S NOTE: I would like to acknowledge Jeffrey C. Alexander for suggesting the title for this chapter.

21

generalizable. They are procedural and/or analytical rather than being substantive. In my view the linkage of Habermas's communication theory to political practice cannot be accomplished using any other set of concepts and escape relativism or dogmatism (cf. Dallmayr, 1976, 1981; Bernstein, 1978, 1983).

Four propositions elaborate this thesis and orient the discussion to follow.

(1) Habermas will continue to be unable to link his communication theory to collective practice until he mediates both theory and practice specifically with Fuller's *empirical* principles of *procedural* legality and Parsons's extension of those principles to the generalizable social functions performed by the collegial *form* of organization. The latter are unique concepts in two respects. First, they are procedural and do not violate the integrity of Habermas's idealized procedural standard of non-distorted communication. They do not compromise the latter's claim to represent a generalizable standard of reason "more comprehensive" than the narrow norm of formal rationality. Any proposed *substantive* mediation, by contrast, would necessarily violate Habermas's standard. In so doing it would fall victim to Habermas's critique of Neopositivist copy theories of truth (1968; 1973b; 1982: 274-8) and/or mark a regression from Habermas's clear advance beyond the substantive absolutes offered by Marxism or the Frankfurt school (1981, Chap. 4). It would, in other words, presuppose direct access to, an ability to "copy," true states of affairs or reasoned action as a substantive way of life.

In Habermas's view, Marxism and the Frankfurt school's first generation of theorists fail to fully appreciate that in modern pluralistic societies, characterized by actors' normative and conceptual relativism, the very recognition of substantive truths or reasoned actions must be mediated by maintaining the integrity of procedures of communication among actors. In the absence of this procedural mediation, the common recognition of "truth" or "reason" can only be imposed by either manipulation or force.

Second, the concepts provided by Parsons and Fuller permit Habermas's *idealized* standard of true or reasoned consensus to be specified in terms of irreducible threshold conditions: *empirical* procedures of common recognition and conduct, and a form of organization of that recognition and conduct. The latter conditions can be directly institutionalized and upheld with sanctions. These sanctions, in turn, can be justified as being reasoned in terms of Habermas's communication theory, By contrast, if Habermas's ideal standard is imposed without mediation, or if it is aspired to by self-selected participants in any way that encroaches on or violates the integrity of Fuller's and/or Parsons's threshold standard, the result would necessarily be arbitrary power and bureaucratic-authoritarian domination rather than emancipation or communicative action.[1]

(2) Habermas, Parsons, and Fuller each address the following problem: How can norms (i.e., standards of practical conduct other than the norm of formal rationality or purposive rationality) be recognized, understood, and acted upon *in common* by pluralistic believers, despite modern functional differentiation and concomitant value-relativism? The synthesis proposed in this chapter pushes the problem another step: If instances of common recognition, understanding, and action can also be shown to represent irreducible conditions necessary for any possible realization of reasoned action, then these conditions can be imposed as society-wide duties or institutions. It would be necessary to uphold such society-wide duties with sanctions, just as any possible institutions are ultimately upheld with sanctions. But these particular sanctions would not, in principle, involve arbitrary power. Rather, the exercise of power in this particular case would itself be reasoned or communicative in Habermas's sense.

(3) The resulting generalizable standard of reasoned procedural restraints on arbitrary power is not only non-Marxian and non-Frankfurtian, but also decidedly non-Liberal. It is distinct from, and unhesitatingly critical of, Liberal contract theory or rational natural law from Hobbes and Locke to John Rawls (1971) and Robert Nozick (1974, cf. Ackerman, 1977, 1980). It updates and extends the radicalism of 17th- and 18th-century *governmental* constitutionalism in the common law tradition (i.e., Fuller's procedural legality) by providing a philosophical grounding by which common law principles can escape relativism (i.e., Habermas's communication theory) and also a sociological extension beyond the narrow focus on the formal institutions of government to groups and institutions in the socioeconomic and cultural orders (i.e., Parsons's collegial form of organization).

The result can best be termed *societal* constitutionalism: The form of organization and empirical procedures that must be established and maintained by at least some groups and institutions if pluralist believers (whether participants or observers) are to have the possibility of recognizing in common, and then the opportunity to act in common on the basis of the sharp distinction between authoritarianism based on arbitrary uses of collective power (even if temporarily popular and/or benevolent) and reasoned authority based on fiduciary or responsible uses of collective power. Societal constitutionalism points to a framework of *specific* empirical institutions that *sharply* differentiates between manipulated or coerced legitimation and reasoned authority.

(4) The proposed synthesis can be accomplished without distorting or reifying any of the three theorist's own framework of concepts. Parsons himself carried out part of the proposed synthesis by directly appropriating Fuller's legal theory rather than any competing alternative, whether some variant of legal positivism (e.g., Weber, Hans Kelsen), liberal contract theory or rational natural law, or civil morality (e.g., Robert Bellah).[2] Parsons's partial synthesis in fact gave his functional social theory a critical edge; when the latter is grounded on Habermas's procedural communication theory, the result is societal constitutionalism.

THE PROBLEM: SUBSTANTIVE RELATIVISM AND PROCEDURAL GENERALITY

Unlike their contemporaries in social theory who employed empirical typologies or sought a substantive concept of reason (whether, for example, Merton, Horkheimer, Adorno, or Marcuse), Habermas and Parsons offer *analytical* concepts and/or *procedural* categories. The latter are intended to be generalizable. Each theorist's project, in other words, is to establish an updated Archimedean point—regardless of their different approaches to philosophy, their indebtedness to quite different theoretical traditions, and their different ideological commitments.[3]

Weber's view of the potential pathologies accompanying the expansion of rationalization sets a major part of the agenda in Habermas's and Parsons's independent efforts to develop a generalizable social theory. Parsons saw Weber's work suggesting a parallel to the second law of thermodynamics, the law of entropy: the drift of social change from normative relativism to nihilism, with the likely modern response of bureaucratic-authoritarianism imposing norms on pluralist believers (1937, pp. 751-753, 624-635, 675-677; 1941, p. 81). Habermas sees it as marking "the decentering of worldviews" and the undermining of the critical potential of the concept of substantive rationality that Lukacs and the Frankfurt school had taken from Weber (1981, pp. 1-3, 66-76, 102-141, 246-250, 267-271; 1982, pp. 226, 235, 251, 276-277).

Habermas proposes a *procedural* Archimedean point of reasoned communication and reasoned action in response to the defects of Marxism and critical theory, and the empirical resilience of advanced capitalism, despite the expansion of Weberian rationalization (or what Horkheimer and Adorno called instrumental reason). His project is to critically study the continued fragmentation of belief in authority, or legitimation crisis. As pluralist believers in modern societies question institutions, it will become apparent that the latter's normative foundations are not based on reasoned justifications ("communicative action"), but, rather, are based on manipulation ("teleological action," or "normatively regulated strategic action"). The latter functions to distort rigorous questioning (1973a, 1974, 1977, 1981, pp. 10, 84-93, 279-280; 1982, pp. 227, 236-238, 263-267, 269, 315). Only subinstitutional networks of actors that can somehow maintain the procedural integrity of communication within their communities have the opportunity to inform or initiate social movements seeking emancipation from manipulation and distortion (e.g., 1971, pp. 25-40; 1981, pp. 86, 100-101, 275, 285-286, 336, 418 n.19; 1982, pp. 220-228, 254-263).

Habermas's project, long the goal of Marxism and critical theory, is to ground his descriptions and evaluations of modern social life so that they are not dismissed (or relativized) as ideological. A grounded critical theory at least potentially can be recognized by both observers and participants to be reasoned in a sense broader than the one-sided, narrow formal norm of purposive-rationality or instrumental reason. For instance, Habermas rejects Weber's position that modern "rational-legal" legitimation may ultimately be reduced to the circular relationship between effective bureaucratic domination and the absence of manifest rebellion (1981, pp. 254-271; 1973a, pp. 97-98; 1977, pp. 205-212).

Parsons developed an *analytical* Archimedean point in response to Weber on the entropic pressures of rationalization (e.g., 1937, pp. 751-753, 624-635, 675-676); Durkheim and Pareto on the tension between moral solidarity and normative breakdown (e.g., 1937, pp. 685-686, 710); and the contemporary empirical integration of advanced societies in the face of rationalization, functional differentiation, and normative relativism (e.g., Parsons & Smelser, 1956). Parsons established his analytical framework of concepts in three stages. First, he established the relationship between the distinct analytical concepts of voluntaristic, rational, and nonrational action. Second, he established the relationship between the analytical pattern variables of normative possibilities and the empirical thresholds already crossed by evolutionary universals of functional differentiation. Third, he established the relationship between the analytical AGIL functionalism, the four ideal types of organizational forms (competitive, bureaucratic, democratized, and collegial), and Fuller's procedural standard of threshold conditions of legality.

Parsons's project was never to link theory to practice in Habermas's sense. He never directly addressed whether the normative foundations of society are reasoned. He never sought a concept of procedural reason "more comprehensive" than the norm of formal rationality. Rather, Parsons's project was to provide an analytical framework for empirical and ideal-type research and to render research findings cumulative and mutually understandable across the social sciences rather than remaining compartmentalized or seemingly unrelated (Bershady, 1973, Chap. 1). In Alexander's term, Parsons's goal was ecumenicism (1983). Yet, Parsons's analytical and generalizable category of voluntaristic action, coupled with his differentiation since the early 1960s between procedural-generalizable norms and substantive-relativistic norms within that category, allowed Parsons to accommodate the most critical or radical potential of Habermas's communication theory.

PARSONS'S THREE STAGES OF THEORY CONSTRUCTION: FROM ANALYTICAL CONCEPTS TO A CRITICAL EDGE

Parsons's critique of Utilitarianism and materialist determinism was one tack in his move to "the voluntaristic means-end schema." But how he steadily distanced himself also from Idealism and value determinism remains obscured or misunderstood in the literature. Materialist determinism involves the overemphasis (reification) of the norm of formal rationality, along with purely material or coercive sanctions, as the basis for social action and order. Value determinism involves the overemphasis of nonrational substantive norms, along with purely moral sanctions of conscience or accepted punishment, as the basis for social action and order.

Parsons rejected materialist determinism with his critique of Utilitarianism and proposed "voluntaristic action" as his alternative. *All of Parsons's voluntaristic concepts are nonrational, or not reducible to the norm of formal rationality or to material and coercion sanctions.*[4]

Therefore, the more important issue is how Parsons kept his voluntaristic concepts distinct from value determinism, or the hypostatization of pluralist actors' supposed common internalization of substantive beliefs. His successful critique of idealism is not familiar because Parsons's eventual differentiation, *within* his category of voluntaristic action, between substantive norms and procedural norms has not been presented either by proponents or critics. Yet, Parsons's debt to Fuller's procedural approach to law (or, more accurately, to normative action as such) is an important symbol of how Parsons's social theory, beginning in the late 1950s and early 1960s, developed his approach of the 1930s while departing markedly from his approach of the late 1940s and early 1950s.

Actors' common recognition and understanding of substantive norms (e.g., the qualities of family, neighborhood, community, religious congregation) are always relative to time and place. It is largely self-enforced (i.e., habitual) by way of group-specific socialization processes and actors' internalization of common beliefs about *a* proper way of life. However, actors' common recognition and understanding of procedural norms (e.g., not only the norms of formal rationality and formal equality, but also Fuller's procedural legality and Parsons's mid-1960s concept of the collegial form of organization) may be, at least potentially, generalizable. It can be other-enforced by the common recognition of violations of procedures, despite actors' otherwise pluralistic substantive beliefs and interests. *Like Habermas's communication theory, Fuller's procedural legality and Parsons's collegial form can filter violations of the procedures and form, but cannot specify what policy content must (or should) be undertaken within the form or consistent with the procedures.* In order to follow his critique of idealism, I first define Parsons's early trichotomy of distinct concepts of action and then devote most of the discussion to Parsons's later differentiation of norms within the category of voluntaristic action.

PARSONS'S TRICHOTOMY OF ACTION CONCEPTS: THE FIRST STAGE OF CRITIQUE OF CLASSICAL SOCIOLOGY

Finding that Utilitarianism attempted to account for social action solely in terms of the somehow concerted action of rational, calculating individuals, Parsons insisted in the 1920s and 1930s that any possible empirical social action in the modern world would necessarily be composed of three *analytical* or pure-type components.

(1) Rational action, or "the intrinsic means-end schema." For Parsons this pure type involves *means* that are efficient or effective. They are instruments or causally repeatable techniques. The *ends* of rational action, in turn, are both empirical *and quantifiable.* They comprise a chain of utilities, a ceaseless series of utilitarian consumables divorced from any and all standards of quality (1937, pp. 56ff., 133, 645, 653-658). Thus the analytical means and ends are *intrinsically* interrelated; there is no possible ultimate end consistent with the pure type of rational action.

In the pure-type case (i.e., action-oriented by common adherence to the *generalizable* norm of *formal* rationality), the quantities of utilities produced can be counted as a final arbiter of disputes over the efficiency of means (1935, pp. 287-293). Thus social action consistent with this formal norm of rationality is directed exclusively to quantity, that is, to abundance as such, to the perpetual effort of accumulation of utilities indistinguishable in quality. The most prominent *empirical* illustrations of the pure-type case are the enterprises of production, formal organization, and scientific technique (not scientific theory-construction, nor scientific "fact-finding"). However, it must be kept in mind that *empirical* enterprises necessarily involve nonrational *analytical* components as well.

(2) Nonrational action, or "the symbolic means-end schema." For Parsons this pure type involves *means* that are symbolic or normative. They are habitually repeatable rituals that are inherently noninstrumental or nonefficient. The *ends* of nonrational action, in turn, can neither be empirical nor quantifiable; rather, they are transcendental, ultimate ends. They are pure ends in themselves, habitually recognized in common (internalized beliefs) as "sacred" or more significant (meta-empirical) than unmediated, formally rational action (1935, pp. 300-305; 1937, pp. 209-218, 257-264, 673-677). Thus the analytical means and ends are *symbolically* interrelated; there is no possible standard of efficiency or effectiveness consistent with the pure type of nonrational action.

In the pure type case (i.e., action oriented by common adherence to an always *relativistic* set of *substantive* norms, to some particular way of living valued above all others), whether the transcendental end is secured can never be recognized empirically at all. For instance, whether devout actors really are rewarded with salvation or sacrilegious actors really suffer damnation cannot possibly be verified.

> In so far as the common system of ultimate ends involves transcendental ends, it is then to be expected that it will be expressed in common ritual actions. From the empirical point of view the question whether such actions in fact attain their ends is irrelevant, for there is no possible means of verification. (Parsons, 1935, p. 303; 1937, pp. 565-566)

Thus the strict (habitual, ritualistic) conformity to the means is the only factor of nonrational action that can be empirically recognized in common, whether in retrospect or while the action is ongoing (1935, pp. 293, 300-305; cf. Luhmann, 1984, pp. 8-10). Furthermore, this assessment of strict, proper conformity to ritual is always a qualitative judgment made by authorities; it can never be rendered quantifiable, nor can it be verified or falsified scientifically. The most prominent empirical illustrations of the pure-type case are the enterprises of traditional ways of life, especially fundamentalist religious ways of life. Again, however, the *empirical* enterprises necessarily involve efficient or rational *analytical* components as well.

(3) Voluntaristic action, or "the voluntaristic means-end schema." For Parsons this pure type involves *means* that are also symbolic or normative. Although they are noninstrumental and nonefficient, however, they are also not routinely repeatable or habitual. Rather, they are contingently or only temporarily recognized and acted on in common, whether they are internalized (self-enforced) or institutionalized (other-enforced). The *ends* of voluntaristic action, in turn, are *necessarily* both empirical *and qualitative.* They are neither pure ends in themselves nor pure utilities but, again, are contingently or only temporarily recognized and acted on in common as more significant *empirically* than unmediated, formally rational action (1937, pp. 11-12, 81-82, 439-467, 572-576, 700-720, 753-762).

> The voluntaristic conception of action implies that there is resistance to the realization of the rational norm. . . . This problem of control [of collective action toward securing qualitative ends] tends to be met by the subjection of action in pursuit of immediate non-ultimate ends to normative rules which regulate that action in conformity with the common ultimate value-system of the community [i.e., sub-group of society]. These normative rules both define what immediate ends should and should not be sought and limit the choice of means to them in terms other than those of efficiency. Finally, they also define standards of socially acceptable effort. This system of rules, fundamental to any society . . . is what I call its institutions. They are *moral* norms, not norms of efficiency. (Parsons, 1935, pp. 298-299)

For Parsons, the analytical means and ends are more contingently interrelated—more voluntaristic in their interrelationship—than is the case with either formally rational (intrinsic) or nonrational (symbolic) action. In the pure-type case of voluntaristic action, which lies between the purely generalizable-procedural norm of formal rationality and the purely relativistic-substantive norms of nonrational action, the means and "the immediate, nonultimate ends" can *potentially* be recognized in common, both in retrospect and while the action is ongoing. This is the case because the means and the ends are empirical, though qualitative rather than quantifiable.

Parsons did not call this middle category "voluntaristic" because he wanted to convey that actors somehow volunteer or subjectively will their obedience to (or disobedience of) such norms in *common*. Rather, he wanted to emphasize *that modern pluralistic actors' common recognition of and adherence to such norms is always contingent; it is inherently temporary*. Neither actors' common recognition and understanding of the norms nor their common recognition and understanding of action consistent with the norms is routinely (causally or habitually) established or maintained (either by scientific laws or moral authorities). The possibility of permanence is eliminated by the fragmenting pressures of rationalization, that is, the functional differentiation of material interests and the normative pluralism and relativism of beliefs. Niklas Luhmann (1976, 1984) and Jan Loubser (1976) come closest to capturing Parsons's concept of voluntarism with their own concepts of contingency. But the secondary literature, across 50 years of commentary, has grievously simplified Parsons's most important early concept by treating it as a synonym for either free will in particular or normative action in general.[5]

Parsons's early thesis was that modern social life is inherently voluntaristic. Any given set of social arrangements in any given modern society is at the very best only temporarily institutionalized or stabilized.

> The further these immediate ends are removed in the means-end chain from the system of ultimate values sanctioning the system of rules, the more the rules will tend to appear to the individuals subject to them as morally neutral, as mere conditions of action. And since the ends *of the great majority* of practical activities are *very far* removed from ultimate values, there is a strong tendency to evasion. (Parsons, 1937, p. 401; 1935, 287-289; emphasis added)

The category of voluntaristic action (and the problem of institutionalization), therefore, must be the most important category of social theory rather than remaining, as it has been for the classical sociologists, a mere residual category. The analytical components comprising voluntaristic action must be specifically differentiated, rather than being collapsed into a purely residual category (the nonrational realm) or into a broad and analytically unilluminating category (normative action). Parsons's theory construction since 1937, in turn, was a steady and persistent effort to comprehensively *specify* empirical manifestations of voluntaristic action, while simultaneously avoiding the conceptual relativism of empirical social science.

THE PROBLEM OF VOLUNTARISTIC ACTION: MOVING TO THE SECOND AND THIRD STAGES

Parsons's reasons for emphasizing the concept of voluntaristic action were consistent with his formulation of the Utilitarian dilemma: Formally rational action alone can never account for *social* action or *order*. Action undertaken in common by pluralist believers cannot permanently rely on either effective coercion or unavoidable material sanctions. Parsons had pointed out repeatedly in the 1930s that even if we attempted to reify the norm of formal rationality to the ultimate norm of modern social life, when pluralist believers merely question what the ends of rational action *are*, or question whether their ongoing activity is actually becoming more or less rational, *they are already no longer acting rationally* in the pure-type case. Questioning and deciding what the ends of social action are or will be, or whether ongoing social action is becoming more or less rational, are not the most efficient or effective means to secure quantities of utilities. Rather, questioning and deciding are more akin to the interpretation of a text than to efficient production—questioning and deciding, literally, what the text *is*, what it *means*. What are the most effective or efficient ways to interpret a text? Hermeneutics may be rigorous and methodical, but it is never effective and efficient, formally rational, or scientific.

Parsons insisted that formally rational action in the pure-type case necessarily represents a very narrow norm of reason. It is an *analytical* component of social action. It will always be realized empirically through some nonrational framework, through some set of norms drawn from the broad residual category of the nonrational realm. That framework, in turn, will always restrain the full realization of formally rational action. In short, Parsons saw in the 1930s what the philosophy of science has in the 1960s and 1970s popularized: The enterprise of science, like any other possible empirical social action, can never *be* rational. At best, it can incorporate more and more formally rational components:

> An act may be described as having a certain degree of rationality, of disinterestedness, etc. It is these general[izable] attributes of concrete [relativistic] phenomena . . . to which the term "analytical realism" will be applied. Such analytical elements need not be thought of as capable of concrete, even hypothetical, existence apart from other analytical elements of the same logical system. . . . We may say that such and such an act is rational (to a certain degree) but never that it *is* rationality, in the sense of a concrete thing. . . . An analytical element . . . is an

abstraction because it refers to a general[izable] property. (1937, pp. 34-35)

Parsons saw that modern social action and order are becoming more and more voluntaristic. They are inexorably becoming more and more subjected to the contingency of establishing and maintaining actors' common recognition and understanding. Parsons's very concept of voluntaristic action conveys this lack of stabilization or ultimate temporariness of any possible common action in modern societies. First, voluntaristic action means collective action that is *always* more contingently institutionalized than either rational or nonrational action. Second, voluntaristic action means that *specific* empirical institutions consistent with the analytical definition or pure-type case could not be selected on the basis of Parsons's first theoretical schema as more or less likely candidates for stabilization. On the basis of Parsons's first general theory, we *must* treat *all* specific empirical qualities as potential bases of institutionalization or as candidate-qualities should any ongoing attempt at stabilization seem to be failing.

The problem that Habermas poses with his communication theory (namely, whether the qualities of the means or ends are being acted on geniunely or willingly rather than due to manipulation or distorted understanding), therefore, is quite secondary to the more fundamental problem posed by Parsons across his 50 years of publications. Parsons asked, How is *common* understanding and *common* action as such even temporarily stabilized among pluralist believers? How can qualitative means and ends be even temporarily recognized and acted on in common?

Regarding *substantive* norms that are empirical and qualitative and thereby consistent with the pure-type case of voluntaristic action (e.g., particular beliefs regarding family, neighborhood, community, "the good life"), actors' common recognition and understanding does require their common socialization and internalization of common beliefs within at least some major (functionally important) groups in society. But regarding *procedural* norms that are empirical and qualitative, and therefore also consistent with the pure-type case (e.g., Parsons's later "*symbolic* media of interchange," and especially Parsons's collegial *form* as the organizational embodiment of Fuller's *procedural* legality), actors' common recognition and understanding of violations or normative breakdowns are possible *even when* their socialization and internalized beliefs are extremely pluralistic, incommensurable, and (always potentially) conflictual.

The easiest course Parsons could have taken, having elevated the problematic of contingent institutionalization, would have been to hypostatize contemporary instances of social order. Parsons could then treat them as products of actors' presumed common internalization of substantive norms and goal-priorities. In his "middle period" of theory construction, from the 1940s through the mid-1950s, up until his collaboration in 1956 with Neil J. Smelser on *Economy and Society*, Parsons tended to follow that course. This tendency was capped by *The Social System* (1951), a work that Parsons himself later refuted or fundamentally amended in print on repeated occasions especially by sharply differentiating normative *motivations* from normative *orientations* (e.g., 1963a, p. 395, n. 15; 1961, pp. 331-332; 1969, p. 486, n. 15; 1971c, pp. 383-385; 1978, p. 367, n. 38; cf. 1974, pp. 40-43). Yet, it is this middle period, coupled with a longstanding unsatisfactory appreciation of what Parsons had already established as the foundation of his theory construction by coining the term "voluntaristic action," that has until very recently led to the caricature of Parsons as a consensus theorist, or a conservative apologist unable to account for change.

With *Economy and Society* Parsons reconsidered the basis of his theory of social action and order. Parsons and Smelser reconsidered even economic processes in terms of nonquantifiable, institutionalized norms that actors need not internalize in common as their own substantive beliefs or motivations (self-enforced by conscience). Yet, these institutionalized norms, which also cannot be reduced to their support by effective coercion or purely material sanctions, mediate the enormously detailed functional differentiation and dynamic change of economic activities. They restrain actors' pluralistic material interests and substantive beliefs by broadly framing the situation that neither conforming nor rebellious actors can escape or ignore, regardless of actors' interests or motivations.

> Economic growth in the quantitative sense constitutes *one* aspect of the rationalization process. Over the longer run, however, economic growth merges with change in institutional structure which can be neither economic nor purely quantitative change. . . . It cannot be purely quantitative because differentiation must be balanced by new processes of integration unless it is to disrupt the system. (Parsons & Smelser, 1956, pp. 292-293)

From 1956 onward Parsons did not hesitate to again face the implications of Weber's theory of rationalization. "We have tried to carry the analysis of institutional change a little farther than Weber did" (Parsons & Smelser, 1956, p. 293). Parsons from 1956 onward faced the following important issue: The process of the internalization of substantive norms may just as likely increasingly *contribute to* rather than ameliorate the fragmentation of belief because future socialization-internalization processes will very likely involve increasingly differentiated norms. Like all other substantive ways of life, the qualities of marriage, family, neighborhood, child rearing, and schooling can be expected to be understood and to be acted on in quite differentiated ways rather than in terms of some implicit or intuitive common recognition, common understanding, and resulting common activity.

What in advanced societies are the qualities by which a child should be raised that are readily recognized and understood in common? What are the qualities of family life? On what qualities should marriage be based? What are the qualities of a neighborhood; are neighborhoods either important or desirable for social life (see essays by Wellman, Dentler, & Suttles, reprinted in Warren, 1977)? Merely posing these questions already suggests a great plurality of responses rather than some overarching, substantive commonality. Because these questions address the immediate spatial locus of socialization, they indicate that the qualities being internalized as normative are likely to be quite pluralistic. Furthermore, we cannot assume that the *ranges* of possible substantive qualities will be narrow enough to account for consensus in a multiethnic society, especially those in the West and non-West characterized by communal or ethnic sections (e.g., Despres, 1967; Kasfir, 1976; Lijphart, 1977; Young, 1976). Valued qualities of the larger social world of economics, politics, civic affairs, and cultural mores certainly cannot be assumed to fall automatically and conveniently within a narrow range of consensus.

Methodically addressing these problems, Parsons in time moved to the function performed in at least certain modern societies by (1) procedures and symbols for the common recognition and understanding of violations of the integrity of qualitative norms and goals and (2) forms of organization for sustaining common action based on such recognition among pluralist believers. Procedures and forms can potentially overarch the material differentiaiton and normative relativism of modern societies. They are potentially generalizable. When Parsons linked procedures and forms to substantive societal functions that he defined analytically, he rendered his entire social theory generalizable. He established an Archimedean point in the face of modern drift and relativism.

In this effort to escape relativism, Parsons was already approaching, and open to directly appropriating, Lon Fuller's principles of procedural legality.[6] Once he worked Fuller's specific approach to law into his analytical social theory, Parsons (1977, pp. 21-31, 43-49) had completed his longstanding rejection of (1) Weber's and legal positivists' reduction of legality to effective enforcement, institutionalized in bureaucratic formations; and (2) legal idealists' reduction of legality to common internalized beliefs regarding morality, institutionalized in a particular substantive way of life presumed to represent "a natural identity of interests," "democratic will-formation," or, in Victor Lidz's (1979, pp. 16ff.) phrase, "a propensity to observe the law." Parsons's position on law cannot be interpreted narrowly; rather, it symbolizes Parsons's procedural approach to normative action as such. This is why, in my view, none of Parsons's references since the late 1950s or early 1960s to politics, power, government, organizations, professions, stratification, or law—his references to social action as such—can be consistently understood without his "procedural turn" being kept in mind. Unless Fuller's legal theory is kept clearly in mind when reading any of Parsons's essays on the social system, the achievement of his mature social theory becomes hopelessly obscured or distorted. Furthermore, no other approaches to law, and especially those offered by Durkheim and Weber, can be read into Parsons's social theory *without distorting that social theory as a whole*.

By the late 1960s (e.g., 1969, pp. 505ff.) Parsons saw that Fuller's procedural legality was institutionalized or stabilized in what Parsons called collegial formations, rather than in either democratic or bureaucratic forms of organization (Parsons & Platt, 1973; Parsons, 1977, pp. 54, n. 9). Parsons's great insight since the late 1960s, anticipated much earlier by his work on the professions, was that the *institutionalized* value commitment characteristic of the *collegial* form of organization is not only a distinctive normative *orientation* analytically. It is also becoming functionally more important in those pluralist societies that are not manifestly authoritarian. Parsons's emphasis was on the broad orientation characteristic of the distinctive and generalizable collegial *form* as such, not on the specific motivations or substantive interests of personnel within or actors outside the formation. Actors' motivations and substantive interests are in principle largely relative to time and place.

For Parsons, the collegial form is distinctive. To the extent that the integrity of the formation itself is maintained vis-a-vis both bureaucratic top-down chains of command and democratized one member-one vote blocs of opinion,[7] its voluntaristic value comitment or normative orientation will necessarily be in evidence. The formation's very presence in the social system necessarily functions as a restraint on the one-sided expansion of rationalization and on the increasing resort to arbitrary power by governmental or socioeconomic agencies in order to maintain social order.

The importance of Parsons's distinction between *internalized normative motivations* of actors and *institutionalized normative orientations* of organizational forms or procedures must be emphasized. This distinction enabled Parsons to account for integration within pluralist societies without hypostatizing common conditions (coercion, material sanctions) and/or common internalized beliefs (conscience, ideal sanctions). He was able to do so by analytically separating the internalized motivations of actors, which are in principle unlimited in variation and also unstable over time, from the institutionalized orientations distinctive to each of only four possible forms of organization. Thus actors' motivations and interests *may* be mediated short of conflict and/or short of the imposition of social control by arbitrary, bureaucratic-authoritarian enforcement due to distinctive normative orientations institutionalized in forms of organization.

The very possibility of bringing Parsons's analytical framework to empirical research hinges entirely on his successful turn, beginning in the late 1950s and early 1960s, to *symbolic* media and to *generalizable* procedures and forms of organization. In order for Parsons's analytical social theory to escape relativism, the latter as well must not only be generalizable but also comprehensive: There can be no other possible media, procedures of common normative recognition and understanding, or forms of organization than those systematically presented in the AGIL schema. Parsons's seemingly familiar AGIL functional schema for the social system actually has yet to be considered by empirical researchers in the social sciences in ways that are not reifications or distortions. I close this section by offering a few suggestions for reconsidering the AGIL schema.

Following the classic European sociologists, Parsons emphasized that the economy and polity subsystems are mere means to ends; the ends, therefore, must be "given" by other subsystems. Both the economy and polity subsystems tend toward (have the normative orientation of change toward) a strict, unmediated bureaucratic form of organization within their analytically defined subsystem functions of efficient production and effective organization. Furthermore, with Weber, Parsons acknowledged that unless this orientation of change and form of organization are mediated, restrained, or redirected by the institutionalization of norms that are distinctively voluntaristic, then the economy and polity subsystems will ceaselessly pressure *society as a whole* toward the broad normative orientation of formal rationality, that is, toward one-sided rationalization and authoritarian bureaucratization. Parsons saw communist systems as being less "advanced" than Western systems precisely because the former had failed to institutionalize voluntaristic norms of mediation, thereby acceding to the drift of authoritarian bureaucratization society-wide (e.g., 1964, 1969, 1971a).

As a *form* of organization in the pure-type case, bureaucracy is the most efficient and effective means to quantifiable ends, that is, the production of utilities and/or the enforcement of regimentation or social control. Unless norms that are not formally rational are institutionalized, the expansion of rationalization will subordinate all social action to a mere means of production and/or regimentation. Bureaucratization will broadly elevate its normative orientation—the norm of formal rationality—above any and all incompatible *motivations* or beliefs of its personnel unless or until that broad orientation is itself mediated by some alternative normative *orientation,* institutionalized in some alternative form of organization. Bureaucratization is, in fact, the attempted superordination of the narrow norm of formal rationality, whether or not this is reasoned in terms of a more comprehensive view of normative social action (Parsons) or a more comprehensive standard of reason (Habermas).

The societal community subsystem, with its broad normative orientation toward formal equality or democratization (1970c, 1971a, Chap. 2), cannot mediate these pressures of the expansion of rationalization (Habermas, 1973a, pp. 74-75). Parsons rejects the optimistic belief that the democratic form may frame individual actor's equality in substance. Michels' iron law of oligarchy eliminates this possibility; Parsons's approach to a generalizable social theory defines away the empirical individual (and the individual's relativistic motivations and interests) by treating social action in terms of sets of analytical roles. For Parsons, therefore, democracy can only mean that within the analytically defined societal community subsystem, the trend or orientation of change, if left unmediated, is toward *formal* equality in the treatment of *all* pluralistic *substantive* norms and material interests—toward unprincipled ordering or relativistic accommodation.

The societal community subsystem cannot mediate bureaucratization and one-sided rationalization. Why? In the face of drift and relativism, the norm of *formal* rationality and concomitant orientation of change toward efficient production and effective control becomes "elevated" to the only norm likely recognized and understood *in common* by pluralist believers. On the one hand, within the societal community subsystem, all nonrational or voluntaristic norms and interests can only consistently be recognized and understood if treated, at least formally, as equally able to compete in influencing the priorities of economic production and political organization. On the other hand, only the *generalizable,* purely formal norms of rationality (formal efficiency) and equality (formal relativism) are available to broadly frame or orient the policy process of substantive debate (e.g., 1962b).

On this point Parsons is supported by the vast literature on interest group politics or pluralist theory (e.g., Truman, 1951; Dahl, 1956, 1961, 1967; Polsby, 1963), including the major criticisms that have been lodged against the implications of pluralism. Theodore J. Lowi, for instance, demonstrates that U.S. pluralist politics reduces *all* norms—even those of "public authority"—to the drift of the perpetual accommodation of groups' substantive interests. For the pluralist literature, in fact, the only due process considered necessary to escape authoritarianism or arbitrary power is the competition between group interests ("countervailing power") within a framework of formal equality (Lowi, 1969, Chaps. 3, 5, and 10). Along with Grant McConnell (1967), Peter Bachrach and Morton S. Baratz (1970), E. E. Schattschneider (1960), and Isaac Balbus (1971), Lowi demonstrates that this seemingly formal equality actually favors business (economy subsystem) interests, interests most efficiently responding to the pressures of the systemic expansion of rationalization, rather than nonbusiness groupings having interests based on normative standards other than formal efficiency.

This is why, for Parsons as for Michels, democracy is primarily a *form* of organization that frames the competition *between* group interests, rather than a quality of decision making to be found *within* any empirical organization. Neither proponents nor critics of U.S. pluralism have attempted to systematically confront Michels on this point (including Bachrach, 1967; Pateman 1970; cf. Dahl, 1970). According to Parsons and the literature of the pluralism debate, unless there are unique normative standards involving means and ends that are qualitative and thereby inconsistent with the normative standards of formal rationality and formal equality, but yet generalizable rather than completely relative to any particular moment of bargaining between substantive policy interests, democratization will broadly elevate its normative *orientation.* The normative orientation of unprincipled, brokered selection of policy priorities will no longer be evaluated or restrained by any other normative standard. Democratization is the attempted superordination of the narrow norm of formal equality, whether or not this is reasoned in terms of a more comprehensive view of normative social action (Parsons) or a more comprehensive standard of reason (Habermas).

Finally, Parsons saw that in certain advanced societies *part* of the latency or pattern-maintenance subsystem, that part removed from the immediate spatial locus of socialization, *may* become organized in the distinctive collegial form. Parsons had long argued that the professions are distinct from bureaucracies in business and governmental agencies (e.g., 1939). But it was only with his isolation of the collegial *form* of organization, developed from and extending Fuller's principles of procedural legality, that Parsons's previous arguments and his first two stages of theory construction came together into a generalizable social theory with a critical edge escaping relativism: "societal constitutionalism" (e.g., 1969, 1970a, 1971a, 1971b, 1973, 1975, 1977, Parsons & Platt, 1973; Parsons & Gerstein, 1977).

The institutionalization or stabilization of the collegial form *necessarily* restrains the drift of one-sided rationalization and the arbitrariness of society-wide bureaucratization and/or democratization (also see Lowi, 1969, on "juridical democracy"). This is the case because both the means and the end involved are inherently qualitative: (1) Fuller's procedural legality as the means, rather than bureaucratized commands or democratized votes; and (2) the end of maintaining the integrity of the collegial form itself against the systemic pressures of social change toward formal rationality and formal equality. Neither this procedural means nor end-as-form can be subordinated to *any* substantive project, whether to more efficiently secure quantifiable ends or to more equally treat substantive qualitative ends. If subordinated, the collegial form itself is necessarily abandoned in favor of the bureaucratic or democratized forms. Arbitrary exercises of collective power in the name of formal efficiency or subjective legitimation, then, increase in regularity and become cumulative (see Fuller, 1969, pp. 92ff.).

For Parsons that part of the pattern-maintenance subsystem that does maintain that integrity of the collegial form restrains the manifestations of one-sided or arbitrary expansion of rationalization from increasing and becoming cumulative. Collectivities already organized at least in part in the collegial form—such as the university, professional associations, research communities, and intellectual networks, in addition to common law courts, legislatures, and review boards—necessarily bear a *fiduciary* responsibility that is generalizable or society-wide and assume normative authority based on that fiduciary responsibility. Both the responsibility and the authority exist, regardless of the motivations and substantive interests of the personnel within such collectivities, as long as the integrity of the collegial form is being maintained. The collegial form institutionalizes an irreducibly voluntaristic *orientation* of restraint on one-sided, arbitrary social change.

But how do pluralist believers and bargainers recognize in common whether the collegial form is being maintained rather than being feigned? How do they recognize when seeming fiduciary authority is false, a mere veil for more sophisticated modes of arbitrariness, that is, manipulation rather than manifest coercion? Just as Parsons turned to clearly recognizable empirical thresholds of evolutionary universals in order to specify the possible analytical pattern variable combinations, Parsons saw that Fuller's eight principles of procedural legality had already established the clearly recognizable empirical thresholds marking whether or not the integrity of collegial formations is being maintained even minimally in any given instance.

> Every freedom has to be protected by constraints operating to control and counteract forces tending to undermine it. Such constraints operate at the boundaries of the academic system in relation to tendencies to distort the pattern. They must also operate at the boundaries between the levels within it. . . . One set of internal constraints from the point of view of the effective implementation of the pattern of academic freedom is the procedural norms for the conduct of intellectual discourse. (Parsons & Platt, 1973, pp. 154-155)

> Regulated enforcement requires some mode of determining the actual fact, agency, and circumstances of the infraction of norms. Among the specialized agencies that operate in this connection are courts of law and the legal profession. A complex normative order requires not only enforcement, however, but also authoritative interpretation. Court systems have very generally come to combine the determination of obligations, penalties, and the like for specific cases with interpretation of the meaning of norms, often a very general problem. [Parsons footnotes the following: "Extremely suggestive in this regard is Lon Fuller, *The Morality of Law* (New Haven: Yale University Press, 1964)"]. Less developed societies tend to reserve the latter function to religious agencies, but modern societies entrust it increasingly to secular courts. (Parsons, 1971a, p. 16)

In his characteristic fashion, Parsons followed Fuller in linking actors' common recognition of the integrity of the collegial form to their compliance with minimal, irreducible criteria of reasoned action. Yet Fuller (1969, pp. 184-186) saw the need to move to *some* communication theory in order to ground his procedural criteria (against the charge of relativism, or ethnocentric preference for common law practices). Parsons never addressed this issue and certainly never considered moving, with Habermas, to idealized requirements of nondistorted communication ("the ideal speech situation").

HABERMAS'S TWO STAGES OF THEORY CONSTRUCTION: CRITICAL THEORY DIVORCED FROM COLLECTIVE PRACTICE

Habermas explores the implications for social theory of the necessary mediation of any possible access to factual truth or to substantive reason by the quality of communication within researchers' or actors' communities. Because that quality of communication cannot be directly evaluated by any standard that is itself substantive (whether "substantive rationality" or "Gemeinwesen") without recapitulating the problems of a copy theory of truth, *that quality must be determined by a procedural standard.* The procedural standard, in turn, represents *an Archimedean point of nonmanipulated or genuinely consensual mutual understanding.* It is an ongoing procedural *mediation,* not a substantive endpoint secured once and for all. It cannot, in principle, establish what factual truth or substantively reasoned action *is.* But it can establish what distorts (manipulates) truth or reasoned action within any given communication community at any given time.

Habermas's communication theory, his proposed consensus theory of truth or "procedural rationality," therefore, established the ultimate ground of his critical theory of society. The importance of that critical theory to research in the social sciences, even the most purely descriptive or most nonideological research, cannot be overemphasized: Habermas's procedural standard of reason allows the social sciences for the first time in their history to differentiate potentially between manipulated domination and genuinely consensual ordering, even in instances when manifest coercion is not in evidence. Habermas is the first theorist to isolate manipulation, and not simply coercion, within the larger categories of social action and social order. More specifically, Habermas's communication theory is a methodical, grounded restatement and specification of Marxism's and the Frankfurt school's vague and speculative category of false consciousness.

Thus, like Parsons, Habermas elevates to the forefront of social theory the problem of determining how actors' common recognition and understanding of norms is established and maintained. But unlike Parsons, Habermas operates on a dual level of analysis in attempting to specifically locate manipulation within social action and order. On one level, shared with Parsons, Habermas explores how *any* instance of empirical recognition and understanding of norms is established and maintained. This involves the study of each society's institutions and cultural traditions. On a "deeper" level of analysis, however, a level never explicitly pursued by Parsons but established by Habermas's ultimate procedural requirements for the *reasoned* recognition and understanding of norms, Habermas explores the ways in which a society's very institutions and normative traditions may themselves violate reason, regardless of surface popularity or subjective legitimacy.

With this dual level of analysis, Habermas accepts the contributions of the "surface" or empirical hermeneutics of the first level of analysis. But he provides in addition what at times he calls "a depth hermeneutics." The latter does not specify *the* truth or *the* reasoned set of substantive norms; rather, it locates skillful threats of force or even instances of subtle manipulation that necessarily distort any common enterprise of recognizing truth or reason. Stated more positively, Habermas's communication theory elaborates procedures that allow social actors to repair disrupted empirical agreements, agreements disrupted by one-sided rationalization and normative relativism. It offers those actors the opportunity to establish a new basis for agreement based on reasoned consensus. The latter agreement may be established by extended discourse or "argumentation" consistent with the procedural framework of the consensus theory, rather than social order being based only, by default, on coercion or manipulation in the face of pluralist believers' questioning and bargaining.[8]

Habermas acknowledges that full mutual agreement among participants on the validity of pragmatic claims "is not a normal state of linguistic communication." But his universal pragmatics offers "an unreal" or "counterfactual" standard (1976, 1977, 1981, 1982). It offers pluralist believers the opportunity to consistently describe and evaluate distortions and manipulations in empirical communication communities, regardless of their relativistic social contexts, substantive beliefs, and material interests. It establishes a procedural, although idealized, Archimedean point.

Habermas's central thesis since the early 1970s is that this Archimedean point, although idealized or unreal, is not only generalizable but is immutable. Given this procedural (validity claims) and formal (ideal speech situation) Archimedean point, it would seem but a short step for Habermas to turn to *empirical* procedures (Fuller's procedural legality) and a form *of organization* (Parsons's collegial formation) consistent with Habermas's rigorous, idealized grounding but more closely linked to political practice. Fuller's empirical procedures and Parsons's form for organizing common recognition and understanding allow reasoned common action to be sustained and institutionalized, within and across collectivities, rather than remaining merely ad hoc and contingent moments of common action restricted to serial interpersonal networks. The latter procedures and form, that is, mark *thresholds* of *irreducible* conditions for *any possible* realization of Habermas's procedural reason by collective or institutionalized action.

Rather than taking this short step, however, Habermas himself has continued to speak of understanding as rooted in speakers' and hearers' "intuitive competencies" and to couple this with Kohlberg's theory of moral development. As for his most recent emphasis on the phenomenological concept of *Lebsenswelt* (i.e., actors' immediate arena of lived experience), it merely rephrases the sociological hypostatization of a presumed common internalization of norms (e.g., 1981). Habermas merely sees "reflective" norms being internalized rather than the "habitual" norms of the conventional stages of socialization (e.g., 1981a, pp. xli-xlii, 33, 69-71, 121-124, 228-237, 278; 1982, pp. 226, 235-238, 268-271, 278-382).

Habermas must turn, as did Parsons, to a third stage of theory construction. He must turn to the minimal procedural threshold conditions necessary for any possible common recognition of norms within and across collectivities, aside from resorting to arbitrary power (i.e., Fuller's procedural legality), and to the form of organization necessary for any possible *reasoned* action based on that common recognition and understanding (i.e., Parsons's collegial formation). Neither the procedures nor the form, to be sure, can guarantee that communicative action in Habermas's sense will be realized. But it can be *guaranteed* that if communicative action is to be realized by a collectivity or organization, the latter will honor the integrity of both the procedures and the form. Groups or organizations that appear to be collegial in form but that violate Fuller's procedural legality are necessarily feigning the form; any reference to communicative action in situations in which either the integrity of Fuller's procedures or of Parsons's collegial form are being violated is a neologism.

CONCLUSION

Although Parsons never explicitly employed the two levels of analysis that characterize Habermas's critical theory—the surface and the depth hermeneutics—Parsons's theory nonetheless picked up a critical *edge* when Parsons extended Fuller's procedural legality. The only reason that Parsons's work of the 1960s and 1970s is not today considered to be a full-blown critical theory is that neither Parsons himself nor any of his students or commentators has seen that the ground of Fuller's legality and Parsons's collegial form is, ultimately, Habermas's communication theory and standard of procedural reason. Yet Fuller's legal principles cannot be elevated above the relativism of common law traditions without the grounding of Habermas's theory; and if Fuller's principles are reduced to relativistic prejudice, Parsons's social theory cannot sustain its own claim to generalizability, or to ecumenicism. Rather, it becomes as relativistic or ideological as Weber's or Marx's social theories (Alexander, 1983, explores this in great detail).

Habermas's communication theory and procedural standard of reason pushes Parsons's category of voluntaristic action much further toward a critical standard of evaluation than Parsons himself saw, regardless of Parsons's own view of the prospects of, or the need for, a critical social theory. On the other hand, Parsons's category of voluntaristic action, and especially his later differentiation of procedural norms within that category, pushes Habermas's communication theory even further away from Marxism's absolutist critique of ideology and alienation and the Frankfurt school's absolutist critique of advanced capitalism than Habermas may wish. This is the case even though Habermas has already distanced himself markedly from both Marxian and Frankfurtian concepts by moving to a procedural category of reason and to an increasing reliance on functional concepts (e.g., 1981, pp. 144-145, 150, Chap. 4; 1982, pp. 220-228, 231-232, 238-241, 253-254; cf. Heller, 1982).

NOTES

1. Because Habermas has never offered threshold conditions for realizing his communication theory, conditions that are procedural but yet empirical rather than idealized, critics have argued that his social theory as it stands contains authoritarian or dogmatic elements (e.g., Nielsen, 1979, pp. 278-279; Gadamer, 1967, pp. 32-33, 40-42; McCarthy, 1978, pp. 211-213; White, 1980; Ottmann, 1982, pp. 94-97; van den Berg, 1980, pp. 470ff.). Habermas's response to the charge has been decidedly very weak. He emphasizes the integrity of actors' "motivations," or "intuitive competences," and/or amenability to "therapeutic critique" to rehabilitate improper motivations.

2. Parsons's direct references to his appropriation of Fuller's procedural legality can be found in many of his writings (1968, 1969, 1970a, 1970b, 1971a, and elsewhere). Furthermore, Parsons's *use* of Fuller's legal theory pervades *all* of his work in social theory from at least 1966 onward; Parsons's own developments in social theory since the mid-1950s, furthermore, anticipated his collaboration with Fuller in the mid-1960s. A clear instance in which Parsons anticipated Fuller's legal theory was Parsons's first (1964) presentation of his evolutionary universals. Two clear instances in which Parsons used Fuller's legal theory were Parsons's insistence (1971a, pp. 86-137) that the United

States is "the lead society" rather than the Soviet Union and Parsons's critique (1977) of any and all attempts—even by his own student Robert H. Bellah—to reduce the importance of law's procedural standard of integrity to any other factors. Parsons rejected the reduction to economic factors (e.g., Marx or Milton Friedman), political or enforcement factors (e.g., Weber), sociocultural ideals of substantive "justice" (e.g., Roberto Unger), or to civil morality ideals of substantive "community" (e.g., Bellah). Parsons's 1977 article leads off a special two-issue number of *Sociological Inquiry* devoted to law and sociology; the second article is contributed by Fuller.

(3) See Jay (1974) on Archimedean point in this restricted sense. Bernstein (1983) and Nielsen (1979) correctly reject the Cartesian attempt to locate an absolute, substantive grounding.

(4) Another way of phrasing this point is that all of Parsons's concepts and categories of voluntaristic action function to restrain or mediate the most immediate realization of formally rational action, or the most immediate accommodation of the expansion of rationalization in Weber's sense. What Habermas is getting at with his standard of procedural reason that is "more comprehensive" than the norm of formal rationality is whether any noninstrumental factors can be said to be *reasoned* restraints or *reasoned* mediations. Commentators have not appreciated the great complementarity between Habermas's and Parsons's responses to the relativism of Weberian rationalization because, in part, each theorist has placed a subtle obstacle in the way. Habermas sees communicative action at times as complementing or merely balancing one-sided, Weberian purposive-rational action. The former is not then seen as necessarily being a restraint on the realization of the latter. Parsons, for his part, never addressed whether any aspects of voluntaristic action may be reasoned, as determined by some standard broader than the norm of formal rationality.

5. I review the 50-year literature on voluntarism, comparing it to my reading, in a forthcoming work (Sciulli, 1985b).

6. I cannot discuss Fuller's reasoning here, aside from the following schematic remarks. For Fuller, laws, or any other set of norms to be potentially acted on in common by pluralistic believers, aside from the norm of strict formal rationality, are not simply automatically recognized and understood in common; nor are they acted on in common, unless imposed by arbitrary power. Rather, they *may* be recognized and understood in common without being imposed by arbitrary power if eight procedures of rule-making or norm-setting are honored by authorities: (1) Involve general rules (rather than ad hoc dicta); (2) be publicized and made available to all affected; (3) be normally prospective (rather than retroactive); (4) be clear and understandable (at least to those trained in the law); (5) be free from contradiction, or demanding opposite actions from the citizenry; (6) be physically possible to perform by the typical citizen; (7) not be frequently changed; and (8) be congruent with the actual administration of enforcement (Fuller, 1969, pp. 46-84). Fuller's thesis is that enforced commands (bureaucratic) or subjectively acceptable votes (democratized) are not the law proper, or even potentially reasoned as norms, if they fail to conform fully to all eight procedures. Thus Fuller insists on the sharp distinction between the effective enforcement or purely subjective legitimation of rules and the governance of citizens assumed to be, at least potentially, reasoning and responsible agents. Commands or votes may be merely cues to enforcers, the latter controlled by the chain of command, to establish and maintain social control vis-à-vis actors not considered to be capable of reason or responsibility. In fact, Fuller's thesis is that as soon as any of the eight principles are violated, the latter view of actors is *necessarily* taken by enforcers, whether explicitly or implicitly. Why conform to the eight at all if

those being ruled cannot be expected to follow even clear rules or to take responsibility for violations? Conversely, why fail to conform to all eight procedures if one is attempting to govern reasoning and responsible citizens? Thus Fuller updates the common law "commonsense" understanding of when *the government* has become rebellious (i.e., has violated the rule of law); citizens who actively oppose such a government, in turn, are not rebels but, rather, are upholders of the law, whereas those citizens who do not oppose such a government are not reasoning and being responsible but are instead accessories to unreasoned rebellion (see Sciulli, 1985).

7. Parsons extends Fuller's standard of procedural legality in two important ways. First, any voluntaristic action, if it rests on some degree of mutual understanding, must conform to Fuller's eight principles or else it must be unambiguously internalized in common. Violations of any of the eight principles are a clear, empirical signal that even potential understanding (among citizens) is being subordinated to effective enforcement (by personnel against unruly human "means") or to purely subjective legitimation (unprincipled appeal to unquestioned, internalized affects). Second, any empirical collegial formation that maintains the integrity of that form against the pressures toward bureaucratization and/or democratization will *necessarily* institutionalize the upholding of the integrity of the eight principles as *the most minimal* fiduciary responsibility to its voluntaristic normative orientation. This can be put bluntly: *Any empirical organization that violates any of Fuller's eight principles could not possibly qualify as a collegial formation in Parsons's sense,* regardless how it recruits its personnel or deals with its personnel otherwise. If the eight principles are not being upheld within what *appears* to be a collegial formation (e.g., a university, a research or intellectual network, or a court proceeding), that is clear empirical evidence that either (1) voluntaristic norms are being imposed, with the collegial form actually being subordinated to the bureaucratic form, or (2) voluntaristic norms are being treated as arbitrary or decisionistic choices indifferently selected by the equality of opinion, and the collegial form is being subordinated to the democratized form. Within the limitations of this chapter, I can provide only a negative definition of the collegial form as restraining or mediating both bureaucratization and democratization; in other works I offer a positive definition and discussion.

8. Habermas's repeated reply to those who argue against the generalizability of his communication theory is to ask why they provide arguments at all, unless they too are *presupposing*—regardless of the content of their counterargument—that truth or rightness can be based on reasoned consensus. See, for example, the discussion sections in Geraets (1979) after the contributions by Apel, Habermas, and Kai Nielsen. To oppose Habermas's position without falling into this dilemma of conceding Habermas's case by even attempting to reason with counterarguments, one would have to resort to manipulation or force rather than to arguments. Of course, once one has made that latter choice, it is very easy to decide also to violate any and all of Fuller's eight principles and/or the integrity of Parsons's collegial form.

REFERENCES

Ackerman, B. A. (1977). *Private property and the constitution.* New Haven, CT: Yale University Press.

Ackerman, B. A. (1980). *Social justice in the liberal state.* New Haven, CT: Yale University Press.

Alexander, J. C. (1978). *Formal and substantive voluntarism in the work of Talcott Parsons:* A theoretical and ideological reinterpretation. *American Sociological Review,* 43, 177-198.

Alexander, J. C. (1983). *The modern reconstruction of classical thought: Talcott Parsons: Theoretical logical in sociology* (Vol. IV). Berkeley: University of California Press.

Bachrach, P. (1967). *The theory of democratic elitism: A critique.* Boston: Little, Brown.

Bachrach, P., & Baratz, M. S. (1970). *Power and poverty. Theory and practice.* New York: Oxford University Press.

Balbus, I. (1971). The concept of interest in pluralist and Marxian analysis. *Politics and Society,* 2, 151-177,

Bernstein, R. J. (1978). *The restructuring of social and political theory.* Philadelphia: University of Pennsylvania Press.

Bernstein, R. J. (1983). *Beyond objectivism and relativism: Science, hermeneutics and praxis.* Philadelphia: University of Pennsylvania Press.

Bershady, H. J. (1973). *Ideology and social knowledge.* New York: John Wiley.

Dahl, R. (1956). *Preface to democratic theory.* Chicago: University of Chicago Press.

Dahl, R. (1961). *Who governs? Democracy and power in an American city.* New Haven, CT: Yale University Press.

Dahl, R. (1967). *Pluralist democracy in the United States.* Chicago: Rand McNally.

Dahl, R. (1970) *After the revolution?* New Haven, CT: Yale University Press.

Dallmayr, F. R. (1976). Beyond dogma and despair: Toward a critical theory of politics. *American Political Science Review,* 70, 64-79.

Dallmayr, F. R. (1981). *Twilight of subjectivity: Contributions to a post-individualist theory of politics.* Amherst: University of Massachusetts Press.

Despres, L. A. (1967). *Cultural pluralism and nationalist politics in British Guiana.* Chicago: Rand McNally.

Fuller, L. L. (1969). *The morality of law.* New Haven, CT: Yale University Press.

Gadamer, H. (1967). On the scope and function of hermeneutical reflection. In *Philosophical hermeneutics* (pp. 18-43). Berkeley: University of California Press.

Habermas, J. (1968). *Knowledge and human interest.* Boston: Beacon.

Habermas, J. (1971). Some difficulties in the attempt to link theory and practice. In *Theory and practice* (pp. 1-40). Boston: Beacon.

Habermas, J. (1973a). *Legitimation crisis.* Boston: Beacon.

Habermas, J. (1973b). A postscript to knowledge and human interests. *Philosophy of the Social Sciences,* 3, 157-189,

Habermas, J. (1974). Legitimation problems in the modern state. In *Communication and the evolution of society* (pp. 178-205). Boston: Beacon.

Habermas, J. (1976). What is universal pragmatics? In *Communication and the evolution of society* (pp. 1-68). Boston: Beacon.

Habermas, J. (1977). Aspects of the rationality of action. In T. F. Geraets (Ed.), *Rationality today* (pp. 185-212). Ottawa: University of Ottawa Press.

Habermas, J. (1981). *The theory of communicative action, Vol. I: Reason and the rationalization of society.* Boston: Beacon.

Habermas, J. (1982). A reply to my critics. In J. B. Thompson & D. Held (Eds.), *Habermas: Critical debates.* Cambridge: MIT Press.

Heller, A. (1982). Habermas and Marxism. In J. B. Thompson & D. Held (Eds.), *Habermas: Critical debates* (pp. 21-41). Cambridge: MIT Press.

Jay, M. (1974). The Frankfurt school's critique of Karl Mannheim and the sociology of knowledge. *Telos,* 20, 72-89.

Kasfir, N. (1976). *The shrinking political arena: Participation and ethnicity in African politics, with a case study of Uganda.* Berkeley: University of California Press.

Lidz, V. M. (1979). The law as index, phenomenon, and element: Conceptual steps toward a general sociology of law. *Sociological Inquiry, 49,* 5-25.

Lijphart, A. (1977). *Democracy in plural societies: A comparative exploration.* New Haven, CT: Yale University Press.

Loubser, J. J. (1976). General introduction. In J. J. Loubser et al. (Eds.), *Explorations in general theory in social science: Essays in honor of Talcott Parsons* (2 vols. pp. 1-23). New York: Free Press.

Lowi, T. J. (1969). *The end of liberalism: Ideology, policy and the crisis of public authority.* New York: W. W. Norton.

Luhmann, N. (1976). Generalized media and the problem of contingency. In J. J. Loubser et al. (Eds.), *Explorations in general theory in social science: Essays in honor of Talcott Parsons* (2 vols., pp. 507-532). New York: Free Press.

Luhmann, N. (1984, August). *Society, meaning, religion—based on self-reference.* Paper presented at the American Sociological Association annual meeting, San Antonio, TX.

McCarthy, T. (1978). *The critical theory of Jürgen Habermas.* Cambridge: MIT Press.

McConnell, G. (1967). *Private power and American democracy.* New York: Knopf.

Nielsen K. (1979). Reason and sentiment: Skeptical remarks about reason and the "foundations of morality." In T. F. Geraets (Ed.), *Rationality today.* Ottawa: University of Ottawa Press.

Nozick, R. (1974). *Anarchy, state and utopia.* New York: Basic Books.

Ottmann, H. (1982). Cognitive interests and self-reflection: The status and systematic connection of the cognitive interests in Habermas' knowledge and human interests. In J. B. Thompson & D. Held (Eds.), *Habermas: Critical debates.* Cambridge: MIT Press.

Parsons, T. (1935). The place of ultimate values in sociological theory. *International Journal of Ethics, 45,* 282-316.

Parsons, T. (1936). Pareto's central analytical scheme. *Journal of Social Philosophy, 1,* 244-262.

Parsons, T. (1939). The professions and social structure. In *Essays in Sociological theory* (pp. 34-49). New York: Free Press.

Parsons, T. (1941). Max Weber. In *Essays in sociological theory: Pure and applied* (pp. 67-147). New York: Free Press.

Parsons, T. (1951). *The social system.* New York: Free Press.

Parsons, T. (1960). Pattern variables revisited: A response to Robert Dubin. In *Sociological theory and modern society* (pp. 192-219). New York: Free Press.

Parsons, T. (1961). The point of view of the author. In M. Black (Ed.), *The social theories of Talcott Parsons: A critical examination* (pp. 331-363). Carbondale: Southern Illinois University Press.

Parsons, T. (1962a). Law and social control. In W. M. Evan (Ed.), *Law and sociology: Exploratory essays* (pp. 57-72). New York: Free Press.

Parsons, T. (1962b). Review of "Law and social process" by Hurst. *Journal of the History of Ideas, 27,* 558-565.

Parsons, T. (1963a). On the concept of political power. In *Politics and social structure* (pp. 405-438). New York: Free Press.

Parsons, T. (1963b). On the concept of influence. In *Politics and social structure* (pp. 405-438). New York: Free Press.

Parsons, T. (1964). Evolutionary universals in sociology. In *Sociological theory and modern society* (pp. 500-514). New York: Free Press.

Parsons, T. (1968). Law and sociology: A promising courtship? In A. E. Sutherland (Ed.), *The path of the law from 1967* (pp. 47-54). Cambridge, MA: Harvard Law School.

Parsons, T. (1969). Polity and society: Some general considerations. In *Politics and social structure* (pp. 473-522). New York: Free Press.

Parsons, T. (1970a). The impact of technology on culture and emerging new modes of behavior. *International Social Science Journal, 22,* 607-627.

Parsons, T. (1970b). On building social system theory: A personal history. In *Social systems and the evolution of action theory* (pp. 22-76). New York: Free Press.

Parsons, T. (1970c). Equality and inequality in modern society, or social stratification revisited. In *Social systems and the evolution of action theory* (pp. 321-380). New York: Free Press.

Parsons, T. (1971a). *The system of modern societies.* Englewood Cliffs, NJ: Prentice-Hall.

Parsons, T. (1971b). Belief, unbelief and disbelief. In *Action theory and the human condition* (pp. 233-263). New York: Free Press.

Parsons, T. (1971c). Commentary. In H. Turk & R. L. Simpson (Eds.), *Institutions and social exchange: The sociologies of Talcott Parsons and George C. Homans* (pp. 380-399). Indianapolis: Bobbs-Merrill.

Parsons, T. (1973). Some reflections on post-industrial society. *Japanese Sociological Review, 24,* 109-113.

Parsons, T. (1974). Essay review of Harold J. Bershady: Ideology and social knowledge. *Sociological Inquiry, 44,* 215-221.

Parsons, T. (1975). Social structure and the symbolic media of interchange. In *Social systems and the evolution of action theory* (pp. 204-228). New York: Free Press.

Parsons, T. (1977). Law as an intellectual stepchild. Sociological Inquiry, 47, 11-58.

Parsons, T. (1978). A paradigm of the human condition. In *Action theory and the human condition* (pp. 352-433). New York: Free Press.

Parsons, T., & Gerstein, D. R. (1977). Two cases of social deviances: Addiction to heroin, addiction to power. In E. Sagarin (Ed.), *Deviance and social change* (pp. 19-57). Beverly Hills, CA: Sage.

Parsons, T., & Platt, G. M. (1973). *The American university.* Cambridge: Harvard University Press.

Parsons, T., & Smelser, N. J. (1956). *Economy and society.* New York: Free Press.

Pateman, C. (1970). *Participation and democratic theory.* Cambridge: Cambridge University Press.

Polsby, N. W. (1963). *Community power and political theory.* New Haven, CT: Yale University Press.

Rawls, J. (1971). *A theory of justice:* Cambridge: Harvard University Press.

Schattschneider, E. E. (1960). *The semi-sovereign people: A realist's view of democracy in America.* New York: Holt, Rinehart & Winston.

Sciulli, D. (1984). Talcott Parsons' analytical critique of Marxism's concept of alienation. *American Journal of Sociology, 90*(3), 514-540.

Sciulli, D. (1985a). *Toward societal constitutionalism: Principles from Habermas on legitimation crisis and Fuller on the problem of arbitrary power.* Paper presented at the annual meeting of the American Sociological Association, Washington, D.C., August.

Sciulli, D. (1985b). *Voluntaristic action: The reconstruction of a distinct concept.* Unpublished manuscript.

Sciulli, D., & Gerstein, D. R. (1985). Social theory and Talcott Parsons in the 1980s. In R. H. Turner (Ed.), *Annual review of sociology* (Vol. 11). Palo Alto, CA: Annual Review.

Truman, D. B. (1951). *The governmental process.* New York: Knopf.

Van Den Berg, A. (1980). Critical theory: Is there still hope? *American Journal of Sociology, 86,* 449-478.

Warren, R. L. (Ed.). (1977). *New perspectives on the American community: A book of readings.* Chicago: Rand McNally.

White, S. K. (1980). Reason and authority in Habermas: A critique of the critics. *American Political Science Review, 74,* 1007-1017.

Young, C. (1976). *The politics of cultural pluralism.* Madison: University of Wisconsin Press.

Chapter 2

PROLEGOMENA TO ANY FUTURE THEORY OF SOCIETAL CRISIS

MARK GOULD
Haverford College

A SOCIETAL CRISIS may be said to exist when there is the possibility that social disorder will lead to the transformation from one stage of societal development into another. It is the major contention of this chapter that *a theory of crisis can be successfully enunciated only within a conceptual framework that encompasses three dimensions: the functional, structural, and developmental.* In this chapter I present a snapshot discussion of each of these dimensions, tying my analysis to the theoretical traditions from which I draw. To further elucidate my argument I will suggest the relevance of this theory to one historical situation, that of early seventeenth-century England. Finally, I will explain why this three-dimensional framework allows for the formulation of a theory of societal crisis that is useful in examining a society even when we have no examples of societies more advanced in developmental progression. I do not articulate a theory of societal crisis in this chapter; instead I specify the tasks that must be completed if such a theory is to be successfully formulated.

FUNCTIONAL, STRUCTURAL, AND DEVELOPMENTAL ANALYSES

Concepts by themselves are neither true nor false; rather, they are useful (or not useful) in specific types of analysis. Thus a good concept is not "correct"; instead it helps, when used as an element in a proposition, to elucidate a relationship. Within the social sciences the most useful concepts have three foci: functional, structural (interactional), and developmental dimensions. The concepts used in a viable theory of societal crisis possess these three dimensions; such a theory is articulated across all three modes of analysis.

AUTHOR'S NOTE: A number of substantive footnotes were dropped from this essay owing to space limitations. These may be secured by writing the author at Haverford College, Department of Sociology-Anthropology, Haverford, PA 19041.

Units conceptualized for sociological analysis must be defined in terms of their function, that is, the consequences of their actions for the social system under analysis when that social system is taken as a whole. Our task is not to identify seemingly "objective," directly observable properties of the unit; "the objective forms of all phenomena change constantly in the course of their ceaseless dialectical interactions with each other. The intelligibility of objects develops in proportion as we grasp their function in the totality to which they belong" (Lukacs, 1971, p. 13) The proletariat, for example, must be defined with reference to the consequences of its actions for the capitalist system (cf. Marx, 1967, p. 182); the proletariat cannot be defined by noncontextual, "objective" attributes.

The second focus of good social concepts is interactional. This involves the identification of the unit's relational network, that is, its interactions with other units at the same level of analysis. Within certain contexts this may involve the specification of the organizational patterns with which these interactions occur; then this conceptual framework may be referred to as "structural." The proletariat is defined within the context of its interactions with the bourgeoisie, within the context of the sanctioned patterns that constrain this interaction.

The final focus of good social concepts is developmental. This reference involves a consideration of the potentialities of structural transformation inherent in the unit, forcing us to categorize it within the context of this potential for development and within the context of its past transformations. In other words, it is essential that we are able to conceptualize the stages of development for our units; in analyzing a particular manifestation of that unit, we must characterize it as falling within one or another of these stages. One asks with regard to a particular proletariat, at what stage in its development as a class is it to be found? Within a highly simplified two-stage model, is it a class in itself, or a class for itself?

The second level of conceptualization, the structural, deals with patterns of social interaction, where violation of the pattern implies (in the ideal case) a negative sanction (see Gould, 1979, pp. 10-11; Durkheim, 1964, p. 424). These patterns may be differentiated according to the stage of social development arrived at by the system under analysis; that is, each stage is said to be constituted by a specific structural pattern. The second and third foci are intimately related.

Structures will be analyzed within the context of a more general functional frame of reference. This does not involve functional, teleological explanations, but rather the provision of a coherent, analytically defined set of concepts within which it is possible to discuss social interactions.

Functional analysis is, to use economists' term, a form of macroanalysis (Ackley, 1961, Chap. 20). Units are categorized according to the consequences of their actions for the system as a whole, without reference to their organizational characteristics. Thus yearly production within the American economy consists in the sum of the production of all producing units, from independent artisans to General Motors.

When an analysis relates solely to one stage of social development, structural and functional analyses may be congruent. Here, in dealing with concrete social formations, we may restrict ourselves to discussing organizations characteristic of a particular stage. For example, so long as one discusses economically productive units only insofar as they are organized in a capitalist fashion and ignores productive units not so organized, even if found within the most highly developed "capitalist" economy, one's discussion will be congruent in its structural and functional dimensions. For all productive units within the discussion will be, by definition, of one type; thus an aggregative analysis—that is, "summing" these units—will not differ from a "structuralist" analysis, as the integrity of the organization is maintained in both cases.

Structural and functional analyses will differ in those cases in which an analysis is undertaken of a "concrete social system." As noted, functional analysis will treat all "productive organizations" alike, owing to their common, functionally defined consequences for the economy under examination. A structural analysis of the same system will focus upon the tendencies constituted by specific patterns of interaction between economic units. Both abstract from the concrete system, but the procedure of abstraction differs in the two cases. The focus of a functional analysis necessitates that the concepts be defined at a level of abstraction enabling them to encompass all varieties of social organization that might fall within their purview. The focus of a structural analysis involves the introduction of concepts that allow the articulation of an underlying structure, a structure not apparent upon a surface examination of appearances.

Thus although structural analyses are couched within a functionalist framework—the units are defined, in part, in terms of the consequences of their actions for the total system—they also involve the specification of an organizational context. They are, therefore, defined more narrowly than their functional counterparts. Propositions using functionalist concepts are "societal (social) universals" meant to be valid for all societies (social systems) (see Gould, 1976); propositions using structural concepts are meant to be valid only for the type of society (social system) to which they refer. Thus although functionally defined theory is valid for all stages of societal development, structuralist theory is valid for only one specific stage.

SOCIAL DISORDER AND SOCIAL CRISIS

Social disorders are motivated actions in violation of one or another institutionalized normative code within a society. They may result in attempts to redefine some component of social action or they may be constituted as violations of institutionalized norms without any attempt to reconstruct the system attacked. For example, deviance is a violation of a legal code within what Parsons calls the societal community. The deviant makes no attempt to redefine any component of the assaulted system; this is the case even when the deviance is subculturally legitimated. In contrast, revolutionary actions are violations of the political authority code that seek to redefine one or another component of the polity (values, norms, collectivities, or role relations). These attempts at reconstruction need not seek to, nor have the consequence of, transforming the stage of social development of the structure attacked.

The term "crisis" may be applied to the social system in which a particular form of disorder is occurring or to the disorder itself. In the latter case, a crisis is something more than a form of social disorder that endeavors to reconstruct the system under attack; in addition, the attempted reconstruction must have as a possible consequence the transformation of the system from one stage of social development into another. Only when this structural development is an objective possibility, whatever the goals of the actors under discussion, will I use the concept "crisis." Thus a crisis is a subset of social disorder; a crisis may be said to occur when there is the possibility that social disorder might lead to the structural transformation of a social system from one stage of social development into another.

The successful articulation of a theory of crisis is dependent upon our capacity to integrate functional, structural, and developmental perspectives. A structure describes a tendency of development. Marx, for example, retains the Hegelian "notion" within the context of his analysis of each stage of social development. His characterizations of these stages are tendential, specifying the constrained pattern of development, the logic of progression within a stage. These patterns are, of course, subject to countervailing pressures within the same logic, as well as to conjunctural imbalances and exogenous dislocations. Nonetheless, a structural analysis is necessary if we are to assess the constancy of the crisis. Is the conjuncture definitive of the crisis fortuitous and thus capable of successful, long-term amelioration? Or is the crisis a necessary consequence of the natural, patterned unfolding of the structure? In order to determine the answer to these questions we must be capable of specifying the natural, tendential development within the extant structure; this specification is the goal of a structural analysis.

The next question we must ask concerns the consequences of this tendential development. Will the natural unfolding of the system give rise to social disorder? In order to answer this question we must rephrase it; we may argue that a crisis is present only when the tendential development of a system gives rise to the necessary and sufficient conditions leading to a disorder "severe" enough to reconstruct the social formation. To make this argument we must have a theory of internal disorder, a theory that is couched in functionally defined concepts and is valid for all social formations. Only with such a theory is it possible to get outside of the structural, tendential model to define the meaning of an irresolvable contradiction.

Finally, most social disorders, even if they involve the reconstruction of some component of a social formation, do not lead to the transformation from one type of social formation to another. In order to assess this possibility we need a theory of societal development that allows us to order social formations as stages in the development of societies. Such a theory will allow us to determine when, for example, a revolution might lead to a new stage of society. If this theory is to be of assistance in evaluating the crisis potential of specific conjunctures in capitalist societies, it must be defined within a functionally conceptualized framework. If it is so formulated it will be possible to find empirical anticipations of postcapitalist societies in social systems of smaller scope than societies, social systems conceptualizable within the same framework we use to analyze societies. Thus it will be possible to formulate a quasi-empirical theory of future events, events of which we have no societal examples. It will, in other words, be possible for us to specify the type of social organization that would have to be created to secure the institutionalization of a new social order, an order marking an evolutionary development in the adaptive capacity of the system.

FUNCTIONAL ANALYSIS:
THE THEORY OF INTERNAL DISORDER

Theory using functionally defined concepts formulates societal (social) universals, propositions intended to be valid for all societies. Premised on the understanding that any system requires specifiable resources to adequately function, it asks about the consequences of the "withdrawal," for whatever reason, of one or more of the functionally defined inputs. Thus no claim is made that the resources are always present; rather, questions are asked about the consequences of the relative dearth or plethora of one or another of these inputs (see Gould, 1976).

A theory of internal disorder may be formulated within the context of this simple assertion. It is possible to enunciate a theory of subsystem output for each of the four functionally defined subsystems Parsons has identified. Elsewhere I have argued that determinant consequences occur when inputs to any of these subsystems fall out of balance. For example, if the "real" inputs to the polity exceed in scope the symbolic inputs to that subsystem, a deflation of power will occur. In this situation "governmental" coercion will be used in an attempt to maintain order. Power deflation will channel a possible social disorder toward the political system (cf. Gould, 1976).

A theory of internal disorder couples an analysis of imbalances affecting the generalized media of social action (including money, power, influence, and value-commitments) with a theory of social strain. Each of the four functionally defined subsystems provides factors of production to the other three subsystems (facilities from A, motivational resources from G, normative justifications from I, and evaluations from L); an imbalance steming from any of these imputs will generate social strain for the receiving subsystem. Depending on the location of strain, disorders will be directed at one or another of the components of social action (role relationships, collectivities, norms, and values). Depending on the location of the media imbalance, the disorder will be directed toward the affected subsystem. For example, a strain affecting goals, when coupled with a deflation of power, will generate a political disorder (revolution or riot) directed to the collectivity structure of the polity.

Internal disorders are categorized within a three-axis framework. First, the disorder will be directed toward the institutional structure centering on one of the four subsystems of the society under discussion. Second, the disorder will be directed at one or more units of social action within the institutional structure attacked. Third, disorders are classified as to whether they attempt to restructure the institution under "attack." Is the disorder solely negative or does it demand a positive redefinition of the extant system?

It is possible to specify the necessary and sufficient conditions leading to each of these 32 types of disorder. These variables are ordered within a value-added model (see Smelser, 1962; Gould, 1981b). As indicated above, the type of strain present among the prospective participants determines the level of action within the institutional structure that will be attacked: Strain at the level of facilities will result in an attack upon the structure of role relationships; strain at the level of goals implies an attack directed to collectivities; strain at the level of norms directs the attack to norms and value strain toward value orientations. The disorderly movement will be directed toward the institutional structure within which the medium deflation occurs; for example, influence deflation will direct the movement toward the societal community (*I*).

Participants in internal disorders may pass through a two-stage sequence in the commission and legitimation of these actions. Those is a situation of strain, in which power (or some other generalized medium) is deflated, will be prepared to commit riotous or revolutionary actions (or some other form of disorderly actions). They form a sub-culture of revolution (disorder). They have neutralized the commission of revolutionary (disorderly) acts. Those who have committed and legitimized revolutionary (disorderly) actions will form a revolutionary (disorderly) subculture (cf. Cloward & Ohlin, 1960; Matza, 1964). This legitimation is necessary if the actions and their advocacy are to be regularized. In a situation of potential crisis, the revolutionary sub-culture will provide direction for undertaking revolutionary actions, perhaps "motivating" their occurrence.

This theory of internal disorder—which can only be schematically presented here (see Gould, in press, Chaps. 2-3)—makes no reference to the organizational attributes of the system under examination. It is intended to be valid for all types of societal systems. Thus it seeks to specify the necessary and sufficient conditions for internal disorder for all societies. It makes no statement about the origin of these conditions and the capacity of the society to reconstitute itself. Thus it is possible that the genesis of a particular source of strain (or some other necessary condition) might be found in some exogenous, quite transitory, impingement on the system under examination. To assess the seriousness of the threat to the system, we must have some sense of the systemic nature of the variables involved. For this we must look toward a structural analysis.

STRUCTURAL ANALYSIS:
THE TENDENTIAL DEVELOPMENT
OF A SOCIAL FORMATION

As I noted above, a structural analysis seeks to articulate the tendential development constituting one stage in the development of societies.

TABLE 2.1
Types of Disorders

Type of Strain Present Within the System	Component at Which Disorder Is Directed	Is the Component Redefined?	Medium Deflated			
			Money	Power	Influence	Value-Commitment
At the Level of Values	Values	Yes		Total Revolution (REVOV)		
		No		(RIOTV)	Deviant Retreatism (DR)	
At the Level of Norms	Norms	Yes		Normative Revolution (REVON)		
		No		(RIOTN)	Deviant Conflict (DC)	
At the Level of Goals	Collectivities	Yes		Rebellion (REVOG)		
		No		(RIOTG)	Deviant Aggression (DA)	
At the Level of Facilities	Facility-Roles	Yes		"Faciliatory Rebellion" (REVOF)		
		No		(RIOTF)	Deviant Innovation (DI)	

NOTE: Only the disorders discussed in Gould (1979, and in press) are included.

Such an analysis is intended to be valid only for that stage; thus it is difficult to provide a general picture of this form of theory. Rather than trying, I will endeavor to encapsulate my analysis of one particular structure—that characterizing a manufacturing social formation. Later in the chapter I will saw a few words about the structural analysis of "late capitalism." (The three classic examples of this form of analysis are Marx, 1967; Lenin, 1960ff.,v. 3; and Weber, 1958.)

The early seventeenth-century English social formation was constituted in terms of a manufacturing economy, interpenetrated with rationalizing values and regulated by a patrimonial political structure. A manufacturing economy (in both agriculture and industry) is characterized, in its early phase, by the formal, but not the real, subsumption of labor under capital (see Marx, 1976, pp. 1019-1038). In other words, while the extraction of surplus value is the mode of appropriating surplus labor and product, the actual labor process characterizing precaptialist production is not altered. Increases in surplus value must come as increases in absolute surplus value or through increases in what I have labeled iterative surplus value. The latter merely refers to the multiplication of the units of production, allowing for increases in the amount of surplus extracted, but not altering either the rate of surplus value or the rate of profit.

This process is characterized by constant returns to scale; thus the competitive pressures that motivate capital accumulation in machine capitalism are not present. Thus it is possible that manufacturing organizations (i.e., economically productive units characterized as units of manufacture) might stagnate, rather than constitute the dynamic of the system. It is only when a primitive manufacturing economy is interpenetrated with a rationalizing set of values that the process of capital accumulation will be systemic for the affected actors. Here a tendential development of the system will be constituted; in the first instance characterized by the accumulation of iterative surplus value. The interpenetration of the Protestant Ethic with a manufacturing system (see Gould, 1981b) defined the economic mode of production predominant in seventeenth-century England.

Predominance may be interpreted in this context to suggest that the manufacturing mode of economic production constituted the structured path of development of the English economy. In other words, insofar as the economy developed along the path charted by its patterned constraints and controls, a secular process of capital accumulation was to be expected. In early seventeenth-century England, this system of economic production was regulated by, and in conflict with, a patrimonial political structure. It was the contradiction between these two structures that constituted the crisis of the English Revolution.

In early seventeenth-century England the political system was legitimized in terms of traditional values while nontraditional economic activities were predominant within the economic system. In patrimonial political structures, the ruler's powers are viewed as legitimate insofar as they fall within the confines of what are understood to be traditional values. This tradition does not entail the constant repetition of customary practice, but it does necessitate a legitimation of innovation in terms of perceived past practice. In response to innovations outside his or her control, a patrimonial ruler seeks to consolidate his or her powers by including extrapatrimonial areas within the realm of his or her "patriarchal" power. To do this it is necessary to develop a set of "servants" and a loyal "administration" whose use is at his or her discretion.

As Weber emphasizes, "The liturgical meeting of the ruler's political and economic needs is most highly developed in the patrimonial state. . . . For the ruler liturgical methods mean that he secures the fulfillment of obligations through the creation of heteronomous and often heterocephalous associations held accountable to him" (Weber, 1968,v. 3, p. 1095). This process may entail the establishment of economic monopolies as vehicles establishing political control over economic processes.

Both with regard to fiscal and administrative processes, patrimonial structures are characterized by an element of arbitrariness, which is claimed as a right (Weber, 1968,v. 1, p. 238). This arbitrariness is one element that comes in conflict with a developing manufacturing economy. Organizations based upon the systemic extraction of iterative surplus value—and thus a rational organization of formally free labor-producing commodities for sale to autonomous consumers—depend upon the capacity to calculate the consequences of specific actions and the regularity and impersonality of the responses to these actions. Thus although economic innovations were possible within a patrimonial political structure to an extent not possible in a strictly traditional structure, they were always in a precarious position under patrimonial rule. If your daily actions are subject to arbitrary sanction, the capacity to plan rationally, free from interference, is always subject to challenge. Even those persons in privileged situations are in a position in which the loss of favor brings ruin and destruction (Weber, 1968, p. 1099). Politics of this sort did not provide the conditions in which the new manufacturing economy could blossom.

Paradoxically, this situation of contradiction between political and economic structures resulted in increased demands being placed upon the polity and, correspondingly, in increased needs for economic resources by the polity. The latter led to attempts at extensive regulation and control over economic processes, both via administrative procedures and tax policies. Whereas a nascent capitalism seeks to establish an administration of honoratiores, subject to the influence of their peers and liable to negative economic sanctions when acting against the interests of their class, a patrimonial regime seeks to establish an administration dependent upon itself (p. 1091). In this context the continued domination of a patrimonial state continually ran counter to the private interests delimited within the manufacturing structure; but in England it did not succeed in appropriating these interests. Thus the manufacturing structures continued to create pressures for the expansion of economic production within the context of poltical controls upon that growth. These controls, inhibiting the opportunity for effective economic action, created strain at the level of goals for those controlling the economic organizations within the manufacturing structure.

At the same time, demands for greater political control over economic resources and activities resulted in a situation of power deflation, impinging upon the same socially structured positions. In the English case, not only was the level of economic resources sought by the government enhanced, but this occurred in a situation in which a primary source of political legitimation came from a state church discredited in the eyes of the nascent manufacturing bourgeoisie. Thus, to put it very simply, the economic resources sought by the government far exceeded the scope of authorization granted to governmental actions by a powerful segment of the population. As the contradiction between the two grew, power deflation grew in severity.

In the last two paragraphs I have introduced concepts from a functional analysis; strain at the level of goals and a deflation of power are two of the necessary conditions for the occurrence of a revolution seeking to reconstruct the collectivity structure of the polity. Without the functionally defined theory there is no way to assess the possible consequences of the structurally constituted tendential development I have presented. From the structural analysis we can conclude that "contradictions" exist in the system, but there is no way to assess the consequence of these contradictions. The logic of structural theory does not allow us to get outside of the structure it delimits.

Thus many Marxists have fruitlessly sought for the final crisis of machine capitalism when they were really looking at a series of business cycles, each of which in time created the conditions for the renewal of economic activity and capital accumulation. If our analysis remains within a structural model, we have no way to determine the resolution of events we may label "crises"; we have, in other words, no way to differentiate between crises (as I have used the term in this chapter) and cycles, where the latter are integral in the continued tendential development of the system under examination. But even with an integrated structural and functional theory, we still have no way of determining whether the predicted disorder will result in the transition from one stage of social development into another; to determine this we require a developmental theory.

DEVELOPMENTAL ANALYSIS: THE TRANSITION FROM ONE STRUCTURE TO ANOTHER

The developmental theory I have constructed generalizes Piaget's discussion of the stages of moral development. It articulates the structural relationships characteristic in each stage of this sequential progression. In the analysis of both cognitive and social systems the theory focuses upon structural relationships (not as in Kohlberg and Habermas, on normative principles). Here I will present only a very truncated picture of the theory, emphasizing its generality and its applicability to the situation of "late capitalist" social formations.

Piaget (1962) has articulated seven stages wherein children learn the practice of rules and become conscious of the significance of rules. My contention is that this theory can be generalized and made relevant to all "action systems," allowing us to elucidate empirical examples of stages that extend beyond contemporary societal development. The first stage in each sequence overlaps; thus the composite series has six periods. Stage Three in the sequence (Piaget's second stage of consciousness of rules) articulates hierarchical relationships, legitimized in terms of traditional values. Stage Four (Piaget's third stage in the practice of rules) is a stage of incipient cooperation. It involves innovations that anticipate the fifth stage; these are legitimized in terms of traditional values, drawn from the third stage. Stage Five (Piaget's third stage in the consciousness of rules) articulates formally egalitarian relationships. The structure of normative regulation is formally rational, wherein the justification of claims is made within the context of specifiable procedures.

The logic of this model is the same in dealing with societal development as in analyzing the structure of games in which moral judgment emerges. The following is a partial representation of societal development within this stage sequence model (see Figure 2.1).

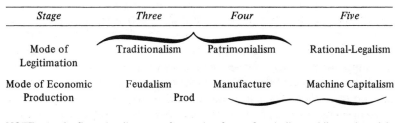

Stage	Three	Four	Five
Mode of Legitimation	Traditionalism	Patrimonialism	Rational-Legalism
Mode of Economic Production	Feudalism Prod	Manufacture	Machine Capitalism

NOTE: As the figure implies, manufacture is a form of capitalism, while patrimonialism is a form of traditionalism.

Figure 2.1

Piaget speaks of one additional stage (six), which he views as a codification of the norms defined in Stage Five. In fact there is also a seventh stage. While Stage Three concerns the institutionalization of hierarchical controls, identified with tradition, and Stage Five the institutionalization of egalitarian controls, identified with rational-legal legislation, Stage Seven institutionalizes equitable controls, which we will learn to recognize, at the societal level, as focusing upon the scientific, nonarbitrary control over decision making.

Equity is not based on formal equality; instead the definition of equitable "rights" involves a consideration of the different statuses of individuals. Although Piaget does not characterize a stage of development in terms of equitable relationships, he does comment that "in the domain of distributive justice it means no longer thinking of law as identical for all but taking account of the personal circumstances of each. . . . Far from leading to privileges, such an attitude tends to make equality more effectual than it was before" (1962, p. 317) Thus equitable structures transcend hierarchical and formally egalitarian relationships, as they maximize substantive equality along specifiable dimensions of social interaction. In this process the demand for homogenization that often accompanies formally equal norms is no longer prevalent. Thus equitable structures allow for the inclusion of a wider variety of actors within a given system, allowing for judgments upon their performance capacity rather than ideological characterizations of their abilities.

Within an organizational context characterized by equitable relationships, the basis for the evaluation of actors is their performance capacity. The substance of this evaluation, and thus the ranking of actors, must be specific to the situation under examination. But in every instance the principle of equity must be maintained and control over a situation vested in those able to act in ways capable of successfully implementing system goals. Thus although expertise is respected, it is understood to be reciprocal. For example, in a client-professional relationship, ultimate control over the quasi-experimental, clinical process must remain in the hands of the client, as he or she possesses greater expertise vis-à-vis the attainment of the process's collective goals.

I do not mean to imply that in Stage Seven all organizations will be guided at all times by equitable regulations. Rather, it is clear that there will be situations in which hierarchical and egalitarian relationships are appropriate in terms of the performance capacity of the system. In such cases, these types of relationships will be the natural consequence of equitable structures. What places equity higher in a series of developmental progression than either hierarchy or egalitarianism is that the reverse process of genesis is not possible within these earlier structures. When an equitable system has greater performance capacity it will not be generated by either egalitarian or hierarchical systems (cf. Parsons, 1961, 1966, 1971, 1977, Chap. 11).

SEVENTEENTH-CENTURY ENGLAND AND LATE TWENTIETH-CENTURY UNITED STATES

Within the context of our three-dimensional framework we can see why the English revolutions of the seventeenth century had the potential to generate the transformation from one form of social formation into another, more advanced in the system of social development. The manufacturing bourgeiosie (in agriculture and industry) took a leading role in the crucial stage of the revolution. These were the same persons who assumed a leading role in the process of capital accumulation, which led to the transformation of manufacture to machine capitalism. Whereas the former was grounded in the formal subsumption of labor under capital, the latter entailed the real subsumption of labor under capital. Thus machine capitalism involved revolutionizing the labor process that constituted the forces of economic production. This development altered the economic foundation that limited the form of political and other social structures that might be constructed on its base. Crucial in this process of economic transformation was the position of the nascent bourgeoisie. This class's capacity to accumulate capital within the predominant manufacturing economy was constrained by a patrimonial political structure. This impingement helped to generate the conditions necessary and sufficient to "motivate" revolutionary action. In addition, this developing bourgeoisie constituted a class with a future in the construction of an evolutionarily viable social formation. This coincidence did not ensure the progressive nature of their revolution, but it made possible its progressive consequences.

Put somewhat differently, in the seventeenth century, the manufacturing bourgeoisie could enunciate its views as universal principles. Because it was a class with a future, its focus was not primarily on the defense of traditional privileges; rather, it could state demands within an unstated problematic that necessitated the eventual articulation of universal rights (even when it was not so used by the revolutionaries themselves). Thus when the necessary and sufficient conditions leading to a revolution impinge upon groups with a future in the construction of the next stage in the developmental progression, they may legitimize a revolution in terms of progressive, universalistic demands; when they impinge on groups without such a future, they will enunciate reactionary, particularistic demands, usually entailing the preservation of some privilege. The former groups may work toward the reconstruction of the society in a progressive direction; the latter will most generally work toward goals that do not have this consequence.

In the space that remains I want to say a few words about the current situation in "late capitalist" social formations. It is easy to see that Figure 2.1 might be extended to include Stages 6 and 7, which we might label socialism and communism (see Lenin, 1960ff., v. 25, pp. 384-497). Socialism entails actions anticipating communism, legitimized in terms of the egalitarian values of Stage Five. Communism entails the construction of an equitable society.

Does the three-dimensional theory I have outlined enable us to say anything about the likelihood and nature of the crisis that will lead us into socialism? More specifically, what is the position of the proletariat in "late capitalism?" And does this position necessitate, or at least make possible, progressive activities? Insofar as the political actions derivative from the proletariat's position are variable, what can those of us who consider ourselves part of a socialist (or politically progressive) subculture do to help guide workers into progressive actions, actions that will help to reveal the true, oppressive nature of capitalism and manifest our capacity to transform it?

I have argued elsewhere (Gould, 1981a) that the relative isolation of American capitalism from competitive pressures in the post-World War II world allowed for a revaluation of American labor-power. This process included what I have labeled "credentialing," the utilization of more complex labor-power than that which is productively most optimum; in other words, credentialing involves the utilization of complex labor-power when simple labor-power is equally productive, or where the proportional difference in productivity is not equivalent to the proportional difference in complexity. Further, this revaluation included an increase in the bundle of commodities that were deemed socially necessary for the worker. Thus both the maintenance and reproduction components of the value of labor-power were increased.

This revalued labor-power became the socially necessary—the "normal, average"—labor-power used in production. As such, the value added in each hour's labor increased with the revaluation of labor-power; this entailed an increase in both the value of labor-power and in surplus value, and was thus in the mutual interest of both capitalist and worker. These were not purely "nominal" increases because of the continued growth in productivity within the American and international economies and owing to the fact that these processes were concentrated in the relatively monopolistic sectors of the American economy, characterized by considerable unionization. Thus income was redistributed to these sectors.

In the late 1960s these circumstances began to alter. As American hegemony waned in the international economy, an integrated economic system grounded in increasingly competitive production relations emerged. Within this new structure the most efficiently producing "monopolies" of an increasing number of American industries were challenged and socially necessary labor-power came to be redefined within the international system. In consequence, American labor-power that had previously been upgraded in value, to the benefit of both worker and capitalist, now appeared as high wages above its newly lowered value, to the detriment of capitalists. This situation, which is systemic and nonconjunctural, has generated a series of pressures to "devalue" American labor-power, pressures that will exacerbate in time. We have already witnessed real wages falling with inflation and the increased inclusion of a second or third family member into the labor force. The services workers receive from the state have declined while their percentage of the tax burden increases. Their unions are under siege; in some instances they have watched as their shops have moved from the Northeast and Upper Midwest to the less unionized sun belt or to non-American locales within the international economy. They watch as their schools fall under attack, at primary, secondary, and college levels. These and other pressures are not discrete; they are symptoms of the secular tendency to "devalue" labor-power. (I have analyzed some of these pressures in Gould, 1981a, parts of which I have paraphrased in this discussion.)

It is not yet possible to determine exactly what types of strain and deflation will be generated for the proletariat by these structurally constituted tendencies, as our analysis must first be placed within the context of the "late capitalist" social formation. Thus it is not yet possible to state categorically that these tendencies will result in a societal crisis. I believe, however, that they are likely to generate goal strain and a deflation of power among large sections of the proletariat, especially for those within primary labor market, unionized jobs. Goal strain will be manifest as opportunities for effective attainment of social goals diminish and power deflates, when and if political structures lose their legitimacy as they come to be seen as complicit within this process. The latter is a more speculative conclusion given the resiliency of parliamentary democracy. In order for widespread power deflation to occur the governmental structure must be held accountable, not merely as some set of incumbents.

These contradictions can result in reactionary as well as progressive movements. One might well want to argue that the pressures that I have described will lead to the genesis of particularistic movements seeking to preserve the relatively privileged position of the organized proletariat within American society. In what follows I am concerned to show that the proletariat should be viewed as a class with a future and not, as some "progressives" argue, as a class necessarily prone to reaction. I do not claim to have demonstrated that this progressive motivation will occur, but I would suggest that we must act so as to make this "claim" a self-fulfilling prophecy; the alternative is truly barbarism. Thus I will enunciate a set of principles that is consistent with, and perhaps deducible from, the discussion of the constituitive elements of a theory of social crisis; my hope is that these principles will command the allegiance of all progressives, nonsocialists, and socialists alike. If they do, it will be possible to form a progressive movement as the subculture within which a proletarian party might emerge.

There are three principles that must guide our actions: (1) We must recognize that workers are caught up within the ideational structures of the capitalist social formation; thus we must help enunciate programs that workers view as in their own interest within this structure. (2) These programs must be universalistic and inclusive; they must emphasize the need to include those previously excluded from, for example, primary-sector jobs in the work place. They must involve struggles against racism and sexism in order to allow persons to attain and freely use their performance capacities. (3) They must articulate, as a matter of principle and as a condition for success, the necessity of changing the institution under examination in the direction of an equitable structure, rather than focusing upon the transformation of those to be included. These principles entail a recognition of the structural constraints impinging upon the proletariat, the possible disorders that might emerge from these constraints, and the possibility that this disorder might emerge as a societal crisis. The actualization of the latter will require the proletariat's channeling its actions toward the construction of a new social formation. Thus each principle is derivative from one of the elements integral to a theory of societal crisis; only when they are grouped together as guidelines for political action will actions have the potentiality of concluding in the construction of a new social order. Unlike structural transformations in the past, the construction of an equitable social order will entail the conscious direction of social actions in the construction of equitable relationships, which will in turn provide the institutional base for further, more intelligently articulated action.

Rather than arguing these principles in the abstract I will conclude with an illustration of them. Some progressives argue for the necessity of job retraining programs to prepare previously excluded "underclass" Blacks and Hispanics for inclusion into primary-sector labor force jobs. Such a proposal, focusing on those excluded, has every potential for putting primary-sector white workers on the defensive and mobilizing them into reactionary coalitions against what most of my readers will agree is a desirable goal. However, if we redefine the process by which this goal is to be attained, the potential for including white, primary-sector workers into the coalition, while working to transform the structure of their work situation, will be manifest. The difference will be seen as between a course of action that unintentionally defines primary-sector, largely white and male workers as (1) reactionaries, guarding privileges, or as (2) members of a class articulating universalistic, progressive demands, a class with a future in the construction of a new social order.

It has been suggested that "underclass" Blacks and Hispanics would not be capable of adapting to the disciplined structure of the normal American labor process without considerable "retraining," being unaccustomed to such circumstances and responsibilities. But what if we imagine that labor process as constituted by small, worker-controlled, equitably structured task groups. Here loyalty is to the group; it is in the interest of the group to secure the adequate performance of each member. Thus responsibility for each and every group member's success is a group concern and the successful performance of the tasks assigned to each and every member a group necessity. In general, "underclass" Blacks and Hispanics will have had considerable experience in small-scale peer groups and will thus understand the forms of loyalty requisite for successful functioning in such groups. There is no reason to assume them incapable of assimilating the skills requisite for entry-level tasks within primary labor markets.

The goal I have defined is not merely the inclusion of previously excluded persons, but also the restructuring of the labor process in the direction of equitable forms, so as to allow for their inclusion in a manner making likely both their successful performance and the enhancement of the performance capacity of the group. It involves not merely an adaptation of the new workers to work, but an accommodation of the structure of work to the new workers. This accommodation involves meaningful benefits for those workers already working, benefits that can be made palpable in terms of both the conditions of work and wages (insofar as such task groups increase productivity and strengthen working-class solidarity). In addition, such actions against racism may make it easier for workers to legitimize other desirable consequences that may flow from these actions. At the most fundamental level these might include the preservation of jobs within the Northeast and Upper Midwest, where there are heavy concentrations of both unionized workers and Blacks and Hispanics. Thus these goals allow workers to act progressively, not only in regard to their already constituted interests (trade union consciousness) and vis-à-vis those marginalized within American society, but in regard to the transformation of the structures that constitute the society.

This program is not inconsistent with the extant structure of capitalist relationships. Currently most "worker control," "worker participation" programs are instituted by management to generate greater flexibility and productivity within the work place. Further, a consistent governmental pressure for the inclusion of Blacks in primary labor market jobs is not necessarily contradictory to capitalists' interests. Thus the proposals that I've described may be said to fall within the structure of the capitalist mode of production, a requisite for their success as reforms.[1]

I am not suggesting that the transformation of the labor process is a vehicle for the genesis of socialism. I am suggesting, however, that socialists (and other progressives) must learn to articulate goals and programs that are both progressive and in the immediate interests of workers. These goals must be geared to the accommodation of our institutions to those currently excluded, as a vehicle for constructing equitable organizations, which within the capitalist social formation will remain incomplete anticipations of socialist structures. But these organizations will also provide a social base from which further demands may be articulated by a more unified working class.

I am also suggesting that the secular tendencies currently impinging upon American workers will make them willing to listen to such programs. The potential for societal crisis in late twentieth-century United States is real. In time these pressures may place workers in a neutral position toward a potential revolution, at which point socialism and the transcendence of the capitalist social formation may become a realistic goal. It is clear that as we articulate this goal we will be competing with others who are already dangling reactionary programs before the proletariat.

CONCLUSION

I have argued in this chapter that a three-dimensional perspective is necessary if we are to construct a viable theory of societal crisis. Implicitly I have suggested that such a perspective must draw upon the work done by Marxists, Parsonian functionalists, and (Piagetian) developmentalists, among many others. If done successfully, this project can provide us with explanations for the crisis in seventeenth-century England that led to the emergence of the machine capitalist social formation (see Gould, in press); it can also provide insights into the form of social organization and political practice that will enable us to transcend the capitalist social formation. These explanations and insights are possible because the dialectical integration of the three perspectives allows for the transcendence of the problems inherent within each to be taken separately.

NOTE

1. This example emerged from discussions with Eric Abrahamson and Richard DiCarlo, two of my students.

REFERENCES

Ackley, G. (1961). *Macroeconomic theory.* New York: Macmillan.

Cloward, R., & Ohlin, L. (1960). *Delinquency and opportunity.* New York: Free Press.

Durkheim, E. (1964). *The division of labor in society.* (G. Simpson, Trans.). New York: Free Press. (Original work published 1893)

Gould, M. (1976). Systems analysis, macrosociology, and the generalized media of action. In J. Loubser & R. C. Baum (Eds.), *Explorations on general theory in social science: Essays in honor of Talcott Parsons.* New York: Free Press.

Gould, M. (1977). *Development and revolution in science.* Unpublished manuscript, Max Planck Institute, Starnberg, West Germany.

Gould, M. (1979). *The coming of the English revolution.* Unpublished doctoral dissertation, Harvard University, Department of Sociology.

Gould, M. (1981a). The devaluation of labor-power. *Berkeley Journal of Sociology, 26.*

Gould, M. (1981b). *Marx? Weber: The role of ideas in social action.* Paper presented at the annual meeting of the American Sociological Association, Toronto, Canada.

Gould, M. (1981c). Parsons versus Marx: An earnest warning. *Sociological Inquiry, 51*(3-4).

Gould, M. (in press). *Revolution in the development of capitalism.* Berkeley: University of California Press.

Lenin, V. I. (1960). *Collected works.* London: Lawrence & Wishart.

Loubser, J., & Baum, R. C. (Eds.). (1976). *Explorations on general theory in social science: Essays in honor of Talcott Parsons.* (2 vols.) New York: Free Press.

Lukacs, G. (1971). *History and class consciousness* (R. Livingston, Trans.). Cambridge: MIT Press. (Original work published 1922)

Marx, K. (1967). Capital (3 vols.) (S. Moore & E. Aveling, Trans.). New York: International Publishers. (Original work published 1867)

Marx, K. (1976). Capital (Vol. 1) (B. Fowkes, Trans.). Harmondsworth: Penguin.

Matza, D. (1964). *Delinquency and drift.* New York: John Wiley.

Parsons, T. (1961). Some considerations on the theory of social change. *Rural Sociology, 26,* 219-239.

Parsons, T. (1966). *Societies: Comparative and evolutionary perspectives.* Englewood Cliffs, NJ: Prentice-Hall.

Parsons, T. (1971). *The system of modern societies.* Englewood Cliffs, NJ: Prentice-Hall.

Parsons, T. (1977). *Social systems and the evolution of action theory.* New York: Free Press.

Piaget, J. (1962). *The moral judgment of the child.* (M. Gabain, Trans.). New York: Collier Books. (Original work published 1932)

Smelser, N. (1962). *Theory of collective behavior.* New York: Free Press.

Weber, M. (1958). *The Protestant Ethic and the spirit of capitalism.* (T. Parsons, Trans.). New York: Free Press. (Original work published 1904-1905)

Weber, M. (1968). *Economy and society.* Kansas: Bedminster. (Original work published 1922)

Chapter 3

PREDICTING TECHNOLOGICAL INNOVATION THROUGH A DIALECTIC REINTERPRETATION OF THE FOUR-FUNCTION PARADIGM

INO ROSSI
St. John's University

THE READER OF this chapter should not expect a disquisition of "straight" Parsonian thinking, but rather an idiosyncratic application of some Parsonian ideas heavily influenced by a dialectic view I have been developing in connection with and in reaction to certain strains of structural and poststructural semiotics (Rossi, 1974, 1982b, 1983). My attempt has been prompted not only by theoretical convictions stemming from a long reflection on apparently odd paradigms, but also by that open-mindedness I have always appreciated in Talcott Parsons on the occasion of his participation in sociological sessions I have organized on continuities among presumed "odd paradigms"; he gladly and promptly agreed to contribute to a volume I put together on the interface between classical sociological traditions and modern French Structuralism as a follow-up to those sessions (Rossi, 1982a). It is in continuation of that spirit and in the memory of an "ecumenical" and great sociologist (especially in a seminal sense) that I write this chapter, apparently so different from his sociology, but in fact so close, I think, to its spirit.

Let me state at the outset that I can somewhat relate to the neofunctionalist paradigm as described by Jeffrey Alexander in a past issue of "Perspectives" (1983, p. 2). According to Alexander, the essential requirements of the neofunctionalist paradigm are the following: (1) society must be conceived as an intelligible system whose parts interact without a priori or monocausal determinism; (2) the attention of the sociologist should be on the regulation of means by ends and (3) on integration as well as deviance.

In this chapter I will argue in reference to Alexander's first point that I do not concur with the Parsonian cultural determinism (even in its cybernetic version) because I see the four subsystems of action, or rather the components of the four-function paradigm, in dialectical-constitutive interaction with each other. As to the third point, I suggest that by

73

adopting a dialectical interpretation of the four-function paradigm, one cannot focus on integration without focusing also on internal tensions. In fact, the very possibility and dynamics of any action system rests on the reciprocal dialectical-constitutive tension of its four systemic functions. I may add that Alexander himself speaks about tensions produced by the interpenetration of the subsystems of action.

At the same time, I feel in a more generous mood than Alexander does because I am willing to add to his list of the essential components of neofunctionalism the four-function paradigm. I agree with Alexander that "Parsons' functionalist theory is highly ambivalent, even contradictory"; I agree with him even more when he describes the emerging (hoped for?) neofunctionalism as a "broad intellectual tendency" that reaches out "to incorporate elements of purportedly antagonistic theoretical strands" (Alexander, 1983, p. 2). I suggest that a dialectical perspective, at least as I define it, is not antagonistic to the action frame of reference because it enables one to reconcile and develop, respectively, diverse and inchoate elements of the Action Theory. I have to qualify that I am not talking of a dialectic of opposites but of what in a recent work I have called a dialectic of mutually constitutive oppositions (Rossi, 1983, pp. 14 ff.). Not only is such a dialectical orientation consistent, at least in a developmental sense, with Parsons's orientation, but, as I shall argue, it seems also substantiated by Parsons's own substantive analyses.

As I have already mentioned, the ultimate justification of the thrust of this chapter lies in my theoretical orientation. Having recently glanced through the Alexandrian quatrilogy, I have pleasantly realized that both of us have been moving in parallel directions. Like Alexander (1982, pp. 5ff.), during the last 10 years I have been reacting against a positivistic conception of science. Having undergone empiricist training in this country first, and a French structuralist exposure next, I strongly sympathize with Alexander's contention that we need to formulate a "synthetic, multidimensional epistemological position" (Alexander, 1982, p. 68). For Alexander a multidimensional understanding is necessary to grasp the relationship between subject and object and to overcome the dichotomies of idealism versus materialism, and voluntarism versus the primacy of external conditions—dichotomies that have pervaded our sociological tradition (Alexander, 1982, pp. 67ff.). I have proposed a synthetic approach myself but not of a multidimensional nature. Rather than proposing a "multiple or universal or integrated paradigm" (See in Rossi, 1983, p. 1313), I have formulated a dialectical perspective that keeps distinct but complementary the objective and subjective principle; hence structure and subjectivity are seen in a mutually con-stitutive relationship (Rossi, 1983, p. 32). Alexander correctly sees the need to avoid the dualism implied in the acceptance of either the materialist or idealist position and to integrate elements of both into a synthetic approach. I had myself originally accepted Levi-Strauss's epistemological position to avoid the empiricist dualism of subject and object, but subsequently I have attempted to avoid the staticity of Levi-Strauss's universal deep structures with a dialectical integration of struc-ture and subjectivity, somewhat inspired by the phenomenological and Marxist semiotics of poststructuralist orientations.

Alexander and I agree on the need for a synthetic approach but perhaps not on the dialectical nature of such an approach. Alexander argues that because social action is "in part voluntary, in part determined" we can conceive it as composed of an interpenetration and combination of both elements (Alexander, 1982, p. 67). My question is how such combination and interpenetration is possible if the normative and con-ditional components of social action are, as Parsons states, in a state of tension (Parsons, 1937, p. 732)? Are we to understand the notions of "interpenetration" (for a recent statement see Münch, 1981, 1982; Alexander, 1978) and "differentiation" in a dialectical rather than in a multidimensional sense? As presented, the notion of "multi-dimensionality" seems to imply the combination (or juxtaposition?) of two dimensions, each one of which is self-contained and intelligible in-dependently of the other. To me such an interpretation would represent a typical example of dichotomous-positivistic thinking, which renders impossible an integrated synthesis of subsystems because of their very conceptualization as analytically self-intelligible and self-sustaining sub-systems. For this reason I maintain that neither the subjective or the objective principle is intelligible and/or possible without the constitutive opposition of the other.

Under Alexander's suggestion I have agreed to scrutinize the notion of "code" as used by Parsons and recent action theorists to see what light this notion may shed on this issue.

ON THE TRADITIONAL VIEW OF
THE FOUR SYSTEMS OF ACTION

Parsons and the Cybernetic Hierarchy of Control

I have already stated that I find useful Parsons's distinction among the four subsystems of action but that I prefer to dialecticize their rela-tionship. Let me briefly point out some Parsonian elements that seem to imply, or at least find, a resolution in a dialectical view. In their 1965 work Parsons, Shils, Naegel, and Pitts referred to the cultural and social system as follows: "However empirically interdependent they may be, [they] should be kept analytically distinct" (1965, p. 34); the two systems are well integrated and interpenetrated through the mechanism of institutionalization, which makes "the relationship between the two so intimate." The structure of social system "consists in institutionalized patterns of normative culture. It consists in components of the organisms or personalities of the participating individuals only so far as these . . . interpenetrate . . . with the social and cultural systems, i.e., are internalized in the personality and organism of the individual" (p. 36).

The interpenetration of the subsystem takes place through "a hierarchy of relations of control." For instance, "the social system . . . controls . . . the personality system" in a twofold way: through various social actors composing the situation and by making the individuals internalizing "institutionalized patterns of normative culture" (p. 36). The control of the social system is so pervasive that even "individuality and creativity are, to a considerable extent, phenomena of the institutionalization of expectations" (p. 38). Here Parsons seems to hint at an element of tension in the relationship between the personality and social systems, but he does not elaborate on it. In fact, the hierarchy of control is so pervasive that it characterizes not only the relationships among the four subsystems but also the relationship among the components of each subsystem. For instance, the cultural system is composed of a "four stage hierarchy of ultimate grounds of meaning" (p. 971). Parsons finds support for the notion of hierarchical control in the morphemic, lexical, syntactical, and phraseological levels of language (p. 975), language offering a model for the analysis of culture (p. 974).

Once again, Parsons seems to sense the inherent limitations of cultural determinism in dealing with voluntaristic social action. For instance, in his 1965 work, he often states that among the four subsystems of action there is no one-way influence but an interaction and "complex feedback effects on each other" (p. 979). Parsons, however, roots these feedbacks in maladjustments within the system; they consist in "the pressure of strains in the personalities and of the society" and in "tensions involved in commitments and structural strains" (p. 979).

However, these fleeting remarks on tensions and strains take place within the perspective of the hierarchy of control, which, at most, seems only temporarily challenged and reconstituted at a higher level. As Parsons himself states, he is strongly committed to "maintain an ordered cognitive picture of the system." In one of his recent collection of essays

Parsons reinstates the notion of the interdependence and interpenetration of the personality and social system, but he also reiterates that they are analytically independent of each other and allow for personal creativity, autonomy (1977, p. 197), and freedom (p. 131); again, how creativity and autonomy are analytically grounded is not explained.

In Parsons's recent works one finds the notion of "interpenetration" as a recurring theme, but he speaks at the same time of "interactional transaction" among the components of the social action systems (p. 116). He also speaks of "distressingly complex" interactions and of the interrelationship of ideal and real factors (p. 131). Parsons also pays attention to the autonomy of personality, which "is grounded in the personality's interchanges with the cultural and organic level of organization of action" (1977, p. 197). But what is the nature of the interchanges that can take place within such a tight hierarchy of cybernetic control?

In his latest collection of essays, Parsons classifies the four systems of action into a collective component (social system and cultural system) and an individual component (behavioral system and personality system). However, the cybernetic hierarchy of control is still dominant (Parsons, 1978, pp. 374-380, 388, 391, 419) and we are left with the malaise of having to cope with the overarching leviathan of culture, a problem once social scientists had to phase with Kroeber's notion of culture as superorganic (and Kroeber elaborated with Parsons that famous definition of culture).

However, a close reading of some substantive analyses of Parsons generates a less deterministic and a more dialectic view of social action.

Parsons's "Substantive" Dialectic

I focus my attention on Parsons's analysis of the relation between personality and the social system, which is at the heart of my concern. In *Social Structure and Personality* Parsons derives from Freud and Durkheim his views on "the internalization of normative culture in the personality of the individual" (1964, p. 2). Parsons argues that American values provide conceptions of what's desirable for the society as such and "patterns of evaluation of the individual" (p. 277). In American society there is no goal to be attained by the society as a whole. The activities of society are "fundamentally dependent on the capacity and commitments of the human individuals" who have "the liberty to pursue goals which to [them] may seem worthwhile" (p. 278). "For the individual, the primary focus of evaluation is universalistically judged achievement" (p. 279). Does Parsons imply a sort of "societal consensus of individual goals" or perhaps an identity of group goals and individual goals that anthropologists have found to characterize preliterate homogeneous cultures (Lee, 1959)? This position would seem to be implied by his cultural determinism, which appears to ensure that individual freedom and achievement automatically sum up to societal achievement. Parsons explicitly states, "to the individual the most important goal to which he can orient himself is a contribution to the good society" (1964, p. 160). To Parsons this position is a consequence of Weber's "inner-wordly asceticism" whereby "the individual is committed to maximal effort in the interest of valued achievement"; hence, the individual "tends to maximize the desirability of autonomy and responsibility" (p. 159). But he immediately qualifies this by stating, "yet this is an institutionalized individualism, in that it is normatively controlled at the moral level": First, the individual must be committed to a good life not only for himself but for all society; second, "autonomy and responsible achievement" are regulated by normative order or "a moral law that defines the relations of various contributions and the patterns of distributive justice" (p. 160).

But should we assume there is an immutable, once and for all, given image of good society and/or distributive justice? Don't all the efforts of social legislation, constitutional clarifications, and civil rights movements document the continuous redefinitions or at least progressively deeper understanding of the societal image? For this reason we must recognize the importance of individual versus societal tension over what is or ought to be a "good society." Anthropologists have put forward the thesis of the importance of a balance between the "pull" and "press" of culture (Goodman, 1967) and between the integration and individuation of the person in society (Radin, 1971). I shall propose later on the notion that the function of the cultural code should be to ensure the balance of the innovative and conforming capacities of the individuals in society.

In his analysis of the role of youth in American society Parsons appears sensitive to this issue and seems to open up his monolithic cultural determinism: The nature of the American value pattern and the nature of the process of change "makes individual adjustment very difficult" (1964, p. 164). On the one hand, one hears emphasizing personal responsibility and autonomy; on the other hand, one must reiterate the need to conform to collective norms of cooperation. All too often the individuals are relegated to specialized contribution so that "it is not always easy to see their bearing on the larger whole" (p. 164). Parsons himself admits there is a continuous bettering of the standards of minimum welfare and of distributive justice as shown in shifting social and political emphases (p. 164).

In my view these statements, and others that could be quoted, do not represent anomalous Parsonian statements in respect to the purity of the hierarchy of control in the AGIL paradigm, but, rather, they throw light on what the core of Parsonian thinking really is; that is, the cultural code cannot be conceived as a monolithic, unidirectional, and immutable controlling force. Perhaps the cultural code cannot be defined in terms of value content, but rather as a deep structure ensuring the coordination of the AGIL functions in reciprocal dialectical relations (adaptation, goal attainment, integration, latency). The essential function of the cultural code ought to be to ensure a continuously dynamic achievement of the balance between individual fulfillment and societal welfare.

Parsons himself outlines some of the elements of this reciprocally constitutive dialectic. The most general orientation of the American value system is "instrumental activism," which he explains as follows: "The society is conceived to be not an . . . end in itself. . . . The society exists in order to . . . facilitate . . . the achievement of the good life for individuals" (p. 196). Here we have the first dialectical pole of the cultural code, the constitutive contribution of the personality system by the social system. Then Parsons goes on to state that the American value system places the individual in an instrumental position: "His [individual] goal cannot be self-indulgence or the maximization of the gratification of his personal wishes, but must be achievement in the interest of the good society" (p. 197). This is, of course, the other pole of the constitutive dialectic. Then Parsons immediately concludes as follows: "The society itself does not, however, tend toward a specific goal, but rather to a prospect of progressive improvement of the level of realization of its values." Here Parsons explicitly refers to the dynamic tendency toward the fulfillment of the "ideal" good society and the dialectical tension between the real and ideal societal images as an important propellant toward the realization of societal values.

However, Parsons seems to ultimately uphold an interactional synthesis of the two dialectic poles with a priority attributed to society (hence a nondialectical synthesis). He states that the individual has "the obligation of contribution to the goodness of the society" and "the criteria of what is worthwhile are socially given." On the other hand, he adds that "the implementation of his obligation is left very largely within his own discretion" (p. 198). It is here where Parsons does not go far enough. I am not so convinced of the analytic priority of societal standards because they are continuously redefined and certainly more and more deeply understood; this also happens for the continuous challenges and inputs of individuals. This is what Parsons himself states at the end of his essay on youth in American society: "American society is not doing reasonably well in implementing [his] values" vis-à-vis rapid industrialization, immigration of heterogeneous groups, and shifting power relations with the outside world. "It is impossible for youth to be satisfied with the status quo, which must be treated only as a point of departure for the far higher attainments that are not only desirable but also obligatory" (p. 182). This is a well-taken point that expresses my notion of cultural code as the deep structure (or logic) of the balance between individual fulfillment and societal welfare.

As Parsons states, the ferment of American youth "expresses many dissatisfactions with the current state of society, some of which are fully justified, others are of a more dubious validity" (p. 182). This is precisely the sense in which structure is constituted (tested out and reshaped) by the continuously changing subjectivity, and, conversely, the latter is shaped by existing values. In this sense only a dialectical tension beween structure and subjectivity can guarantee an optimal realization, or at least a striving force toward the realization of the ideal image of society.

But can we argue that this conception of deep structure is contained in the notion of cultural code as proposed by Parsons and recent theorists of action?

Parsons's Cybernetic View of Systems Interpenetration

Not only Parsons's substantive analyses but also certain passages of Parsons's own theoretical works seem to preannounce some elements of the dialectic view I am advocating. The social system and personality systems "interpenetrate in the sense that no personality system can exist without *participation* in a social system, by which we mean the integration of *part* of the social system. Conversely, there is no social system which is not from one point of view a mode of the integration of *parts* of the systems of action which constitute the personalities of the members" (Parsons & Shils, 1951, p. 109). The notion that no system can exist without partial participation in other systems comes very close to my notion of the mutual constitutiveness of subsystems in dialectical interaction with each other. However, this notion of interpenetration has severe limitations. How can a system be a "part," although partially, of another system and still preserve its analytical distinction? It does not make sense to consider a part of a system as a part of a different analytical system because what gives analytical distinctiveness to a "part" (if such a statement can be made at all) is not its "content" but its structural relationship to the other parts; such a structural relationship is not transferable to another system. This amounts to saying that Parsons, like other empiricists, thinks in terms of "content," and not of "structure" as a logical organization of reality (Levi-Strauss, 1976, p. 115).

Parsons and Bales offer further clarifications on this issue: "Personalities and social systems are not directly homologous; they are differently organized about different foci of integration and have different relations to the sources of motivational energy. But they are more than merely . . . analogous . . . they are literally . . . *made of the same stuff* . . . they are not merely interdependent, they interpenetrate. Above all, it is important that the focus of organization of both types of systems lies in certain aspects of the relevant cultural patterns . . . these are not merely . . . *the same kind* . . . of cultural values, they are literally the same values looked and analyzed in terms of different system-references" (1956, pp. 357-358). This explanation seems to contain an embryonic structural explanation because it refers to the "focus of organization," but their perspective led them to insist on "the same stuff," "the same kind" of values, that is, on "content."

Interestingly enough, Parsons and Shils themselves speak of a "homology to refer to certain formal identities between personalities and social systems," but, then, they immediately continue as follows: "When we use the term homology to refer to certain formal identities between personalities and social systems [they] are to be understood in terms of the above considerations" (1951, p. 109), that is, the integration of a part of one system into another. Again, the limitations of the empiricist framework are evident when they conceptualize formal similarities in terms of "partial" integration of content into different subsystems.

In addition to the static perspective implied by these considerations, I also find objectionable Parsons's cybernetic, hence deterministic, view, whereby values are held to control both the social and personality systems. I claim that no value system is possible or even conceivable without the notion of its translatability into normative structures (social system) and its internalization into the personality system. My position is that the four subsystems constitute each other through their distinctive but complementary differences. By definition each subsystem must remain analytically distinct in its organizational focus from the others; but at the same time, the subsystems constitute each other in the sense that no such system is explainable without its reciprocal counteropposition to the other subsystems.

Does Parsons's notion of "code" do justice to or at least is it compatible with the view I am proposing? According to Parsons, social interaction entails a set of interacting units and "a set of rules or other . . . code . . . factors, the terms of which structure both the orientations of the units and the interaction itself" (Parsons, 1977, p. 163). Parsons takes the notion of code from linguistics; any social phenomenon is a mechanism of communication, of which language is the paramount model (Parsons, 1961, p. 972). He refers to the message function and the code function of language; he defines the latter as "a set of rules and forms by which intentions are expressed" (p. 163). From these considerations he draws the notion of code as "the symbolic frame of reference within which meaningful utterances can be formulated" (1961, p. 113). In the latter part of his career Parsons has been frequently postulating a functional analogy between the DNA, the deep structure of language and symbols (Parsons, 1961, pp. 113, 143, 189; see also Rossi, 1982a, pp. 49-65). Parsons even goes as far as using the linguistic notion of "generativity" to suggest that the deep structure can produce an indefinite number of surface structures through rules of transformation (Parsons, 1978, p. 397).

However, the notion of code in linguistics and biology is used in a much more technical and certainly more precise way than how it is used by Parsons. Elsewhere, I have shown that in biology the notion of code has a precise mathematical meaning (Rossi, 1983), as it refers to the dictionary used by the cells to translate through a mathematical formula the four-letter language of nucleic acids into the 20-letter language of proteins; the four letters of nucleic acids read three at a time, produce 64 triplets (Rossi, 1983, p. 167). In *Theories of Society* Parsons makes abundant references to Jakobson and Halle (1961, pp. 971-975; 1977, pp. 113, 245). But, this is how Jakobson defines the code: "a fixed transformation, usually term by term, by means of which a set of information units is converted into a sequence of phonemes and vice versa" (quoted in Bourricard, 1981, p. 173).

There is no one who cannot see the technical and mathematical nature of such a definition in comparison to Parsons's very generic usage of code as a normative structure and cybernetic mechanism of control (on this point see Rossi, 1983, pp. 185, 189). The reason for this vaguely analogic usage of code is that the empiricist (though not exaggerated empiricism [see Rossi, 1983, p. 193]) and dualistic perspectives prevent Parsons from adopting a meta-empirical and mathematical notion of cultural code. This is the same reason why he adopts a definition of code not in terms of structure but of content. In the definition of culture jointly prepared with Kroeber, Parsons refers to culture as "transmitted and created *content* and patterns of values, ideas, and others" (quoted in Bourricard, 1981, p. 175, emphasis added).

At this point it is telling to use the words of an action theorist who qualifies Parsons's notion of code as a jumbled and confused one (Gould, 1976, p. 498). At best, Parsons's notion of code is a vague analogy that does not add any analytical power or corrective to his cybernetic, and hence undialectical and culturally deterministic, perspective.

Do we fare any better when we examine the works of other action theorists?

Neoaction Theorists on the Cybernetic View of Culture and Cultural Code

For V. Lidz "culture consists of the system of stable beliefs . . . that impart enduring patterns to the meanings that may be generated in action process. . . . Cultural beliefs are . . . constraining . . . objects of respect" (Lidz, 1976; 126). Culture "stabilizes in the realm of belief some ground of action to which there can be general and common adherence" (ibid). Hence, culture is a "form of pure meaning," that is, meaning free from embodiment in psychological and interactional contingencies. Social systems refer to "interactive relationships among persons"; it focuses "upon the ways in which constraining social relationships may operate to determine courses of action" (p. 128). Lidz argues that we need "an acute conception of social structure" to understand both the enduring features of social relations as well as "openness to change or transformation" (p. 129). Yet, he continues, Action Theory has focused the treatment of social structure on normative entities. The reasons being that "if individual actions within a social system were in a radical sense truly free to pursue the satisfaction of their own wants and interests in whatever way they found expedient, social life would be profoundly chaotic" (ibid).

In the following discussion Lidz refers to such structural constraints as authority, law, elite, and, in the wake of Durkheim, general "moral constraints" of the social system. Social structure is referred to as "institutionalized normative culture" that establishes stable social constraints; the latter serves as a fixed reference point through which the activities of social actors can be coordinated and "interdependence among discrete pursuits" can be achieved. Lidz's emphasis on the coordination and interdependence of free wills and "disparate pursuits" (ibid.) leaves unaccounted for the uncoordinated, noninterdependent, and conflictual interaction.

When discussing the personality system, Lidz still pays attention to the cultural and social systems that "define enduring models for action and establish constraints upon the possibilities for action"; "personalities serve to select among the many desirable potentialities for action just those projects which may fulfill the needs the desires of individuals" (p. 132). In a word, culture and the social system remain in Lidz's analysis the great leviathan, or a sort of Kroeberian "Superorganic," which controls the range of variations of the personality and social systems. The superorganic view is an inevitable corollary of the cybernetic view whereby "components high in information guide and regulate . . . components low in information and high in energy" (Effrat, 1976, p. 666). Parsons has candidly admitted to be a "cultural determinist," but his followers are no less so. Then, can they develop a more viable notion of code?

Lidz raises the question of how the four subsystems of action communicate with each other and coordinate their processes. Phrased differently, how is it possible for concrete social action to be in simultaneous relationships with all four subsystems? The answer has to be found in the symbolic media of exchange of which language is the paramount model. Lidz refers to Parsons's distinction between code and message that is taken from Jakobsen and Halle (Lidz, 1976, p. 137). But Lidz candidly admits that the code of signs contained in any symbolic mechanism only approximates the Saussurean conception of language. What is even more questionable for me is the antidialectic turn of Lidz's discussion. In fact, he stresses a relationship of continuity from the Cartesian dichotomy between subject and object, to the linguistic categories of subject, object, verb, and modifier, to the Parsonian categories of action (p. 138-139).[1]

Lidz also attempts to make some usage of the Chomskian notions of generativity, deep and surface structures and transformational rules. He sets out for himself the task of analyzing "certain characteristics of the media of the primary subsystems of action" in terms of the linguistic model (p. 141), but he does not succeed in establishing more than generic analogies. For instance, he treats various definitions of the situation as meta-empirical entities or messages that are made possible by stable, institutionalized normative structures or codes (p. 144). Besides the generic nature of this analogy, one can also detect an empiricist or quasi-empiricist interpretation of the notion of transformation. He conceives the deep structure of the situation as made of "simple selective combinations of exemplar of categories of normative social structure"; only few elements of deep structure are selected for inclusion in surface structures (ibid). It is clear that according to Lidz, surface structures are composed of a selective content of the deep structure, whereas in transformational linguistics between deep and surface structures there is a relationship of transformation, not a correspondence of content. At least in my opinion, what matters is the mathematical or quasi mathematical formula that permits the production of a large amount of content in a precise way. In conclusion, Lidz's discussion is an example of another vague analogy because it does not provide the equivalent of precise transformational rules.

I have already stated that besides the empiricist misrendition of transformational grammar, I also find objectionable the lack of dialectic perspective. In my view a definition of the situation is an outcome of the interaction of structural and subjective forces that operate within the framework of culture, the latter in turn being sustained and modified by the interactive tensions brought to bear by structural and subjective forces. We must credit Lidz with having called attention to a very much needed development in the theory of action; but because he shares the empiricist and dichotomous assumption of the master, he cannot bring his programmatic intent to fruition.

A quick glance at other action theorists will readily show we cannot fare much better regarding their efforts either. R. C. Baum defines the code "as a set of rules delimiting the range of normatively legitimate use and assemblages of symbols into messages" (Baum, 1976, p. 461). A similar definition is provided by B. C. Cartwright and R. S. Warner, who define the code as "the lexicon within which meanings are understood" (1976, p. 640). Obviously, we do not find here the technical notion of rules of transformation.

S. N. Eisenstadt has extended the notion of code so much as to include even Weber's "modes of orientation." However, he clarifies that Weber's Code is not "a purely formal set of signs which organizes sets of abstract, symbolic contents only, but rather a set of orientations toward symbolic, structural and organizational aspects of the basic problems of human and social existence" (1976, p. 789); see also Eisenstadt's essay in my 1982a volume). The accusation of formalism apropos of French structuralism and Chomsky is not new (see Rossi, 1983, passim), especially on the part of empiricist social scientists. Eisenstadt's empiricism is evident in the emphasis he places on symbolic content. Because symbolic content continuously changes and evolves, I find more useful to focus on the dialectical forces of this change and on the higher-order code that ensures the balance among dialectically interacting forces.

The recent presentation of Parsonian theory by R. Münch contains some useful insights. For instance, Münch states that the cultural code "undergoes continuous modifications through the course of its history by means of its interpenetration with the social and personality systems. Its function is to provide for the possibility of variation while preserving the specific cluster of values which characterize the action system (pattern consistency)" (1982, p. 776).

Münch clearly formulates the notion that the interaction (in my view, mutually constitutive opposition) between the two subsystems makes the cultural code an ongoing entity. However, Münch's analysis falls short when it attempts to link the concept of variation and stability as follows: "This cluster or pattern of values must therefore be sufficiently generalized to permit a given type of action system to adjust to new conditions without having to alter its fundamental structure" (ibid). Münch provides a solution in terms of the "generality" of the code, which is, of course, a quality of its "content." Then what kind of generality is necessary to still preserve a specific orientation of the value system and why are there delimiting parameters of the allowed variability and continuity?

I will attempt to propose a more viable dialectical notion of code that entails a structural balance of opposing complementary forces (continuity) and hence is compatible with and generates continuous changes.

A DIALECTICIZED FOUR-FUNCTION PARADIGM AND THE PREDICTABILITY OF TECHNOLOGICAL INNOVATION

Let me go back to an early development in Parson's thought that emerged in 1953 out of a convergence between theoretical reasoning (the notion of four-pattern variables) and the empirical study of small group processes by R. F. Bales. I refer to Parsons and Bales's notion that "systems of action generally could be exhaustively analyzed in terms of processes and structures referable to the solution—simultaneously or in sequence—of the four functional problems that we called 'adaptation,' 'system (not unit) goal-attainment,' 'integration,' 'pattern-maintenance and latent tension-management' " (Parsons, 1970, p. 844). As Parsons himself has said, this notion has remained fundamental throughout his works, up to the very end of his career (ibid; see also Parsons, 1978, passim).

A dialectic view of the four-function paradigm and technological innovation. In Parsons's own words, the "four-function paradigm" refers "to an attempt at a conceptually formal statement of the primary elements of a theoretical scheme and their relations to each other " (1978, p. 353). At this fundamental level, Parsons is very helpful and amenable to interesting developments, not necessarily of an empiricist and static kind. A "code" is "a set of rules for the use, transformation, and combination of [the elementary components of the system]" (Parsons, 1977, p. 189); hence, the logic governing the relationship among the four functions can be seen as constituting the fundamental code of decision making at the firm level.

The key elements of my position are the following: (1) The business firm is considered as a microsocial system that cannot function without a satisfactory solution to the four aforementioned organizational parameters. (2) A functional decision (from the point of view of the firm) on technological innovation is best derived on the basis of the simultaneous or sequential evaluation of the interactive balance among the innovation-laden dimensions of the four organizational parameters. (3) Because the four parameters can be attended to sequentially, they are empirically, although not analytically, independent of each other; hence, the direction of the innovation-laden dimension of each parameter cannot be deduced from the innovation valence of the other three parameters. An analogous statement is made by Parsons apropos of the four basic components of any concrete system—namely, values, norms, collectivities, and roles—which play, respectively, the functions of pattern-maintenance, integration, goal attainment, and adaptation (Parsons, 1969, p. 21). (4) Although each one of the four parameters represents a separate and distinct factor in innovational decision making, their decisional value is constituted through the reciprocal opposition and feedback relationship to each other. (5) This notion of mutual constitutiveness entails the assessment on the part of the owner or manager of a twofold dialectical relationship; first, the dialectical tension and reciprocal conditioning of the innovation-laden dimensions of the four organizational parameters; second, the dialectical tensions among the factors constituting the innovation-laden dimension of each parameter, such as possible conflicts between managers, technical staff, and labor unions on the assessment of the benefits to be expected from a given innovation, and so on. (I purposefully speak of "organizational parameters" rather than systemic functions or needs to avoid the trite objection that systems do not have needs. In reality, there is a need for the manager to consider all of the four organizational parameters in organizational decision making.)

The reason for the existence of the latter type of dialectical tension is intuitively obvious, but the same is not true for the first kind of dialectic on which the whole thrust of my predictive model of innovation depends. Why must we conceive of the four basic organizational parameters of any system as in dialectic relationships with each other? Both theoretical reasoning *and* empirical research provide an answer to this question.

To begin from the theoretical argument, we know that the four-function paradigm was derived from a cross-classification of two dichotomous axes of the social system: the external-internal axis and the instrumental-consummatory axis. The very notions of external versus internal and instrumental versus consummatory problems consist of two sets of binary oppositions, whereby each pole of the opposition entails (and hence constitutes) its own opposite; this is the core notion of what I call *a constitutive dialectic of complementary oppositions* (for an early formulation of this notion see the conclusion of Rossi, 1983). A similar argument can be derived from the classification of pattern variables in terms of their functional primacy—namely, diffuseness (internal dimension) versus specificity (external dimension)—and universalism (instrumental dimension) versus particularism (consumatory dimension; see Loubser, 1976, p. 13). Again these oppositions mutually constitute each other as universalism entails the existence of its own negation,that is, particularism and vice versa. Here one can find a *fundamental similarity between the elementary structure of Action Theory and Levi-Strauss's structuralism* (see Rossi, 1983).

A predictive model of innovation based on the dialectic relationship among the four organizational parameters is shown in Figure 3.1.

Each one of the four organizational parameters is endowed of an innovation-laden valence that can range from a minimum (−) to a maximum (+) valence. *The closer intersection point of the four valences is perceived to be to the positive end of the continuum, that is, the most likely it is that a proinnovation decision will occur.*

Economic, administrative, and social sciences have empirically documented the importance of a variety of factors on innovation decision making, but they have proceeded in a piecemeal fashion and have largely ignored each other's contributions and theoretical orientations. Unfortunately, lack of space prevents me from presenting a dialectical reinterpretation of this literature that would show the interrelatedness and potential complementarity of a large number of apparently heterogeneous findings when they are seen as components and/or indicators of the four organizational parameters. Whereas regressional methodologies would be of no help, the four-function paradigm, reinter-

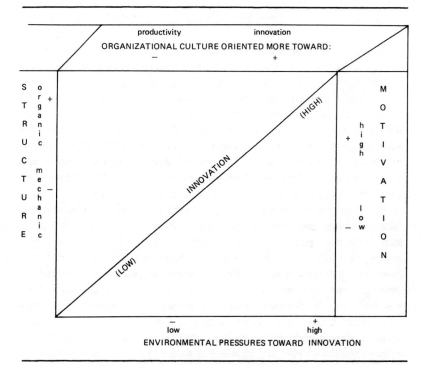

Figure 3.1 A Predictive Model of Firm Innovation

preted in dialectical terms, makes possible a truly interdisciplinary discourse that produces a predictive model of a major social process. In this theoretical chapter, I must present at least some empirical evidence about the plausibility of the dialectical nature of the predictive model.

Empirical Evidence on the Dialectical Interrelationship among the Four Organizational Parameters

After the original intuition that originated this chapter, I have come across some sociological and anthropological review essays of organizational and other studies that seem to support my line of thinking. Although I refer the reader interested in detailed references and studies to the review essays themselves, I will briefly outline in this already lengthy chapter a few emerging themes.

Contemporary anthropologists have criticized early organizational theorists (including Parsonian ones) for having considered factories as integrated systems in stable functional equilibrium. They have also attributed analytical priority to stable structure and a subordinated importance to the individual, whose role presumably consists of becoming integrated and submissive to the whole; conflicts and tensions were assumed to be disruptive of the systemic equilibrium and to prevent efficient productivity. Recent anthropological case studies have reacted to these structural and static biases with a variety of approaches, among which I mention the focus on the strategizing behavior existing in factories and network analysis (Holzberg & Giovannini, 1981, pp. 328-332).

Insofar as the notion of culture is concerned, the sociologist Gary A. Fine has stated that "organizational culture" has emerged as a major thrust in organizational theory and that some studies have demonstrated that a *flexible* culture is a prerequisite of an effective organization (1984, pp. 239, 244), a notion very different from the "given" and determining characteristics of Parsons's notion of culture; after all, culture mirrors society (Peterson, 1979, p. 141). Moreover, unlike early functionalists, contemporary sociologists consider expressive symbolism, rather than values and norms (à la Parsons), as the most important aspect of culture; in fact, symbols serve as a code for creating and recreating society in social interaction and from generation to generation (Peterson, 1979, p. 138). This interactive notion of culture is echoed by a dialectical notion of culture propounded by some contemporary anthropologists: *"The constant tension between individual experience and the collective means for expressing and interpreting that experience is the dynamic relationship by which culture comes to be and through which it is constantly changing"* (Dougherty & Fernandez, 1981, p. 413). Some studies have shown that culture is constrained by structure (Fine, 1984, p. 247); others have shown that a strong culture can dismantle organizational structure and effectively motivate people (p. 255).

References and studies reacting against the primacy and the static notion of structure are frequent, especially in social interactionist literature. Organizational structure does not consist of the organizational chart, but, rather, of the meaningful interactions among members; hence, structure is continuously constituted and reconstituted; it is both a producer and a product (Fine, 1984, pp. 240, 256; Maines, 1977, p. 256).

As to the role of the individual, various studies have shown the influence of the social actors on their organizational environment (Fine,

1984, p. 242). Other studies have pointed out the influence of factors external to organizations on individuals' attitudes (see references in Holzberg & Giovannini, 1981, p. 328). For a systematic study of such interactive-dialectic relationships, Chad Gordon's paradigm might be useful; he hypothesizes a parallelism between the functional problems of adaptation, goal-attainment, integration, and pattern-maintenance, on the one hand, and the "competence," self-determination," "unity," and "moral worth" aspects of the sense of self, on the other. In turn, the latter aspects of self would be paralleled by the symbolic rewards of "approval," "response," "acceptance," and "respect" (Gordon, 1976, p. 410). These few references (and the many more contained in the review essays I have cited) are sufficient to show the shortcomings of a deterministic view of the four systems of action and the plausibility of an interactive and dialectic view of the four-function paradigm.

I omit the discussion of a typology of inter- and intrafunction dialectical tensions, which is easily conceptualizable on the basis, let us say, of various degrees of clarity and valence of the organizational culture on goals and strategies, and their interrelationship with motivational states in reverse order of clarity and valence as they are needed (hence constituted) to arrive at innovational decisions. The same could be done for each one of the other organizational parameters (labor versus manager interests, and so on).

CONCLUSION: THE BASIC TENETS
OF THE NEW DIALECTIC

The overall thrust of this chapter clearly shows how and in what sense the four-function paradigm is a useful, and even a predictive, device of a major social *process*. The crucial issue is not to conceive of the four functions as independent and self-constituted functions and in hierarchic relationship to each other. Alexander's notion that reality cannot be conceived only as an object without considering it also as a human activity, as praxis (see Alexander, 1982, pp. 64ff) is a step beyond static Action Theory. However, Marx's dialectic entails much more than a mere simultaneity or copresence of subjective and objective principles. In a passage that I have quoted elsewhere (Rossi, 1983, p. 49), Marx clearly establishes what I call the principle of the mutually constitutive dialectical interaction: "An objective being acts objectively, and it would not act objectively if objectivity were not part of its essential being. It creates and establishes only objects because it is established by objects, and because it is fundamentally natural."

But again, there are many ways to conceive of dialectical interrelationships. For instance, I disagree with Giddens's position (an author I came into contact with after the publication of my 1983 volume), although he quotes an otherwise enlightening passage of the Grundisse to buttress it: "The conditions and objectifications of the process are themselves equally moments of it, and its only subjects are individuals, but individuals in mutual relationship, which they equally reproduce and produce anew" (quoted in Giddens, 1979, p. 53). Curiously enough, Giddens continues with the comment that according to Marx's standpoint, the notions of action and structure "presuppose one another" and are in "dialectical relation." But what happens to the individual? I know that for Giddens "action has reference to the activities of an agent" (p. 55), but his very definition of structure implies a dichotomy—hence a loss of dialectical relationship—from the acting subject: "Structures are necessarily (logically) properties of systems or collectivities, and are characterized by the absence of a subject" (p. 66). His positivistic-dichotomous view emerges clearly throughout: "Structure is both enabling and constraining" (p. 69), but for me it is also being enabled (constituted) by the interaction with the individuals.

I agree with Giddens's intention of avoiding the functionalist (and Durkheimian) priority of structure over action and with the equally laudable intention of avoiding the cultural determinism of Parsons, whereby social actors are mere cultural dopes (pp. 51-52). The reason is that "a theory of acting subject" is an indispensible component of what Giddens calls "a theory of structuration" or "philosophy of action" (pp. 1-2). However, curiously enough, Giddens posits another structural priority: "According to [my] conception, the same structural characteristics participate in the subject [the actor] as in the object. Structure forms 'personality' and 'society' simultaneously" (p. 70). Obviously, any reference to a reciprocally forming influence is missing. From this structural (undialectic) bias derives Giddens's incomplete notion of structure as "a virtual order of differences produced and reproduced in social interaction" (p. 3). I certainly agree that the decisional structure consists of the relational differences among the four functions, but those differences are not just "given"; they constitute each other through their oppositional tensions and are constituted by the mediating role of the actor (decision manager) who evaluates, manipulates, and counterbalances one against the other. At the same time, the decision maker is constituted itself as a decisional actor by the very interrelated set of parameters he must evaluate.

Correctly, Dean Gerstein, in his comments to the oral presentation of this chapter at the ASA 1984 meeting, placed the key contribution of my reformulation of the four-function paradigm in the combinatorial aspect of the decisional structure; this makes the paradigm predictive, a genuine breakthrough in functionalist thought. However, I am not proposing a mathematical, impersonal combinatorial activity as one that is mediated and activated by the subject, who, in turn, is called into being by the need to assess the interactive "innovation valence" of the four organizational parameters.

The dialectical formulation I have proposed offers the following advantages over a mere Parsonian view: (1) It enables one to capture both the principle of continuity (deep structure) and the change produced by the dialectical interaction built within the decisional code (the four parameters) and the dialectic tensions between the decisional code (structure) and the decision maker (subjectivity). (2) It avoids the shortcomings of dichotomous thought and permits the construction of an integrated and predictive model of a major social process out of a heterogeneous variety of research findings and perspectives put forward by different disciplines.

NOTE

1. Obviously Cartesian thought is the antithesis of dialectic; the other antidialectic source of Parsons's thought is Kant, to whom he repeatedly refers as a source of inspiration (see especially Parsons, 1978).

REFERENCES

Alexander, J. C. (1978). Formal and substantive voluntarism in the work of Talcott Parsons: A theoretical and ideological reinterpretation. *American Sociological Review, 43*(2), 177-198.

Alexander, J. C. (1982). *Theoretical logic in sociology: Vol. I: Positivism, presuppositions, and current controversies.* Berkeley: University of California Press.

Alexander, J. C. (1983). Chair's message. *Perspectives, 6*(2), 1-3.

Baum, R. C. (1976). Introduction. In J. J. Loubser & R. C. Baum (Eds.), *Explorations on general theory in social science: Essays in honor of Talcott Parsons* (pp. 448-469). New York: Free Press.

Bourricaud, F. (1981). *The sociology of Talcott Parsons.* Chicago: University of Chicago Press.

Cartwright, B. C., & Warner, R. S. (1976). The medium is not the message. In J. J. Loubser & R. C. Baum (Eds.), *Explorations on general theory in social science: Essays in honor of Talcott Parsons* (pp. 639-660). New York: Free Press.

Dougherty, J. D., & Fernandez, J. W. (1981). Introduction to"Symbolism and action." *American Ethnologist, 8*(3), 413-422.

Effrat, A. (1976). Introduction to Section V. In J. J. Loubser & R. C. Baum (Eds.), *Explorations on general theory in social science: Essays in honor of Talcott Parsons* (pp. 662-680). New York: Free Press.

Eisenstadt, S. N. (1976). On historical continuity and social change in modernization. In J. J. Loubser & R. C. Baum (Eds.), *Explorations on general theory in social science: Essays in honor of Talcott Parsons* (pp. 788-797). New York: Free Press.

Fine, G. A. (1984). Negotiated orders and organizational cultures. *Annual Review of Sociology, 10,* 239-262.

Giddens, A. (1979). *Central problems in social theory: Action, structure, and contradiction in social analysis.* Berkeley: University of California Press.

Goodman, M. E. (1967). *The individual and culture.* Homewood, IL: Dorsey.

Gordon, C. (1976). Development of evaluated role identities. *Annual Review of Sociology, 2,* 405-427.

Gould, M. (1976). Systems analysis, macrosociology, and the generalized media of social action. In J. J. Loubser & R. C. Baum (Eds.), *Explorations on general theory in social science: Essays in honor of Talcott Parsons* (pp. 470-506). New York: Free Press.

Handy, C. (1980). Through the organizational looking glass. *Harvard Business Review, 58*(1), 115.

Holzberg, C. S., & Giovannini, M. J. (1981). Anthropology and industry: Reappraised and new directions. *Annual Review of Anthropology, 10,* 317-360.

Lee, D. (1959). *Freedom and culture.* Englewood Cliffs, NJ: Prentice-Hall.

Levi-Strauss, C. (1976). *Structural anthropology, Vol. II.* (M. Layton, Trans.). New York: Basic Books.

Lidz, V. M. (1976). Introduction to Part II. In J. J. Loubser & R. C. Baum (Eds.), *Explorations on general theory in social science: Essays in honor of Talcott Parsons* (pp. 124-150). New York: Free Press.

Loubser, J. J., & Baum, R. C. (Eds.). (1976). *Explorations on general theory in social science: Essays in honor of Talcott Parsons.* New York: Free Press.

Maines, D. R. (1977). Social organization and social structure in symbolic interactionist thought. *Annual Review of Sociology, 3,* 235-259.

Münch, R. (1981). Talcott Parsons and the theory of action I: The structure of the Kantian core. *American Journal of Sociology, 86*(4), 709-739.

Münch, R. (1982). Talcott Parsons and the theory of action II: Continuity of the development. *American Journal of Sociology, 87*(4), 771-826.

Parsons, T. (1937). *The structure of social action.* New York: Free Press.

Parsons, T. (1964). *Social structure and personality.* New York: Free Press.

Parsons, T. (1969). *Politics and social structure.* New York: Free Press.

Parsons, T. (1970). On building social system theory: A personal history. *Daedalus, 99*(4), 826-881.

Parsons, T. (1977). *Social systems and the evolution of action theory.* New York: Free Press.

Parsons, T. (1978). *Action theory and the human condition.* New York: Free Press.

Parsons, T., & Bales, R. F. (1956). *Family, socialization, and interaction process.* London: Routledge & Kegan Paul.

Parsons, T., & Shils, E. A. (Eds.). (1951). *Toward a general theory of action.* New York: Free Press.

Parsons, T. Shils, E. A., Naegelt, K. D., & Pitts, J. R. (Eds.). (1965). *Theories of society* (Vol. 1). New York: Free Press.

Peterson, R. A. (1979). Revitalizing the culture concept. *Annual Review of Sociology, 5,* 137-166.

Radin, P. (1971). *The world of primitive man.* New York: Dutton.

Rossi, I. (Ed.). (1974). *The unconscious in culture: The structuralism of Claude Levi-Strauss in perspective.* New York: Dutton.

Rossi, I. (Ed.). (1982a). *Structural sociology: Theoretical perspectives and substantive analyses.* New York: Columbia University Press.

Rossi, I. (Ed.). (1982b). *The logic of culture: Advances in structural theory and method.* South Hadley, MA: J. F. Bergen.

Rossi, I. (1983). *From the sociology of symbols to the sociology of signs: Toward a dialectical sociology.* New York: Columbia University Press.

PART II

Explanation and Social Change

Chapter 4

SYSTEMIC QUALITIES AND BOUNDARIES OF SOCIETIES
Some Theoretical Considerations

S. N. EISENSTADT

Hebrew University of Jerusalem

THE PROBLEM AS TO whether, or to what degree, "societies" and different settings of social interaction can be viewed as systems with clear boundaries that develop internal regulative mechanisms to assure that their different parts contribute to the maintenance of such boundaries has constituted one of the major foci of controversy in sociological theory in the last 20 or so years.

The single focal point of this controversy was, of course, Talcott Parsons's *The Social System* (1951), which signaled the full crystallization of the structural-functional view of societies as social systems. This view was often seen as emphasizing the boundary-maintaining mechanisms of social control, in terms of their contribution to the maintenance of the boundaries of respective social (or personality and even cultural) systems, as well as assuming a basic social consensus around central societal values and goals.

Many, if certainly not all, of the criticisms of the structural-functional school focused on this problem of the systemic qualities of societies (Eisenstadt & Curelara, 1976, Chaps. 8-9; Eisenstadt, 1983).

Thus, in most general terms, Reinhard Bendix (1971) has claimed that there exists two central sociological traditions: the systemic one, ranging from Durkheim to Parsons, and the more open one, focusing on concrete social actions and conflicts, best represented by Max Weber.

In somewhat greater detail, the critics of the systemic assumptions of the structural-functional school claimed that this school took the very emergence and crystallization of some systems for granted. Because of this, the structural-functional school was seen as negating the creative autonomy of groups or individuals in the very construction of social order and as denying the tension between the organization of the social division of labor and the regulation of power and construction of trust and meaning—one of the major emphases of classical sociology.

Closely related to this were several additional allegations. One was that the structural-functional school has in general and Parsons has in particular almost entirely neglected the component of power (and exploitation) in the construction of a social order.

Another criticism was that the structural-functional model was necessarily ahistorical. More specifically, the charge was that in their explanation of concrete historical situations or phenomena, this school neglected past influence and processes in favor of a "static" or "circular" explanatory theory. This was because they were said to explain social phenomena as functionally adjusted to one another through their contribution to societal needs and to assume that there are equilibrating mechanisms in the social system that counteract functional maladjustments or inconsistencies.

This very intense controversy had also some paradoxical aspects. To mention only one such case, it might be worthwhile to emphasize, as Alvin Gouldner has pointed out long ago (1970, pp. 108-116, 157-171), that Marxism is characterized by a very strongly systemic orientation and mode of analysis.

But probably more interesting have been some developments that came out of these different areas of research. One of the most interesting developments of concrete research—starting both from "systemic" and from antisystemic premises and ranging from social psychological and experimental studies to historical ones—has pointed out some interesting potential convergences. Together with the analytical convergences I will describe, these point to fruitful reformations of the problem of the nature of systemic qualities of patterns of social interaction, or of "societies."

Thus more and more stress was laid on the "simple" historical fact that all institutional complexes—as well as so-called formal organizations, the study of which was for a long time informed by strongly systemic premises—are constituted by special social action, as are their concrete boundaries.

At the same time, many social-psychological studies that started from some mode ("individualistic"-"rational") optimizing assumptions or premises have more and more become aware (March & Olson, 1984) that the outlooks of such social actors cannot be fully understood without taking into account the autonomy of some systemic qualities, characteristics, or tendencies of such institutions.

THE POLITICAL SYSTEMS OF EMPIRES:
A REEXAMINATION OF
THE SYSTEMIC PERSPECTIVE

In the following pages I would like to address myself to this problem, that is, whether, in what way, and to what degree, societies or patterns of social interactions are organized and/or systemic. I will do so by going back and extending the analysis I presented of the political system of bureaucratic empires that I undertook in the late fifties and early sixties (Eisenstadt, 1963).

In that work I attempted to analyze the common systemic characteristics of the historically centralized bureaucratic empires, that is, the Sassanid, Roman, Byzantine, Chinese, Caliphate, and Ottoman Empires, and the European states in the period of absolutism, and the development of religious institutions within them

That analysis, as the very title of the book indicates, was based on very explicit systemic premises; that is, it assumed that such empires develop certain specific systemic characteristics, special types of boundaries and "needs," as well as special types of characteristics to assure the continuity of such systems.

Thus to quote one of my earlier formulations (Eisenstadt, 1964):

> Whatever the differences between the aims of various rulers and whatever the attitudes of the various groups, once the major contours of the Empires were institutionalized, various organizations developed within them— mostly through the efforts of the rulers—to implement policies designed to maintain the specific external and internal boundaries of the system, that is, its specific institutional contours and characteristics.

I stressed the coexistence in these empires of traditional, undifferentiated political activities with more differentiated, specifically *political* goals, especially how political differentiation was limited by the former. I argued that, on the one hand, the rulers were interested in the promotion of free resources, particularly in freeing them from commitments to traditional aristocratic groups, and, on the other, that the rulers wished to control these resources for their own use. For example, the rulers' attempted to create and maintain an independent, free peasantry with small holdings and to restrict the big landowners' encroachments on these small holdings in order to assure both the peasants' independence and the provision of resources for the rulers. They also tried to establish colonies and settlements of peasant soldiers to ensure that the state would have sufficient military manpower.

In this early analysis I stressed some aspects of the systemic analysis that had not been predominant in systems analysis up until that time. First of all, I have stressed in many such systems, or at least in these empires, the prevalence of systemic contradictions and possible change. For example, because the rulers were usually unable to transcend the aristocracy's own symbols of stratification and legitimation—the very strata whose influence they wanted to limit—their ability to appeal to the lower strata of the population was obviously limited. Even more important, because of the emphasis on the superiority and worth of aristocratic symbols and values, many middle or new strata and groups tended to identify with them and consequently to "aristocratize" themselves.

Second, I was especially concerned with the possible demise of such systems; instead of taking their persistence for granted, I attempted to analyze the conditions under which they may continue or may disappear. For example, the rulers' tendency to maintain strong control over the more differentiated strata could be come predominant, thus increasing the power of traditional forces and orientations, and sharpening the conflicts between the traditional and the more flexible differentiated strata. In this way, the latter groups were often destroyed or became alienated from the rulers.

The greater the intensity of such internal contradictions and the greater the pressure of external exigencies, the more quickly changes in such societies came about.

I also stressed that the very institutionalization of such a system was not assured in terms of some overall trend to greater differentiation but was dependent on several contingent conditions. First, it depended on the emergence of political entrepreneurs, the emperors and their immediate entourage, who had the vision and ability to create new political entities. Second, it depended on the development of specific collectivities and roles in the major institutional spheres, such that the activities and resources of large parts of the population were freed from ascriptive (kinship, lineage, aristocratic) commitments and could be made available to rulers.

I argued that these conditions developed only in varying degrees in China from the beginning of the Han dynasty, in Byzantium and the Roman Empire in their formative stages, and in the Caliphates at the initial stage of their development. In the Greek city-states, on the other hand, although the broader social conditions did develop, there arose no group of leaders or entrepreneurs capable of forging a new polity. In other historical cases—for example, those of Charlemagne or Genghis

Khan—such leaders did arise, but the broader social conditions were lacking.

IMPERIAL SYSTEMS AND AXIAL AGE CIVILIZATIONS: IMPLICATIONS FOR SYSTEMIC ANALYSIS

In light of work I have done since this project, however, it is clear to me that there were several problems with the systemic analyses of these social systems as they stood at this point. Some of these I touched upon without fully analyzing them; others I barely mentioned at all.

The common denominator of the weaknesses of my earlier approach was that, although I did recognize that political systems (and in principle all social systems) are not simply given but created or constructed, I did not analyze systematically the processes through which each construction, as well as the maintenance of such a system, is effected. Nor did I analyze systematically the implications that no human population is enclosed within any single system, no political (or other social) system is self-enclosed but is, instead, closely related to other social systems, or, in other words, that within this broad setting several more concrete problems have to be singled out.

The first problem is that of the place of various institutional entrepreneurs and their visions in the institutionalization of the imperial systems. Although I did indeed stress the importance of political entrepreneurs in the institutionalization of such empires—and of groups close to them or sharing some interests with them—I did not fully analyze the nature of the coalitions, especially the coalitions of elites, that made possible this institutionalization. Nor did I fully explicate the relation between the visions—religious, political, and civilizational—articulated by such elites and the institutionalization and continuity of such empires.

Second, I did not explicate the differences in the nature of the mechanisms of control as they develop in different types of social systems, especially the less and more differentiated or complex ones.

Last, I barely touched on the problems arising out of the fact that any human population is organized into often competing systems or collectivities.

All of these problems become especially visible in my analysis (Eisenstadt, 1982) of the Axial Age civilizations within the framework of which most, even if not all, of these empires developed.

The term "Axial Age civilizations" was coined by Karl Jaspers to denote the civilizations that developed in Ancient Israel, later on in

Christianity and its great variety; in Ancient Greece; partially in Zoroastrianism in Persia; in early Imperial China; in Hinduism and Buddhism; and, much later, beyond the Axial Age proper, Islam. The distinctive characteristics of these civilizations were the development and institutionalization within them, and particularly in their centers, of basic conceptions of tension between the transcendental and the mundane orders.

These conceptions of tension developed primarily among small groups of intellectuals. Ultimately, these conceptions were, in all the Axial Age civilizations, institutionalized; that is, they became the predominant orientation of both the ruling and many secondary elites, fully embodied in their respective centers or subcenters, transforming the nature of the political elites and making the autonomous intellectual elites relatively independent partners in the central coalitions. Thus the various dispersed groups of intellectuals became transformed into more fully crystallized and institutionalized groups, especially clerics—whether Jewish prophets and priests, the great Greek philosophers, the Chinese literati, the Hindu Brahmins, the Buddhist Sangha, or the Islamic Ulemas.

The institutionalization of these conceptions had far-reaching consequences on the structuring of the major institutional characteristics of these civilizations in general and of the imperial systems that developed within them in particular.

The most general and common of these implications was the high degree of symbolic orientation and ideologization of the major aspects of the institutional structure. This applies in particular to the structure of collectivities, social centers, social hierarchies, and processes of political struggle, and to the construction of worlds of knowledge.

I shall dwell here only on two such institutional aspects or consequences of the institutionalization of these conceptions: the tendency to construct distinct civilizational frameworks and the development of the conception of the accountability of rulers.

Some collectivities and institutional spheres were singled out as the most appropriate carriers of the attributes required to resolve the transcendental and mundane orders. As a result, new types of collectivities were created or seemingly natural and "primordial" groups were endowed with special meaning, couched in terms of the perception of this tension and its resolution.

Two types of such collectivities are of special importance. One is "ethnic," national, or primordial. The other is religious or civilizational, such as the Christian, Hinduistic, Buddhist, Confucian, or Islamic ones.

Both of these types of collectivities can, of course, also be found in nonimperial, less developed (patrimonial) kingdoms, but in a somewhat different mode. In such patrimonial systems, the ethnic or primordial collectivities could indeed be found as distinct from the political ones, but they were not characterized by a high degree of self-consciousness. It was only in the Axial Age civilizations that they tended to develop as more fully self-conscious and ideological collectivities with relatively clear boundaries.

The same was even more true of the civilizational frameworks or collectivities, which on the whole developed as distinct entities above all in the Axial civilizations.

Membership in these collectivities and frameworks tended to become imbued with a strong ideological dimension and to become a focus of ideological struggle.

An aspect of this ideological struggle was the insistence on the exclusiveness and closure of such collectivities and on the distinction between the inner and outer social and cultural space defined by them. This aspect became connected with attempts to structure the different cultural, political, and ethnic collectivities in some hierarchical order; the very construction of such an order usually became a focus of ideological and political conflict.

The crucial analytical point is that these collectivities developed some systemic tendencies and mechanisms of control that were different from those of the empires, and very often also decisively different criteria for membership. Because of such collectivity formation, there developed in these Axial Age civilizations a very strong tendency for the crystallization of autonomous centers that were distinct from the peripheries. These permeated the center and attempted to reconstruct it according to the respective visions carried by autonomous elites.

Closely related to this mode of structuring of special civilizational frameworks and centers, there also took place, in all of these civilizations, a far-reaching restructuring of the relation between the political order and the higher, transcendental order.

The political order, as the central locus of the mundane order, was usually conceived of as lower than the transcendental order and accordingly had to be restructured according to the precepts of the latter, with special concern for overcoming the tension between the transcendental and mundane orders or, to use the Weberian term, the proper modes of "salvation." The rulers were usually held responsible for organizing the mundane political order. At the same time, the nature of the rulers became greatly transformed. The King-God, the embodiment of the cosmic and earthly orders alike, disappeared and a more secular ruler, in principle accountable to some higher order, appeared. Thus emerged the conception of the accountability of the rulers and the community to a higher authority, God, Divine Law, and so forth. Accordingly, the possibility of calling a ruler to judgment emerged. The first most dramatic appearance of this conception took place in Ancient Israel, in the priestly and prophetic pronunciations. A different conception of such accountability, an accountability of the community and its laws, appeared on the northern shores of the eastern Mediterranean, in Ancient Greece. This conception appeared in different forms in all the Axial Age civilizations.

In close connection with these characteristics, there developed, also within these civilizations, new levels of conflicts and change. New dimensions were added to the processes of conflict beyond those that can be identified in the pre-Axial Age societies. The most important were the possible development of new levels of conflicts beyond those of specific "narrow" interests of different groups and elites, and the definition of such conflicts in broader symbolical or ideological terms. The issues of struggle tended to become highly ideologized, generalized, and sometimes even universalized. The struggle itself tended to become organized in relatively autonomous settings. Similarly, there developed linkages between different levels of issues, ranging potentially up to the very principle of legitimation of the social and political order. These new levels of conflict generated new processes of change and continuous reconstruction of the social order.

These new levels of conflict and change were activated by the different elites—often carrying different visions or interpretations thereof—and were most clearly manifest in the movements of protest that developed in these civilizations.

The participation of these elites greatly influenced the post-Axial Age character of protest movements at both the symbolic and organizational levels.

First, there was a growing symbolic articulation and ideologization of the perennial themes of protest that are found in any human society, such as rebellion against the constraints of division of labor, authority and hierarchy, the structuring of a time dimension, and the quest for solidarity and equality and for overcoming human mortality.

Second, utopian orientations were incorporated into the rituals of rebellion and the double image of society. It was this incorporation that generated alternative conceptions of social order and new ways of bridging the distance between the existing and the "true" resolution of the transcendental tension.

Third, new types of protest movements appeared. The most important were intellectual heterodoxies, sects, or movements that upheld the different conceptions of the resolution of the tension between the transcendental and the mundane order, and of the proper way to institutionalize such concepts.

Fourth, and closely related to the former, was the possibility of the development of autonomous political movements and ideologies usually oriented against an existing political center, with its elaborated symbolism and ideology.

Closely related to these changes in the symbolic dimension of protest movements were important organizational changes. The most general change was the growing possibility of structural and ideological links between different protest movements and foci of conflict. These links could be effected by different coalitions of secondary elites, above all by coalitions between "secondary" articulators of models of cultural order and political elites.

Thus, any single protest movement, either in the center or in the periphery, was exposed to possible links with other movements and to more central religious and political struggles. Such movements, moreover, could become connected with the opening up of a relatively wide range of institutional choices that resulted from the institutionalization of the transcendental tension and the quest for its resolution, often impinging on the very basic premises and centers of these societies.

Most of the empires alluded to above—with the exception of the more patrimonial ones in Meso-America, Ancient Egypt, and the Near East—developed within the framework of these Axial Age civilizations.

Indeed, the process of such institutionalization was very closely related to the development of certain characteristics of the Axial Age civilizations; it is impossible to understand the process of these empires without taking into account these characteristics.

First, the very construction of these empires was effected by coalitions of political and cultural elites carrying various transcendental visions. Second, some of the most important institutional characteristics of these empires—such as the development of strong, autonomous centers, the multiplicity of elites and the continuous struggles between them, as well as the numerous and intensive protest movements and processes of change that developed within them—were indeed very closely related to the attempts to institutionalize such visions and to maintain the new imperial frameworks.

Of special importance from the point of view of our analysis is the fact that the differences in the specific institutional dynamics of the different empires were greatly influenced by the transcendental visions and articulated by the different elites and the different coalitions between them.

The Chinese center, for example, was constituted by a coalition between the emperor and the literati and emphasized a strong this-worldly orientation. As a result, it was relatively monolithic, with almost no differentiation between culture and political elite, the literati being both; at the same time, different Chinese economic groups did not have any autonomy. In the Byzantine Empire, on the other hand, a strong tension between this- and other-worldly orientations was predominant. State and church, and civil and military aristocracy, were sharply differentiated. This, combined with the relative autonomy of agrarian and urban groups, created an entirely different dynamic. In the Ottoman Empire the division between "church" and "state" was structured in a different way—ideally it did not exist but was de facto very important—and related closely to the mode of institutionalization of the Islamic vision.

This raises the very important question of the impact of the differences in the relations between the political and the civilizational frameworks, especially in the degree of overlapping and interdependence between them. These were closely related to the nature of their respective civilizational visions and their effects on the dynamics of these societies. The degree of such overlapping and interdependence between these different systems has greatly influenced the relative "survival" of such nonpolitical collectivities. The greater the degree of closed, symbolic, or ideological integration within those empires—as in the strongly this-worldly Chinese system—the smaller the probability that nonpolitical collectivities would survive the downfall of the empires. Compare, for example, the Chinese case with the Islamic or Buddhist ones or different Christians ones. In these latter civilizations, the continuous tension between this- and other-worldly orientations, carried by different coalitions of elites or subelites, created some relative independence and different rates of continuity of the civilizational and political imperial collectivities. These differences are closely related to the nature of the control mechanism that develops in such complex systems.

In an earlier analysis (Eisenstadt, 1982) I have explained to some degree the specific mechanisms of control—especially the means by which bureaucracies implemented the policies of the rulers—through which the political systems of the empires could be maintained. I also described the possible breakdown of such mechanisms through their "aristocratization." However, I did not go in this analysis much beyond these bureaucracies and only hinted at the difference between the nature of such mechanisms in "complex" empires as compared to those of other ("less differentiated") types of political regimes, for instance, the patrimonial ones (e.g., Eisenstadt, 1985). I stress that a close look at such different mechanisms of control does indeed point out that the more complex they are, the more they develop the potential for breakdown, that is, a new level of sensitivity to internal and external pressures and possibly greater internal contradictions.

The relatively greater fragility of the more complex mechanisms that developed in the imperial systems is, of course, very closely related to the fact that within them, as in all Axial Age civilizations, there developed far-reaching movements of protest, levels of conflict, and processes of change; that the various complex mechanisms of control that developed in them were, on the one hand, carried by certain distinctive types of elites who activated the movements of protest; and that these mechanisms of control provided "natural" targets for such movements. Such targets were not as easily visible in less complex societies in which such mechanisms of control were embedded in broader ascriptive collectivities.

ANALYTICAL CONCLUSION:
THE CONSTRUCTION OF SOCIAL SYSTEMS

We may now bring this latter discussion more directly into contact with the issue of the systemic qualities of social interaction of societies.

The starting point of such a discussion is the recognition of the basic fact that the construction of systemic boundaries of patterns of social interaction is part of the human condition; that human social life, social interaction, and the division of labor are continuously organized in some systemic way; that is, there is some tendency to organize such activities in systems, and a crucial part of such organization is the construction of symbolic-institutional boundaries that delineate the relations among any such single system, other systems, and their respective environments.

Unlike, however, the view that can be found in large parts of sociological and anthropological studies—namely, that such social systems are natural or given and that change within them occurs either through some internal processes of differentiation or through the impingement of external forces—it is important to emphasize that such systems are constructed through continuous social process, and that such construction is always very fragile. Thus we should not, on the one hand, underrate these systemic qualities of human interaction and social organization; on the other hand, we should emphasize that such different systems are open and in a continuous process of construction and reconstruction.

Such systems never develop as entirely self-enclosed entities. The populations that live within the confines of what usually has been designated as a "society" or a macro-societal order are not usually organized in one "system," but rather in several different ways and on several levels, the most important of which are political systems, economic formations, different ascriptive collectivities, and civilizational frameworks. These different structures or "systems" evince different patterns of organization, continuity, and change; these structures and patterns may change within the "same" society to different degrees and in different ways in various areas of social life.

All such collectivities, organizations, and systems show, in the face of both external and internal impingements and the relations between these two, some combination of homeostatic tendencies along with tendencies to extend their boundaries, that is, both to adapt to and extend any given environment (which was itself probably created to a large degree by some preceding social creativity) and to create a new one. Thus, in all the empires analyzed earlier, it is possible to identify tendencies, on the one hand, to self-enclosure, to defend the existing geopolitical frontiers and symbolic premises and boundaries, and, on the other, to extend both their geopolitical scope, as well as the symbolic boundaries, as, for instance, through the incorporation of Buddhist symbols in China, "heretic" ones in the Byzantine Empire, or various primordial ones in Islamic countries.

The processes of construction of collectivities, social systems, and civilizational frameworks are processes of continuous struggle in which ideological, "material," and power elements are continuously interwoven. These processes are structured, articulated, and carried out by different social actors and carriers; the boundaries of such different collectivities are constructed by different coalitions of such carriers, different processes of interaction among them and between them, and the various social strata.

It is through such processes that the relations among different social systems and their respective environments are constructed. It is wrong to assume that there exists a natural environment of any society. Rather each society—or rather each concrete pattern of social interaction— constructs its own environment.

Of course, in the construction of environment, any society has some natural "material" to go on. But each "natural" environment provides several possible institutional choices, and even these can be changed through human invention. One or several of these choices are being chosen by the respective social actors, the respective carriers, and they can, of course, be changed through further developments.

Thus the very institutionalization of each of the empires has always implied the delineation of specific geopolitical boundaries, as well as of their respective technical and "natural" conditions, especially the agrarian systems that constituted its relevant environments. Once such choices have been made, they create the limits or the boundaries of the system and generate the systemic sensitivities to environmental changes. These sensitivities however, are created not by the environment as such, or by technology as such, but by social actors in the processes of reconstructing this environment and technology, and of the always fragile and changing boundaries of the respective social systems.

Conflict is inherent in any setting of social interaction for two basic reasons: first, because of the plurality of actors in any such settings; second, because of the multiplicity of the principles of cultural orientations, that is, of power struggles and conflicts between different groups and movements, which any such institutionalization entails.

Accordingly, there exists within any society the possibility that "antisystems" may develop. Although the antisystems may often remain latent for very long periods of time, they may also constitute, under propitious conditions, important foci of systemic change.

The existence of such potential antisystems is evident in the existence, in all societies, of potential themes and orientations of protest of social movements and heterodoxies that are often led by different, secondary elites. We have seen how these themes became much more fully articulated in the Axial Age Civilizations and the empires. Although the potentialities of conflict and change are inherent in all human societies, the concrete development, intensity, and directions of change—and possible decline—they engender differ greatly between different societies and civilizations according to the specific constellation within them of the particular forces analyzed above, that is, different constellations of cultural orientations and elites, the pattern and social division of labor, and political-ecological settings and processes. And such different constellations give rise to different patterns of restructuring of the boundaries of political systems and civilizations.

REFERENCES

Bendix, R. (1971). Two sociological traditions. In R. Bendix & G. Roth (Eds.), *Scholarship and partisanship* (pp. 282-299). Berkeley: University of California Press.

Eisenstadt, S. N. (1963). *The political system of empires*. New York: Free Press.

Eisenstadt, S. N. (1964). Institutionalization and change. *American Sociological Review, 29*, 235-247.

Eisenstadt, S. N. (1978). *Revolution and transformation of societies*. New York: Free Press.

Eisenstadt, S. N. (1982). The axial age: The emergence of transcendental visions and the rise of the clerics. *Journal of Sociology, 23*(2), 294-314.

Eisenstadt, S. N. (1983). Macro-sociology: The state of the art and possible directions. In S. N. Eisenstadt & H.J. Helle (Eds.), *Perspectives of sociological theory, Vol. 1: Perspectives on macro-sociology*. Beverly Hills, CA: Sage.

Eisenstadt, S. N., & Curelaru, M. (1976). *The form of sociology: Paradigms and crises*. New York: John Wiley.

Gouldner, A. W. (1970). *The coming crisis of Western society*. New York: Avon Books.

March, J. G., & Olson, J. P. (1984). The new institutionalism: Organizational factors in political life. *American Political Science Review, 18*, 734-750,

Parsons, T. (1951). *The social system*. New York: Free Press.

Chapter 5

EVALUATING THE MODEL OF STRUCTURAL DIFFERENTIATION IN RELATION TO EDUCATIONAL CHANGE IN THE NINETEENTH CENTURY

NEIL J. SMELSER

University of California at Berkeley

IN KEEPING WITH THE spirit of this volume, my objectives in this chapter are to criticize and revise one of the major ideas associated with the tradition of functional analysis: the idea of structural differentiation as a principle of change in the process of economic, political, and social development. I will illustrate the general points made by reference to the forces that appear to have been most important in shaping the development of primary education in Great Britain and the United States in the nineteenth century.

THE RISE OF FORMAL EDUCATION AS A PROCESS OF DIFFERENTIATION

One historical feature of the process of education (this central term will be defined more formally a little later on) is that it has often taken place in the context of some kind of social structure that may not have education as its primary functional significance. A great deal of education and training has taken place historically in the family; the passing on of agricultural knowledge and skills in a peasant family is an example. The institution of apprenticeship (sometimes also in a family context) is education in the context of a productive economic organization (even though this may be as simple as a cobbler's shop or as complicated as a large newspaper's composing room). Education in a monastery occurs in the context of an organization dedicated primarily to various kinds of religious works. The educational ingredients of "basic training" are imparted in the context of a military organization.

The institutionalization of education on a *formal* basis implies a different kind of social structure. It implies an organization that is dedicated primarily to the process of education *as such* (even though, as I will stress throughout, it maintains linkages with other structural settings in society). It most often is an organization that is formally separated from familial, economic, military, religious, and other educational contexts. It also suggests that its governance and policymaking will also take place in a structure that is in some degree autonomous, that is, not directly controlled by these other kinds of interests, even though it may be influenced by them. It suggests, finally, that specific roles—teacher and student—are defined primarily in their own terms, rather than in the context of some other kind of roles (father-son, journeyman-apprentice, etc.). In short, the one major defining characteristic of formal education is that of *structural differentiation* from other social-structural and organizational forms.

One of the striking features of the "modernization" of the West, as well as the "modernization" of advanced non-Western countries (Soviet Union, Japan) and the aspiring Third-World countries, is that a structurally differentiated system of formal education is part of the package of "modernization." All advanced Western and non-Western nations have developed systems of mass primary and secondary education, even though they have taken very different paths and trajectories and distinctive national differences in educational systems persist. All developing countries envision not only economic, political, and administrative development, but also mass educational development as part of the package that constitutes entry into the company of advanced nations. Standard explanations of this regularity are that education is a kind of institutional contrivance, or even invention, sparked by new demands in other sectors of the society—in particular, by the demands of industrialization, which calls for qualitatively new and higher levels of technical knowledge and skills in the labor force (Halsey, 1973), and mass suffrage in a democratizing society, which appears to call for a more informed and responsible citizenry.

Another aspect of these kinds of explanations are that educational activities that are embedded in traditional familial, community, religious, and economic contexts tend to be less flexible and effective than formal educational systems, presumably because of special constraints imposed by these contexts. The family, for example, is not a very effective formal educational institution because of its limited resources and its commitments to other kinds of functions and activities. Religious organizations are not very effective because of their sectarian commitments, which tie its educational activities to specific religious-moral concerns, likely to produce educational results that are noninstrumental from an economic point of view and divisive from a point of view of generating and sustaining a commitment to societywide integration and consensus. Formal educational arrangements, according to this view, are more effective because they are better able to generate more generalized and flexible knowledge, skills, and commitments that are consonant with industrial and/or democratic societies.

Although the model of differentiation possesses some continuing validity in accounting for the rise of more specialized educational systems, the power of the model appears to be limited, largely because it envisions the main variation in outcome as "less differentiated" or "more differentiated," whereas in fact there are many different variations in educational systems that we might wish to explain that cannot be assimilated to that particular distinction. I will specify some of these lines of variation throughout this chapter. In addition, I will examine a number of the special assumptions associated with the idea of differentiation (including the assumption of "greater effectiveness") as well as a model of how this process comes about. I will now lay some further groundwork for these tasks by developing some ideas about the nature of education in society.

EDUCATION AS A SPECIAL KIND OF SOCIETAL RESOURCE

As a process education must be regarded as a part of and continuous with the socialization process in general. I conceive socialization, moreover, as a process that can be conceptualized simultaneously at the individual, social, and cultural levels. From the standpoint of the *individual,* socialization involves the acquisition of values, ideals, identifications, motivational commitments, interpersonal skills and style, and various kinds of cognitive skills and information. From the standpoint of *society,* the products of socialization are seen as resources that can be allocated to the various activities, roles, and institutional structures that constitute organized social life. And from the *cultural* standpoint socialization is one of the main mechanisms by which values, meanings, and group identity is transmitted from generation to generation, thereby assuring the continuity of a society's cultural heritage.

This series of definitions should not be taken to imply any level of orderliness or neatness of fit among the three levels. At the individual level, the process of socialization sometimes fails, is rebelled against, or otherwise varies. At the social level, the products of socialization may not fit the role and individual demands generated by the social structure, particularly if that social structure has been undergoing rapid change. And at the cultural level, the dynamics of cultural conflict and change in society suggest that the sets of values, ideals, and so forth that are transmitted to one generation may be inappropriate to the next, which may generate its own, different ones. Nevertheless, from the standpoint of the primary intention of the socializers, the process is geared to stress reproduction and continuity at the individual, social, and cultural levels.

According to conventional usage, education is that part of the socialization process that gives primary emphasis to imparting and developing information, knowledge, cognitive skills, and critical skills. Although valid in a general way, this view should not obscure the fact that education as a process is variable in its relation to the more inclusive process of socialization. That is to say, education as a process can never be a purely cognitive process, but it also inevitably involves the exposure to cultural values, ideals, heroes, and villains, as well as normative expectations relating to matters such as personal ambition, attitudes and behavior toward authorities, cooperative behavior, and so on.

The view of education and socialization here advanced is consistent with the formulations of Durkheim (1956). One particular point made by Durkheim is that education is historically variable, reflecting the particular ideals of the home civilization, whether these be values of military valor, religious asceticism, or aristocratic gentlemanliness. To press this view further, it should be acknowledged that—historically, particularly in times of change—for any given society there is no single, integrated set of cultural ideals to be transmitted, but, rather, several sets of ideals in competition with one another. In addition, insofar as society has developed specialized institutional structures—economic, legal, political, etc.—these structures will, to varying extents, have been the structural bases for precipitating groups (classes, estates, ethnic groups, etc.) that are politically significant in the competition over the values, symbols, and ideologies that are consistent with or legitimize their own claims on resources. Because socialization in general and education in particular specialize in the generation and reproduction of these kinds of cultural items, it follows that the content, style, and mode of transmitting them will be items on the social agenda that generate group conflict. Furthermore, because the educational process—like the family process and the religious process—is involved in the transmission of systems of morality from generation to generation, it also follows that conflicts over educational issues are likely to take the form of conflicts over principles, or even conflicts over the definition of the sacred.

Although education, like socialization in general, must properly be regarded as a process that occurs in some degree throughout the life cycle, the educational process in the younger years of the life cycle is particularly significant because of the extreme plasticity of the human organism in its early years and its subsequent long period of maturity. The educational process during these years typically involves the generation of motivational commitments through mechanisms such as imitation and identification, then the inculcation of general skills (for example, literacy and numeracy), and finally the development of more abstract and specialized knowledge and skills. Although a great deal of variation in such a progression is to be expected, the point to be underscored is that, in the early years of education, children are, in their social significance, *generalized* resources; that is to say, they have the potential of being channeled in many different directions with respect to the cultivation of values, outlooks, skills, and information. In fact, education can be seen as an investment in the shaping of these human resources. They are shaped, moreover, with an eye to the future commitment and contribution to different societal exigencies by the recipients of that education. Thus education can be used as a potential military resource if ideas of value, bravery, and martial skills are inculcated; it can be used as an economic resource if scientific and technical skills are given priority; it can be used as a resource for the generation of symbols of national and/or local solidarity, identification, and integration; it can be used as an avenue for generating religious commitment, and in this way as a resource for organized religion; it can be used as a resource to reinforce inequality in society (for example, by conferring status or by cultivating values of deference); it can be used as a means to encourage social mobility; or it can be, and usually is, used to generate resources relative to a variety of mixtures of these purposes.

The fact that education is a generalized resource and can be directed to diverse purposes implies that education can mean or promise different things to different groups and interests in society. The young are thus "fair game" for those sectors and groups in society who are pushing their own interests and values both for themselves and for future generations. Much educational conflict, in fact, will be among the competing demands for the young as a resource, and debate among those groups and classes that have different demands for that resource— business groups, military groups, ruling groups, "intellectual" groups, class groups, ethnic groups, and so on.

EXTENDING THE MODEL
OF STRUCTURAL DIFFERENTIATION

The model of structural differentiation as developed and applied by Parsons, Bales, myself, and others is in my current estimation based on a model of society as an instrumentally oriented, going concern—a problem-solving entity—though that image was not always explicit in the minds of those who worked with the model.[1] Furthermore, the model appears to posit that at the beginning of a sequence of differentiation, things are not working satisfactorily (as evidenced by dissatisfaction) and at the end of the sequence, things are working better (because of new, more differentiated structural arrangements that have been invented after a process of disturbance, handling and channeling, searching, and adaptation).

With respect to the actual initiation of structural change and the typical sequence of events leading to that change, the model was stated—with respect to industrial differentiation—as follows:

> Industrial differentiation implies that under certain market, value, and other conditions, the existing industrial structure becomes inadequate to meet productive requirements. A sequence enters its first stage when elements in the population express dissatisfaction with industrial productivity. This dissatisfaction appears in the form of complaints concerning the misuse of resources, or both. In either case the dissatisfaction is legitimized by reference to the dominant value-system of the time. The immediate responses to dissatisfaction are undirected or misdirected symptoms of disturbance. Initially these disturbances are "brought into line" by a series of holding operations which prevent the outbursts from reaching explosive proportions. Simultaneously there is a reiteration of established values and an encouragement of ideas which promise to carry the implications of these values into practice. These ideas are implemented by inventions and experiments with methods of production. Finally, entrepreneurs turn these suggestions into action to overhaul the productive system. If successful, the entrepreneurial attempts produce a new industrial structure and an extraordinary growth of production, capitalization, and profits. (Smelser, 1959, pp. 2-3)

In my own analysis of social change during the Industrial Revolution in Britain, I attempted to apply the essentials of this model to several different sequences of social change with reference to industrial production and family life. In principle, this kind of model could be applied further to the analysis of the rise of mass systems of formal education.

Out of years of reflecting on the subject of social change and, more particularly, this kind of model of change, and out of years of research on the emergence of the systems of primary mass education in Britain and the United States during the first three-quarters of the nineteenth century, I have concluded that several of the ingredients in this model are problematical and in need of reformulation and extension.

"Dominant value-system of the time." In my empirical work on the Industrial Revolution, for purposes of heuristic assumption, I assumed a dominant value system that remained constant throughout an episode of change and in the light of which various institutional arrangements and situations were judged to be performing more or less adequately or inadequately (Smelser, 1959, p. 16). It is evident that this assumption should be relaxed, so that it is possible to envision a number of value-positions, one of which might indeed be dominant, but which stand in competition or conflict with one another as bases for legitimizing the expression of dissatisfaction. Furthermore, these diverse value-positions may change over time. This means that, for any given set of institutional arrangements or social "facts," there may be a lack of consensus— indeed, disagreement—as to whether these should be regarded as un- satisfactory. It also means that we should expect to find conflict and competition over the definition of the situation itself, that is, whether an unsatisfactory state of affairs actually exists.

With respect to British society around the turn of the nineteenth cen- tury, the dominant value system could be summarized, following Perkin, as "an open aristocracy based on property and patronage":

> A hierarchical society in which men took their places in an accepted order of precedence, a pyramid stretching down from a tiny minority of the rich and powerful through ever larger and wider layers of lesser wealth and power to the great mass of the poor and powerless. (Perkin, 1969, p. 17)

It was a society based on responsibility on the part of the wealthy and ruling classes, answered by deference on the part of the lesser classes. Furthermore, the dominant values of the day legitimized a fusion of status (the aristocracy), power (the governing classes), wealth (mainly landed, but also commercial and mercantile), and religious authority (the established Church of England) at the top. At the same time this dominant value system was being challenged on various fronts: by the Utilitarian value system, which envisioned among other things, a ra-

tional society based on principles of free exchange, not status and obligations; by political radicalism, which envisioned democratic participation
rather than benevolent paternalism; and by religious Dissent, which
argued for religious freedom, toleration, and denominationalism rather
than religious Establishment. With respect to American society, in the
early days of the republic the dominant values could be said to be those
of activist Protestantism republican virtue and democracy (Cremin,
1980), but within these, tensions between democratic and aristocratic
tendencies took different forms in different parts of the country and
among numerous, different religious denominations and sects.

"Elements in the population." In my earlier work I did not specify
which elements in the population were expressing the dissatisfaction,
nor did I explore the possibility that *other* "elements" might not be expressing dissatisfaction or that they might be positively satisfied with the
social arrangements in question and therefore disposed to challenge or
oppose those who were expressing dissatisfaction. One of the points
made by a critic, George Homans (1964), was that the "elements" in
the population were "men" (mostly men engaged in making and selling
cotton cloth), but he did not carry his objection much further than that.
But in any event, it seems advantageous to make the assumption
about "elements" more specific and to identify not only different value-
bases for legitimizing the expression of dissatisfaction (and pressure
to change) but also the specific social categories and groups that
express dissatisfaction.

What are the bases on which such groups are best identified? With
respect to the interest in primary education in both the United States
and Great Britain in the nineteenth century, two bases seem paramount:
primordial and functional. British society was made up of a diversity
of primordial religious (Church of England, Nonconformist, Wesleyan,
Catholic, Jewish) and regional-ethnic (Irish, Scottish, Welsh, and English;
and within the English, various regional specifications, e.g., Cornish)
groupings; in addition, that society was characterized by an increasingly
complex functional (occupational and class) grouping, which tended to
be assimiliated into the hierarchical ordering of British society in multiple
layers. American life was likewise characterized by distinctions along
religious (denominational), ethnic (for example, Scotch-Irish, Pennsylvania German), racial (white, black, and Indian), and regional
(Northeast, Middle Atlantic, South, Midwest, with regional divisions
within each of these and within each state) lines, as well as burgeoning

functional groupings (merchants, planters, free farmers, working men, etc.). It was the vocal leaders of these kinds of groups that expressed satisfaction and dissatisfaction about states of affairs, speaking simultaneously for their groups and toward some higher legitimizing principle. For both countries it appears that primordial and functional groupings overlapped and were in some degree correlated with one another (for example, aristocracy with the established church and Nonconformism with much of middle-class England; Quakers with urban commerce and Germans with independent farming in Pennsylvania), but in many other instances they were cross-cutting (e.g., German independent farmers and Scotch-Irish independent farmers in Pennsylvania) and independent from one another. In general, then, it does not seem justified to regard different primordially based voices only as disguised voices of functional (especially class) groupings. The two sets of groupings had independent significance as bases of group aspirations, group interests, and group conflicts.

In the actual debates over educational proposals, these primordial and functional groups served as a kind of political maze through which proposed reforms, legislation, and expenditures affecting primary education would pass, with the various groups—insofar as they were politically organized and articulate—ultimately taking political stands according to their perceived values and interests.

"Handling and channeling." In the original model a distinction was made between groups involved in protests of various sorts on the one hand and the authority structure that "reacted to" these protests on the other. This distinction should be broken down because, in fact, "the authorities" (political parties, vested interests in governments, etc.) themselves became involved as partisans in defining whether or not a state of affairs is unsatisfactory and in the fashioning of new, presumably more satisfactory states of affairs. In the early nineteenth century in Britain, for example, the Tories and the more moderate elements of the ruling aristocracy were divided on the issue of whether education was even desirable for the poorer classes, the former believing that education fomented dangerous ideas and the latter believing that education made the lower orders more docile, respectable, and responsible. As another example, in the middle of the nineteenth century Tories and middle-class politicians came into bitter conflict over the seriousness of the plight of children and related educational issues. And in a number of American states Whigs and Democrats struggled over public educa-

tion as a partisan political issue. Educational debates, in short, involved political struggles, as well as the management of protest, among partisan groups inside and outside of government.

"Function more effectively in the new historical circumstances." This assessment of the difference between less differentiated and more differentiated structures lies at the heart of the vision of a society or one of its subsystems as a goal-oriented, purposive entity. That specific formulation of "more effectively" also implies that "effectiveness" is the motivating force behind the impulse to develop more differentiated arrangements, that is, a motivating force to make a going concern perform better than it is. The "more effective" functioning, moreover, is assumed to provide the basis for a diminution of dissatisfaction with the previous state of affairs and a motive for establishing a new set of arrangements on a more or less routine basis.

Certainly the effectiveness of the functioning of educational or other arrangements is *one* basis for expressing dissatisfaction and for initiating change. For example, the infant-school movement in various Eastern cities in the United States in the 1820s and 1830s was based on a diagnosis of the inadequate functioning of workers' families with respect to the care of children; the decision to provide government-matching grants to religious bodies in Britain in 1833 was made in part because it was felt that the efforts of these voluntary groups were not effective enough in providing schools, particularly for the urban masses and in isolated rural districts; and in the mid-nineteenth century the Newcastle Commission was created mainly in response to complaints that Britain's primary education for the poor was costing too much and was not educating the young efficiently; the "payment by results" was adopted in part as a way of making that education more efficient (Sturt, 1967, pp. 239-249).

But educational change cannot be regarded solely as an instrumental problem-solving process by which less effective arrangements are replaced by more effective arrangements. Given what has been said about competing systems of legitimization and competing primordial and functional groups, it follows that the creation of new educational structures is *also* a political victory, compromise, or defeat (or all three) worked out in the context of group conflict. A new structure (educational or other) is, among other things, a commitment of resources to certain social arrangements from which a certain group or groups may benefit (or *believe* they benefit) in relation to their pretensions or interests and aspirations while other groups harbor feelings of resentment or defeat. Thus new educational arrangements may or may not be more "effective" according to some performance criterion, but at the same time it may be assessed as being "effective" or "ineffective" in accommodating the demands or pretensions of concerned groups.

There are many examples illustrating this. The initial decision of political authorities in New York City to establish generally philanthropic schools and their later decision to secularize public schools and *not* to establish religious schools (Baptist and Catholic) was based in part on their desire to avoid a competitive scramble among religious groups for public funds (Ravitch, 1974). The decision taken by the British Parliament in 1833 to provide matching funds to voluntary religious groupings interested in establishing schools was a kind of minimalist compromise taken after a long Parliamentary battle in which more ambitious plans for governmental intervention in education had been shot down by various primordial (mainly religious) groups (Craik, 1896). (These more ambitious plans, it might be argued, might have been more "effective" in the sense of increasing the literacy of the poor, but would not have been very "effective" politically because they promised to set off a long season of sectarian squabbling and subversion of the new arrangements.) The decision on the part of various American states in the 1830s and 1840s to provide state educational funds to districts on a voluntary, matching basis was a strategy that avoided a political confrontation that would have resulted if the state had attempted to coerce localities to tax themselves for education. The "shape" of the resulting educational arrangements in each of these examples reflected the presence of actual or potential group conflicts in the process of making these arrangements.

A somewhat different model of change thus emerges from these considerations. According to the "instrumental" model, the new structure, being more effective, renders the old structure obsolete; the latter is dismantled accordingly with varying degrees of pain and resistance. An industrial instance of this would be the obsolescence and ultimate disappearance of craft production in light of continuous technological advances and new forms of productive organization. The contrasting model of change often involves the segementation and differentiation of new structures, but in the context of conflicting group interests. As the new arrangement is "invented" and "consolidated" in the context of competition among political groups, it may not necessarily be more "efficient" than prior arrangements, but is, rather, patched for reasons of accommodation to politically significant groups. This is no reason to assume, either, that the new arrangements will necessarily displace the old ones because they are less "effective." Particularly if old arrangements are thought to serve other groups' interests, there may be active pressure *not* to dismantle the old. The model of change that emerges, therefore, is not one of "more efficient arrangements replacing less efficient arrangements," but, rather, is a model of "proliferation" of new arrangements around a core of vested interests, analogous to "blistering" onto an existing core, which may remain relatively undisturbed despite the appearance of the new arrangements. (In debates over the bill that was to become the Education Act of 1870, W. E. Forster described the projected establishment of state schools as intended to "fill up gaps," that is, to leave undisturbed the existing system of state-supported, voluntary, denominational schooling [Parliamentary Papers, 1870, Col. 44.]) The ultimate "fate" of the emerging structural arrangements, therefore, depends only in part on their relative "effectiveness"; it depends on the kinds and levels of resources that continue to be made available to it and on the relative position and strength of the contending political groupings whose interests are accommodated (and those whose interests are not) by the new structural arrangements. Thus a principle of differentiation along "interest" lines is invoked in addition to a principle of differentiation along "performance" lines. This principle promises to yield a more comprehensive and detailed account of the shape of emerging educational arrangements.[2]

"If successful." To carry forth the reasoning just developed, the criteria for "success" of an institutional innovation are somewhat different than previously noted. Rather than simply positing some level of "satisfaction" with the innovation, note should be taken of the level of "accommodation" that is generated by the innovation and the level of residual "dissatisfaction" that continues to be registered on the part of those groups that remain less than completely satisfied with the innovation, if not actually "defeated." Second, note should be taken of the fact that any new structural innovation itself generates a number of new roles (in the case of education these roles might be "teacher," "master," "student," "pupil-teacher," "parents of students," "inspectors," "school-board member," etc.), *each* of which itself constitutes a basis for the formation of groups that may themselves become political constituencies and part of the very political process that gave rise to the structural innovation. Another part of the definition of "successful," when applied

to a new institution, then, must refer to the efforts on the part of new vested interests generated by that institution to perpetuate it and to protect or advance its interests.

THE STRUCTURAL DIFFERENTIATION OF SOCIETY AS A SOURCE OF OBSTACLES AND OPPORTUNITIES FOR EDUCATIONAL DEVELOPMENT

One fundamental feature underlying the aforementioned view of the rise of primary education in Great Britain and the United States is that in each case the new educational institutions were grafted onto an existing (and changing) society in which the cultural, political, social, and economic institutions constituted a distinctive combination of obstacles and opportunities; the "shape" of the emerging educational arrangements can be largely understood as reflecting these obstacles and opportunities.

The following broad, comparative structural differences between Great Britain and the United States (as of the first quarter of the nineteenth century) can be noted.

(1) Great Britain manifested a stratification system that was based on the layering of "orders," "ranks," and "classes." The system was in part hereditary; even the "openness" of the aristocracy tended to be a two-generational matter (i.e., the acquisition of fortunes in commercial or mercantile activity, then marrying into or buying land). American society in the early Republic, although stratified (planters, merchants, workmen, farmers), had, however, broken through the fixity of class lines both formally (for example, by prohibiting the use of aristocratic titles) and ideologically (with the stress of equality of opportunity and social mobility). Economically, too, the "openness" of the society to the west constituted an opportunity for individuals to "break out" of the stratification system. Several qualifications to this general characterization must be made, however. First, the caste status of the American black slaves constituted an even stricter hereditary "layering" than the British class system. Second, in certain pockets of American society quasi-aristocratic arrangements persisted, particularly in the larger eastern cities (Boston, New York, and Philadelphia) and in parts of the agricultural South (the plantation owners). And third, the possibility of migration (mainly to North America and Australia) also constituted a means whereby some Britons could "break out" of the stratification system.

These contrasting class systems constituted fundamentally different "programs" that would shape the development of the educational systems of the respective societies. For Britain, there was a kind of taken-for-granted tendency to stratify the educational system in such a way that would reproduce the larger stratification system and would work to provide each "class" with what was "necessary" for its station. Furthermore, the primary guiding assumption would be that the education of the poor would be arranged "for" them by the higher classes, whose responsibility it was to do so. (The earliest "voluntary" activities reflected the efforts of landowners, merchants, and clergymen to provide money to establish schools "for" for the poor; the child-labor legislation of 1833 called for industrialists to establish schools "for" the children who worked for them; and as late as the 1850s, the Newcastle Commission blamed the failure of education in remote agricultural areas and in urban centers on absentee landlords and irresponsible merchants and manufacturers who would not provide resources for schools "for" the poor.) This picture is complicated, of course, by considerable evidence of self-education on the part of the poor and by the persistent efforts of the middle classes to break into the exclusive public schools (which traditionally served the artistocratic classes primarily). It is further complicated later in the century when the working-class schools came to be regarded in part as vehicles for social mobility as well as mechanisms for reproducing a stable working class. The primary cultural and ideological thrust in the early American republic was to lay stress on the schools as a community (rather than a class) resource, open to all and constituting an opportunity for personal (rather than class) uplifting. Yet this dominant tendency, too, was qualified in many ways. First, in those areas with more quasi-aristocratic survivals, some efforts were made to provide schools "for" the poor, which, however, gradually gave way to egalitarian pressures to give common access to primary schools. Second, there was the more or less constant tendency for the better-off in large communities to revert to private academies and schools, a tendency that worked in the "British" direction of stratifying education according to class and reproducing class advantages. And finally, in the slave states, blacks were excluded systematically from all schools.

(2) Great Britain was slower in dismantling those political arrangements that restricted political participation by class. By the first third of the nineteenth century, the American states approached universal male suffrage, though some remaining property and racial restrictions still existed. Only in 1832 did the British middle classes gain en-

franchisement; and only in 1867 did a portion of the working classes do so. The hereditary House of Lords continued to play a major political role throughout the century. The decline of patrician republicanism in the Jacksonian era and the rise of popular participation worked in the same direction.

The major differences emerging with respect to educational politics and decision making were that in Britain these politics tended to take the form of different factions within the ruling groups (aristocratic and middle class) fighting among themselves as to what kind of education was appropriate for the poor, though at the same time responding to political agitations by various class and religious groupings in the society. (Sometimes these agitations were not directed at educational issues as such, but concerned issues such as electoral reform and economic hardship, with the ruling groups attempting to deal with them in part through educational reform.) From early on in America, however, the issues of educational reform and educational decision making entered the arena of electoral politics explicitly and became partisan electoral issues. It was only after the extension of the franchise to the working classses that this kind of electoral development took place to a significant degree in Great Britain (for example, in the election of 1874, when Nonconformist outrage at arrangements established by the Education Act of 1870 helped to turn the Gladstone government out of office).

(3) The differentiation between religion and politics had been carried much further in the United States than in Great Britain. This had been accomplished mainly by the First Amendment of the Constitution and by the actions of the various states in their own constitutions in the early years of the republic. In Britain the Church of England was legally established as the national church, was highly privileged, and was actually represented as such in the House of Lords. The religious picture was complicated, however, by the presence of strong forces of Dissent, which had managed to secure toleration and maintained continuous pressure for parity with respect to one issue after another (access in institutions for higher education, marriage ceremonies, etc.). In addition, the religious picture was further complicated by the presence of some Catholics, increasing in number as Irish migration increased throughout the century. From the standpoint of education, one branch of the Church of England maintained that it possessed an exclusive monopoly on the education of the young and that the secular state should in no way be involved in the education of the people. At best, the state could channel resources through the Church, which would retain con-

trol of education. The Nonconformists, on their part, opposed any educational establishment that violated their religious scruples (in particular, the learning and recitation of the catechism) and resisted paying rates to support schools of the Established Church.

With respect to education, the resulting burdens of proof—and the attendant conflicts—were different. In the United States the political authorities were free (indeed, constrained) to take initiative with respect to education without resorting to or going through religious bodies; the shape of the conflict, then, was how to keep religious bodies *out* of public education. In Great Britain the political authorities could *not* intervene in the support of education without resorting to the religious bodies; the shape of the conflict there was how to intervene without at the same time drawing the opposition of one or more of the religious bodies.

Thus in the early nineteenth century the American republic had gone far toward achieving several kinds of differentiation—the differentiation between kinship and class status, the differentiation between class and political participation, and the differentiation between religion and politics—that were underway in Britain, but much further from completion than in the United States. This meant that the political struggles over education would take place on different social and political battlegrounds, and that the results of these struggles—that is, the emerging educational arrangements—would diverge greatly in the two societies.

NOTES

1. It should be remembered that early formulations of the model of structural differentiation grew from empirical study and interpretation of decision-making processes in the solution of instrumental tasks (Parsons & Bales, 1955).

2. The distinction between "instrumental" and "expressive" life has been frequently invoked in the analysis of small groups, as well as the analysis of social systems generally (Parsons & Bales, 1955). Instrumental refers to the accomplishment of system tasks, whereas expressive refers to the process of dealing with members' needs, desires, interests, and so forth within the system. The alternative model I have outlined brings the expressive—which in organized society might read as "political"—dimension into the limelight.

REFERENCES

Craik, H. (1896). *The state and its relation to education*. London: Macmillan.
Cremin, L. (1980). *American education, the national experience, 1783-1876*. New York: Harper & Row.
Durkheim, E. (1956). *Education and sociology*. (S. D. Fox, Trans.). New York: Free Press.

Halsey, A. H. (1973). The sociology of education. In N. J. Smelser (Ed.), *Sociology: An introduction*. New York: John Wiley.

Homans, G. C. (1965). Bringing men back in. *American Sociological Review, 29*, 809-818.

Parliamentary Papers. (1970). Third Series (Vol. CXCIX). London: Cornelius Buck.

Parsons, T., & Bales, R. F. (1955). *Family, socialization and interaction process*. New York: Free Press.

Perkin, H. (1969). *The origins of modern English society, 1780-1880*. London: Routledge & Kegan Paul.

Ravitch, D. (1974). *The great school wars: New York City, 1905-1973: A history of the public schools as a battlefield of change*. New York: Basic Books.

Smelser, N. J. (1959). *Social change in the industrial revolution*. Chicago: University of Chicago Press.

Sturt, M. (1967). *The education of the people: A history of primary education in England and Wales in the nineteenth century*. London: Routledge & Kegan Paul.

Chapter 6

UNEVEN STRUCTURAL DIFFERENTIATION
Toward a Comparative Approach

PAUL COLOMY
University of Akron

SINCE THE LATE 1960s differentiation theory has received unrelenting criticism. The theory has been attacked for its presumed lack of historical specificity, its reluctance to address the causes of differentiation, its failure to examine how concrete groups contribute to the differentiation process, its putative neglect of power and conflict, and its overemphasis on the integrative consequences of differentiation (Nisbet, 1969; Smith, 1973; Rueschemeyer, 1977; Granovetter, 1979). Even at the time of their formulation, these criticisms were not completely justified, and subsequent developments have rendered such charges virtually obsolete.

Building on that recent work, this chapter seeks to elaborate upon the empirical and theoretical scope of differentiation theory in two major ways. First, in an effort to expand differentiation theory's empirical breadth and to lend it greater historical specificity, the concept of uneven differentiation is introduced. Second, it is argued that a satisfactory theoretical explanation of uneven differentiation must incorporate both structural and voluntaristic elements; a provisional model outlining how that might be accomplished is presented. In addition, a few brief observations about the distinctive institutional and systemic consequences of uneven differentiation are essayed. The theoretical argument is interspersed with a discussion of mass party development in the antebellum United States in order to illustrate the potential utility of the general ideas developed here.

AUTHOR'S NOTE: This is a substantially revised version of a paper delivered at the American Sociological Association in San Antonio, TX, August 27-31, 1984. The research reported here was supported by a University of Akron Faculty Research Grant (#840). The author thanks Donald Cressey, Frank Lechner, and Mark Tausig for their valuable substantive and editorial suggestions.

UNEVEN STRUCTURAL DIFFERENTIATION[1]

Contemporary differentiation theory postulates an analytic "master trend" of social change. It asserts that the most theoretically and empirically significant aspect of structural differentiation is the replacement of multifunctional institutions and roles by more specialized units. Parsons (1966, 1971) has described this trend for total societies, arguing that sociocultural evolution has traversed primitive, archaic, intermediate, and modern stages. Combining a similar concern for "general evolution" with a powerful elaboration of Parsons's analysis, Luhmann (1982) describes three broad types of sociocultural evolution: segmentation, stratification, and functional. Several other scholars have documented the trend toward greater specialization in distinctive institutional spheres: Bellah (1964) for religious ideas, institutions, and action; Smelser (1959) for familial and work roles; Keller (1963) for leadership roles; Parsons and Platt (1973) for the modern university; Eisenstadt (1969) for the emergence of historic, bureaucratic empires; Fox (1976) for medical institutions; and Alexander (1980, 1981) for both solidary relations and the mass media.

The postulation of an analytic master trend of social change, as such, is theoretically legitimate. Indeed, the most fertile macrosociological theories of change invariably posit a distinctive master trend. Marx's emphasis on class struggle and the movement toward a classless society, Weber's depiction of rationalization, Tocqueville's description of an irreversible trend toward equality, and Durkheim's discussion of organic solidarity and the "cult of the individual," though differing significantly in their level of generality, represent ambitious efforts to divine a central direction of modern social change. Further, contemporary students of change share with their classic forebearers the same penchant for organizing their analyses around the description of a master trend, for example, convergence theory's description of the increasing similarities across industrial societies (Moore, 1979), world systems theory's discussion of the growth of a capitalist world system and the accompanying tensions between core and periphery (Chirot & Hall, 1982), and conflict theory's depiction of a movement toward power as the primary distributive principle in modern societies (Lenski, 1984).

Despite the central analytic importance of a master trend, the identification of such a trend constitutes only the first step in a fully satisfactory theory of social change. Any theoretical and empirical extension of differentiation theory requires descriptions and explanations of departures from that trend. Consequently, we propose that the postulated trend be treated as an orienting device that establishes ideal-typical starting and ending points. Actual episodes of change can be assessed against the ideal-typical conception. The adoption of this procedure enables the investigator to identify analytically distinct deviations from the master trend. The ultimate product of this approach is a more theoretically variegated and empirically fruitful conception of structural change.[2]

Initial steps toward a more inclusive conception of change have been taken. For example, increasing attention has been devoted to the examination of dedifferentiation, with several studies, including Parsons's (1954, pp. 104-144, 298-322) early work on fascist movements, noting that in response to diverse structural strains social systems may retreat from relative complexity to a less differentiated level (cf. Lechner, 1984; Lipset & Raab, 1970).

The growing interest in "unequal development" represents another important step toward a more variegated conception of structural change. The term refers to the fact that an unequal rate and degree of differentiation across distinct social realms often generate systemic strain.[3] Depending on the specific character of unequal development, the broader structural and cultural constraints of the environing system, and the actions of powerful groups, a variety of responses to that strain are possible including political corruption (Smelser, 1971), a breakdown of modernization (Eisenstadt, 1973), anomie (Rueschemeyer, 1976), and cycles of inflation and deflation (Alexander, 1981).

Uneven differentiation refers to the varying rate and degree of differentiation of a *single* institutional sector or role structure within a given social system. The concept of uneven differentiation thus extends the logic underlying that of unequal development. The principle, then, is that variation in the rate and degree of change becomes manifest within single institutional complexes as well as across social sectors.

Sensitivity to uneven differentiation is particularly important in examinations of structural change in decentralized and heterogeneous social systems. It appears that the greater the dispersion of power and the higher the degree of subcultural and social diversity in a system, the more likely uneven differentiation will occur. Further, in social systems marked by these characteristics, both the rate and degree of differentiation in one single institutional sphere are likely to vary across geographical subunits.

The utility of recognizing uneven differentiation can be illustrated with an example drawn from antebellum United States history. Much American historiography is organized around the discussion of a master trend of political change that occurred during the antebellum period. Specifically, it is asserted that from 1790 to 1840 American political leadership moved from a traditional, deferential pattern to a modern and more egalitarian, mass-party configuration (Formisano, 1974). According to this view, each of the early postrevolutionary American states produced a self-conscious, comprehensive, and relatively cohesive gentry class that dominated the cultural, social, economic, and political life of their region. Although the status of this class was not written into law, its dominance was legitimated, in large part, by an integrated set of traditional values. By 1840, however, the gentry class began to lose its predominant position. Although many individuals of gentry-class origins continued to be leading figures in the nation's history, the comprehensive structure of gentry rule was ultimately supplanted by a more differentiated form of political leadership.

The master trend from traditional, deferential politics to a more modern configuration was marked by two important developments. First, "new men," often of middle- or lower-class origins and responding to relatively more differentiated channels of political mobility, began, in ever larger numbers, to assume positions of political authority. Second, more specialized political organizations and "rules of the game" emerged. Most significantly, mass political parties replaced the personal and "aristocratic" factions and cliques of an earlier era while norms of party loyalty and discipline increasingly displaced the classic statesman ideal.

Note, however, that this master trend of political change was not evenly realized in all parts of the United States. The differentiation was uneven. By 1840, New York had moved closer to the pattern of modern politics than had any other state (Hofstader, 1969). South Carolina, on the other hand, was singular in its virtual total rejection of differentiated political institutions and its near compulsive adherence to traditional forms (Banner, 1974). Finally, Virginia exhibited a pattern of accommodation (Colomy, 1982a). In particular, although listless with regard to local and state matters, political parties oriented toward national elections and ambivalently committed to democratic rhetoric and the new party ethos appeared in Jacksonian Virginia. In short, the transition from deferential politics to a more modern configuration in the antebellum United States is an intriguing illustration of what we have termed "uneven differentiation."

Recognition of uneven differentiation as a distinctive form of change is significant, then, for two reasons. First, it extends the empirical scope of the functionalist conception of social change and propels differentiation theory toward a more comparative and historically specific approach. Second, it encourages those working within this tradition to construct explanatory schemes that can account for both the master trend and patterned departures from it.

ELABORATING THE EXPLANATORY FRAMEWORK

In their early statements, differentiation theorists gave little explanatory attention to how particular societies, institutions, or role systems moved from one level of complexity to another. Subsequent work, however, (particularly Eisenstadt, 1969; Smelser, 1959, 1974) has moved far toward filling that explanatory gap. Our understanding of how differentiation occurs is approaching what may be called a "structural voluntaristic approach." This incipient perspective holds that institutional development is partially shaped, but not fully explained, by such external and constraining social conditions as the predominant economic system (and the tensions it produces), prevailing political structures and the distribution of power, hegemonic cultural codes, and the pattern of solidary relations. According to this view, analysis of these conditions must be supplemented with examination of how concrete, collective, and individual actors, conditioned as they are by these encompassing structural parameters, contribute to the differentiation process. Theorists holding this perspective thus recommend that explanation of institutional differentiation describe the confluence of structural and voluntaristic elements. The phenomenon of uneven differentiation represents a potentially fruitful arena for further theoretical elaboration of each set of elements.

Structural elements. Smelser's (1959, 1962, 1974) theoretical discussions of industrialization, collective behavior, and higher education provide the most theoretically explicit framework for examination of the structural elements affecting differentiation. Smelser identifies three general structural factors—structural strain, structural opportunities and constraints, and institutionalized cultural patterns—that shape the course of differentiation.

The presence of strain indicates either that certain problems are not being met effectively by existing institutions or that certain changes introduced into a system cannot be effectively managed by traditional arrangements. Smelser maintains that strain may derive from changes or conflicts within a given institutional sector, changes in the relations between institutional sectors, tensions within one social sector that are displaced onto another, and/or conflicts generated by intersocietal relations. Thus structural strain is an important impetus to differentiation.

Opportunities and constraints are structural elements that condition the nature and direction of the collective action necessary to realize new levels of differentiation.

Finally, hegemonic cultural code(s) or value pattern(s) and their subcultural refractions shape the direction in which agents of differentiation are likely to carry structural change, as well as the content of responses mobilized against proposed transformations.

Sensitivity to uneven differentiation encourages comparative analysis of how distinctive combinations of these structural elements contribute to varying rates and degrees of differentiation within a system. Within the substantive domain of antebellum politics, Smelser's three structural variables assume the following specifications.

Strain denotes those "cleavage structures"[4] (Lipset & Rokkan, 1967) within and between social spheres and systems that produce integrative problems for the focal system. Examples of cleavage structures include such divisions as conflicting social classes or class segments, ethnic and religious hostilities (often precipitated by mass immigration), and the assorted tensions associated with economic and social modernization.

The greater the number of cleavage structures and the more salient they are to group members and the larger community, the more likely the traditional form of political authority will experience strain. Traditional authority is ideologically premised on the assumptions of consensus and social harmony; intense, open social conflict undermines this authority.

Cross-cutting cleavages, as opposed to reinforcing ones, are a precondition of political stability in established party systems. Nevertheless, the transition from deferential politics, in which relatively few citizens participate, to mass politics, in which the rate of participation is much higher, is facilitated by polarization of the community and a cumulation of cleavages, which, nevertheless, fall short of the erosion of all attachment to the terminal community (Geertz, 1973). The probability that mass parties will emerge is high when polarized social groups become attached to competing elite factions (Huntington, 1968, pp. 416-417).

Second, opportunities and constraints refer to each state's constitutional framework. Significant elements of that framework are provisions about suffrage, regular and genuinely competitive elections, the number of elective offices, and the protection of civil liberties. Generally, the more expansive the constitutional structure—that is, the broader the suffrage, the greater the number of regular, competitive elections, the larger the number of elective offices, and the greater the protection accorded civil liberties—the greater the opportunity for mass party development.

Third, the movement from deferential politics to mass-party politics is more likely when the hegemonic cultural code shifts away from traditional deferential values toward a more egalitarian pattern. As more egalitarian values emerge, the greater the probability that linkages between various competing elite factions, on the one hand, and broad segments of the population, on the other, will be established. Moreover, under the rubric of egalitarianism, people previously excluded from the political community, often consisting of relatively homogeneous social forces (e.g., members of the working class or an ethnic group), tend to create their own political organizations, directed by their own leaders, to promote their political rights as well as their economic and social interests.

Combining the three structural elements yields an orienting structural model: Presuming a minimal level of attachment to the terminal community, the more salient, the greater the number of, and the more reinforcing the cleavage structures; the more expansive the constitutional opportunity structure; and the more egalitarian the value pattern; the greater the probability that fully developed mass parties and a differentiated political elite will displace deferential political leadership.

A preliminary assessment indicates that this model makes good sense of variations in the rate and level of political differentiation in antebellum New York, South Carolina, and Virginia. New York, where a fully modern party system emerged relatively early, was characterized by overlapping cleavage structures, including burgeoning class conflict, ethnic and religious diversity, modernist and antimodernist strands, a relatively expansive constitutional opportunity structure, and an increasingly egalitarian cultural code. On the other hand, Virginia failed to develop fully differentiated parties, though it did move in that direction. Despite salient, overlapping cleavages between the state's eastern and western regions, differentiation was impeded by strong solidary bonds among whites vis-à-vis (disenfranchised) blacks, a relatively restricted constitutional opportunity structure, and the persistence of deferential ethos. Interestingly enough, although South Carolina's structural characteristics were very similar to Virginia's, the Palmetto state, unlike the Old Dominion, remained steadfast in its near total rejection of party.

Thus it appears that our particular specification of Smelser's more general structural model of differentiation contributes significantly to an understanding of a given instance of uneven differentiation. Nevertheless, a comprehensive explanation requires examination of more than just these structural elements.

Voluntaristic elements. Though a necessary condition, a favorable combination of structural elements does not appear to be a sufficient condition for the production of more differentiated institutions. Favorable structural conditions can yield a startling array of responses. To appreciate how differentiation occurs, it is necessary to supplement the examination of structural conditions with an analysis of those concrete actors who mobilize support for or against a specific course of differentiation.

The study of how concrete actors shape differentiation is most fully developed in Eisenstadt's analysis of institutional entrepreneurs. According to Eisenstadt, entrepreneurs are small groups of individuals who crystallize broad symbolic orientations, articulate specific and innovative goals, establish new normative and organizational frameworks for the pursuit of those goals, and mobilize resources necessary to achieve them (Eisenstadt, 1964, 1965, 1971, 1973; Eisenstadt & Curelaru, 1976).

Although Eisenstadt's formulation represents a major theoretical and empirical advance, his conceptualization is analytically restrictive because it is preoccupied with explaining the master trend of differentiation. If the examination of uneven differentiation is to move from a residual category to the center of theoretical attention, we are compelled to generalize the voluntaristic intent underlying Eisenstadt's formulation and to incorporate the notion of institutional entrepreneurs into the more inclusive rubric of *strategic groups*. Analytically, strategic groups are groups whose members assume a leadership role in directing the course of institutional development. Using both substantive and temporal criteria for further specifying the concept, we argue that these groups encompass a wide array of collectivities, ranging from those who assume leadership in introducing new levels of institutional differentiation *(institutional entrepreneurs)*, to those who are enamored with the entrepreneurs' innovations and try to implement similar structures within their own community *(institutional followers)*, to those who take the lead in defending existing levels of differentiation *(institutional conservatives)*, and including those who sponsor working compromises between existing and newly proposed levels of differentiation *(institutional accommodationists)*.

In addition to providing a deeper appreciation for the process of change, the notion of strategic groups also intimates how social units exhibiting virtually identical structural characteristics can generate substantially dissimilar levels of differentiation. For example, antebellum Virginia and South Carolina exhibited similar patterns of strain, possessing relatively intense cleavages in the economic and political spheres that were cross-cut by integrative forces in the cultural and solidary spheres. Moreover, in both states the operative economic and political strains were manifest sectionally in often bitter contests between the eastern and western regions of each state. Finally, both states were encumbered with the most restrictive constitutional opportunity structures in the nation. Still, despite these many structural similarities, the extent of political differentiation in the two states differed significantly. Antebellum Virginia embraced a competitive two-party system *at the level of national politics and issues,* whereas South Carolina violently eschewed the party system at every level. These dissimilar levels of political differentiation were largely due to the distinctive orientations, interests, and activities of strategic groups in the two states.

Although it is useful to subsume the idea of institutional entrepreneurs under the more inclusive concept of strategic groups, there are three respects in which even greater analytic specification is needed. First, although Eisenstadt describes the orientations of institutional entrepreneurs, he does so principally in substantive terms. We shall specify three mechanisms that shape strategic groups' orientations: an institutional project, prototypes, and a generalized value element. Second, Eisenstadt shows little concern for organization of institutional entrepreneurs, especially the presence of divisiveness and conflict. We shall specify the various bases of diversity and coordination within strategic groups. Third, while Eisenstadt examines relations between institutional entrepreneurs and others, he stresses the determinant role of innovative groups in shaping a new institutional order. This emphasis leads him to neglect how groups initially opposed to an innovation can, at later stages, act as agents of institutionalization. A more supple conception of the coalitional and conflictual relations between strategic groups and their allies and opponents is necessary.[5]

Orientations. The activities of strategic groups and their impact on the institutional order are partially determined by their orientations. Those orientations, in turn, reflect a combination of mechanisms. A fundamental component of strategic groups' orientations is adherence to a broad conception of an institutional project. The project is further specified through the employment of past or contemporary institutional models or proto-types. Finally, that project is both elaborated and legitimated by stressing its intimate connection to a generalized value pattern.

An institutional project combines ideological and normative commitments with the self-interested construction or preservation of a social niche. The project identifies the social sector in which change is sought, resisted, or accommodated and specifies the critical social functions to be satisfied by a new or existing institutional pattern. Although sharing these elements, the projects of institutional entrepreneurs, conservatives, and accommodationists have their distinctive features.

Integral to the institutional entrepreneurs' project is a delegitimation of established practices and the creation of new bases of legitimacy. In this regard, the project assumes the character of a "contrast conception" vis-à-vis existing institutional forms and practices, which are denounced as inefficient, ineffective, and inequitable. The proposed new institutional structure is promoted as a remedy for these ills, often as a kind of panacea. Finally, the institutional project identifies a potentially new locus of material interest, for example, the construction of an organizational or professional niche.

Typically, the project of institutional followers is very similar to that of entrepreneurs. In addition to presenting their projects as contrasting alternatives to existing structures, however, followers also maintain that their proposals are faithful reflections of innovations introduced by entrepreneurs.

The institutional conservative's project is organized around a virulent defense of existing practices and a complementary critique of proposed or implemented alterations of these practices. The conservative project also assumes the form of a contrast conception, juxtaposing the institutional and sacred legacy of the founding fathers against the threat represented by the self-interested arrangements advocated by institutional entrepreneurs and their followers. Existing institutional practices are pronounced essential for stability, order, and harmony. Finally, the conservative project aspires to protect the myriad interests endangered by institutional change.

Whereas the projects of institutional entrepreneurs, followers, and conservatives are relatively clear and, in many respects, are mirror images of one another, the institutional accommodationist's mission is fraught with ambiguity and ambivalence. Elements of established practices are condemned and certain reforms are suggested, but the critique is rarely generalized and the reforms are typically piecemeal. Change is proposed so that continuity might be restored. Accommodationists resemble entrepreneurs "with the brakes on." They sponsor change, in part, to protect the interests of those who have traditionally benefitted. Unlike the conservatives, however, they also attempt to broaden the circle of interest, claiming that people previously excluded now have a stake in the modified institutional arrangements.

Again, the theoretical model seems to make sense of the concrete projects of strategic groups in antebellum New York, South Carolina, and Virginia.

The Albany Regency, the political party entrepreneurs in antebellum New York and the leading entrepreneurial group behind the creation of the national Democratic party, promoted parties as the most effective instrument for increased political participation and more voter control over government. This broad conception of party also included concern for more specific activities such as keeping citizens informed about governmental affairs and providing genuine political choices to the electorate. A party was envisioned as a permanent organization independent of any one person, with a leadership responsive to the mass of its members. This institutional project took form, in part, as a contrast conception to the prevailing modes of political organization, which, according to the Regency, were personalistic, temporary, and aristocratic factions allocating political preferment largely on the basis of family pedigree.

The Regency's institutional project acknowledged that significant material interests were attendant upon creating a new institutional infrastructure. The "meritocratic" dispensation of patronage and the election or appointment to leadership positions within the party were primary material rewards available to entrepreneurs and their allies.

In South Carolina, a conservative institutional project was articulated by Calhoun and his faction. Reacting to the successes of party entrepreneurs in other states, these institutional conservatives envisioned a nation ruled by gentlemen. Stability, public order, and the protection of liberty required the enlightened rule of disinterested statesmen.

The Calhounites' defense of a traditional mode of political leadership was partially inspired by a concern for protecting certain material interests. First, these conservatives were the very gentlemen lauded in their approbation of conventional politics. Thus their institutional project was, in part, an assertion of their own interests. In addition, these conservative Carolinians articulated a distinctive southern, regional interest, largely manifest in the protection of slavery and in antiprotective tariff sentiment. In the conservatives' view, traditional politics better protected vital southern interests than did mass-party politics.

In Virginia, a group of institutional accommodationists, the Richmond Junto, articulated an institutional project that "appropriated" many elements of the Regency's innovative institutional vision while tempering the "leveling" edges of that enterprise. The Junto's primary concerns were the maintenance of Virginia's influence on the national polity and the protection of states' rights. To realize those ends, the Junto built party structures to organize presidential and congressional elections and, to a lesser extent, state assembly elections.

Unlike the institutional entrepreneurs in New York, however, the Junto did not couple these organizational innovations with a generalized critique of gentry political domination. In Virginia, mass parties were built alongside the structure of gentry rule and, on occasion, reinforced it and, at other times, opposed it. Moreover, the Junto itself remained oligarchic, closed, secretive, and premised on familial connections.

Materially, the Junto sought to secure federal patronage for Virginians and to preserve Virginia's political influence over national affairs.

Strategic groups' institutional projects are often elaborated by the adoption of an institutional prototype. Prototyping denotes a general process whereby strategic groups draw on institutional exemplars from the past or present to supplement and extend their projects.[6] Prototypes perform both cognitive and legitimating functions. Cognitively, prototypes function as metaphors that give direction to strategic groups' activities and provide potential adherents with an established frame of reference for interpreting the project. Further, institutional prototypes are usually imbued with value, and strategic groups often stress the apparent isomorphism (Meyer & Rowan, 1977; DiMaggio & Powell, 1983) between the prototype and the group's institutional project to attract greater support and to defuse criticism.

For our purposes it is useful to distinguish two types and two phases of prototyping.[7] In the first form of protyping, strategic groups draw on historical, institutional exemplars from their society, thus stressing the continuity between what they advocate and what existed previously. Prototyping, in this instance, often has a revivalistic character to it, with strategic groups claiming that they seek only to resurrect and breathe new life into hallowed forms of the past. The cognitive and legitimating functions of revivalistic prototyping are clear: The older institutional exemplars provide a stable, cognitive frame of reference and their putative sacred character lends legitimacy to the projects of strategic groups.

A second form of prototyping occurs when strategic groups use the institutional arrangements of other spheres within the same society as models. This cross-institutional prototyping is particularly salient in the metaphors used by strategic groups to shape the orientations and participation of adherents to their enterprise. In adopting these metaphors, strategic groups might also alter them, infusing them with new meanings. Nevertheless, the adoption of metaphors and the employment of practices associated with revered institutions imparts a legitimacy to the projects of strategic groups.

In addition to distinguishing between revivalistic and cross-institutional prototyping, we must also identify two phases of prototyping: the innovative and the derivative. In the innovative phase, institutional entrepreneurs, drawing upon both revivalistic and cross-institutional prototypes, begin to construct and implement their vision of a more differentiated institutional order. These entrepreneurs articulate a relatively specific image of the more differentiated institution and take the initial steps in its construction. In the derivative phase, the entrepreneurs' burgeoning structure is taken as a point of reference by other strategic groups. Thus institutional followers, enamored with the new institutional order, employ the structure as a prototype for their own innovative activities. Institutional conservatives, however, view the new structure negatively and therefore seek to repress developments within their own bailiwick that appear sympathetic to the new institutional order. Finally, institutional accommodationists selectively adopt elements of the more differentiated institution and fuse them with more traditional patterns.

The New York Regency employed both revivalistic and cross-institutional prototypes to organize and legitimate their vision of a modern, differentiated party system. Although Martin Van Buren, the acknowledged leader of the Regency, and his associates introduced many significant changes and were the first to build a genuine mass political party, they were forever claiming that their efforts were aimed at the simple restoration of the "old Republican party" (Kass, 1965, pp. 3, 112). The Regency also drew on cross-institutional prototypes to construct a differentiated party organization, often relying on military rhetoric and imagery to shape their vision of modern political organization (Goldman, 1970).

By adopting revivalistic and cross-institutional prototypes, the Regency constructed a mass-party organization and a new style of politics that were clearly differentiated from the traditional structure of gentry domination. Once constructed, New York's Republican party began to serve as a prototype for institutional followers in other states, as the prototyping process entered its derivative phase.

The substantial progress of the master trend of political differentiation in antebellum American is partially due to the large number and relative success of those institutional followers who used New York's Republican party as a prototype for their own institution-building activities. Thus "Regency style politics quickly traversed New York boundaries. The organization code, carried by New York émigrés or imitated by local politicians across the country, powerfully altered the political culture of the middle period" (Wallace, 1973, p. 185).

But in South Carolina the Regency and the new politics it inaugurated served as a negative reference institution. Calhoun and his followers thundered against mass parties. In his correspondence as well as in his *Disquisition on Government,* Calhoun ranted against the "New York School of Politicks" and the vices of party politics. Calhounites contrasted the new politics' celebration of spoilsmen with South Carolina's pattern of gentlemanly rule in which the "best men" exercised public authority.

These institutional conservatives coupled employment of the Regency as a negative reference institution with their own version of a revivalistic prototype. The Calhounites argued that in the era of the founding generation, the dominant pattern of political authority was ruled by enlightened, "natural aristocrats." However, they went on, in the age of Jackson, the philosopher-statesman had given way to the party manager and the demagogue. The Calhounites saw themselves waging a principled struggle to restore the founding fathers' principles and pattern of social leadership.

The Richmond Junto was more receptive to the Regency's conception of party than were the Calhounites. By 1830, "the Richmond Junto had largely accepted Van Buren's view of party" (Dent, 1974, p. 195).

That acceptance was selective, however. In national elections, the Junto employed political strategies and organizational forms that had been refined by the Regency. The Junto also insisted upon a degree of party loyalty and obedience. Unlike the Regency, however, the Junto did not embrace a military metaphor to organize and legitimate political participation, and the Junto and Virginian politics displayed a notably less disciplined politics (McCormick, 1966, p. 185).

In addition to a selective adoption of the Regency model, the Junto's accommodationist vision entertained a distinctive version of a revivalistic prototype. The Junto envisioned itself and presented Virginia's Democratic party to others as the true heirs of the Jeffersonian-Madisonian legacy.

Both prototypes and institutional projects are supplemented with value elements and imagery. By connecting their institutional vision to a society's most fundamental values, strategic groups claim legitimacy for their project and seek to attract a broad base of popular support.

The significance of value elements for institutional change in the antebellum United States is profitably understood in terms of a "cultural refraction" model of culture/society relations (Alexander, 1984). Specifically, during the early national period, republicanism constituted a comprehensive and fairly integrated cultural system that was also subject to conflicting interpretations or specifications by competing social groups and interests.

Republican values shaped the orientations of all antebellum strategic groups. Albany Regency members envisioned their institutional innovations largely in terms of the revitalization of republican sentiment; the latter's antipathy to centralized power was integral to their institutional imagery (Hofstader, 1969, p. 227; Benson, 1961, pp. 216-237). On the other hand, Calhounites, mimicking old republican doctrine, countered that political parties threatened the public welfare and were the artifice of deceitful demagogues (Freehling, 1965). Finally, the twin notions of states' rights and strict construction were the republican tenets the Richmond Junto most frequently drew upon in shaping their vision of Virginia's Democratic party.

Within the expansive context of republicanism, a second, dynamic dimension of culture, which symbolic interactionists call "general movements," also assumed significance. General movements refer to mass preoccupations with certain values, such as equality or liberty. Although general movements lack organizational identity, they do provide broad value orientations to organized groups mobilized in support of or in opposition to change (Blumer, 1939).

The Jacksonian era clearly witnessed the birth of a general movement centered on egalitarianism. As one well-informed student of the age notes, "Egalitarianism expressed the central tendency of the period. . . . After 1815, not only in politics but in all spheres of American life, egalitarianism challenged elitism and, in most spheres and places, egalitarianism won" (Benson, 1961, p. 336).

The Albany Regency employed elements of the egalitarian general movement to level a stinging attack upon the "aristocratic" character of traditional politics. At the same time, Regency members articulated and specified a new institutional order—mass-party structures—in terms of that egalitarian rhetoric.

Equally significant is the tendency for an initial general movement to generate a spirited defense of values and standards threatened by the ascendance of the burgeoning movement (Alexander & Colomy, 1984, 1985). This type of cultural reaction often shapes the orientations of institutional conservatives seeking to revitalize existing organizational and normative frameworks, as well as the orientations of institutional accommodationists interested in fashioning alternative institutional arrangements reflecting a cultural tradition peripheral to or rejected by the dominant general movement.

Although the strong current of egalitarianism placed elitism on the defensive, elements of the older tradition persisted in many areas, especially South Carolina. In that state, the powerful Calhoun faction designed a political organization consistent with the tenets of traditional elitism.

Treading the path toward accommodation, the Junto sponsored a party structure that included elements consistent with both the general egalitarian movement and others more congruent with traditional elitism. On the one hand, several Junto members insisted upon such antielitist measures as a degree of party loyalty and discipline, subordination of individual judgment to the party, the dispensation of state patronage on the basis of party regularity, and legislative instructions to senators. Still, these accommodationists never completely abandoned traditional tenets of elitism: upper-class stewardship, *noblesse oblige,* and statesmanship.

Internal organization. In addition to strategic groups' orientations, their pattern of internal organization also shapes their activities and their contribution to uneven differentiation. Generally, both the creation of more differentiated institutions and the maintenance of traditional structures (in the face of an increasingly realized master trend) require considerable internal cohesion. However, although successful entrepreneurs as well as conservatives are characterized by a high degree of cohesion, the sources of their internal unity often vary. Broadly speaking, entrepreneurs are more likely to rely on generalized commitments and a shared identification with the new institutional order as bases for internal cohension, whereas institutional conservatives are more inclined toward personalistic and primordial sources of solidarity. Institutional accommodationists often exhibit less internal unity; the bases of whatever unity exists often combines primordial and more generalized commitments. These general patterns are found in the internal organization of the Regency, the Calhounites, and the Junto.

Regency men were of middle-class or lower-middle-class origin, often "self-made" men, moderately prosperous and respected, but not rich during their early years and not connected to the leading families of the state (Hofstader, 1969, pp. 240-241). Estranged from "artistocratic" politics and speaking in a voice laced with democratic and egalitarian sentiments, the Regency men began to develop a distinctive social identity: that of the modern, professional politician.

Perhaps the most salient characteristic of the Regency's internal organization was its high degree of cohesiveness: "Unity among the members of the Regency was the single most striking feature in the operation of this political machine. . . . They rarely made important decisions without holding consultations beforehand" (Remini, 1958, p. 350).

Although regular consultation undeniably contributed to internal unity, the latter was also a product of a passion for organization. Even though Van Buren assumed a first-among-equals status, the distinctive feature of Regency organizations was individual subordination to the party.

The preoccupation with an organization deemed independent of any single man's will was reflected in the attention Regency members gave to recruiting new men and promoting them to positions of authority within the party. Specific, impersonal criteria for advancement within the organization began to emerge and political mobility was increasingly separated from the larger-status order (Remini, 1958, p. 349).

Like the Regency, the Calhounites in South Carolina exhibited a high degree of internal unity. The sources of that cohesion, however, were drastically different. The core group of Calhounites was united by familial ties and a common identification with the gentry-planter class and a commitment to its continued predominance.

Within this faction the dominant mode was subordination to Calhoun's leadership. Calhoun expected those who agreed with him to follow his lead. "Those who did not agree were given an opportunity to change their minds, but if they proved obdurate they were eliminated" (Wiltse, 1949, p. 292). Indeed, from 1832 to 1850 John Calhoun was the "almost absolute master" of South Carolina.

Such personalistic authority generated internal tensions. Perhaps most readily apparent was a tendency for jealousy and enmity to arise between Calhoun's lieutenants. Further, personalistic rule and the absence of an independent, permanent political organization produced much disorder in South Carolinian politics after Calhoun's death in 1850.

For the most part, the Calhounites overcame these intrafactional tensions. First, Calhoun insisted upon at least the semblance of unity among his followers and quickly responded to any signs of dissension within his ranks. Internal unity was also achieved through the shared conviction that the Calhounites were protecting vital southern interests endangered by hostile groups from other parts of the country.

In comparison to the Regency and the Calhounites, the Junto is striking for its relatively low degree of internal cohesion. Organizationally, the Junto did not move very far beyond the traditional substratum of familial connections. The inner circle of the Junto resided in Richmond for at least part of the year, but was closely tied to Virginia's planter class and adopted many of its practices (Ammon, 1953, p. 395).

The Junto did, on occasion, discipline its members. "Regarding national candidates and national issues, the Junto assumed the right to speak for Virginia with a single voice and it could be intolerant of dissent" (Harrison, 1970, p. 187). Further, the Junto was able to exercise considerable influence in the state and over its own members through its control of the Democratic party caucus, legislative and state conventions, and the central corresponding committees during presidential campaigns.

Despite these various bases for internal unity, however, the Junto did not exhibit the same degree of cohesion characteristic of the Regency or the Calhounites. Two factors account for the relatively low degree of Junto unity and control.

First, the Junto was primarily oriented toward national issues and presidential elections, not to state issues. The Junto developed no coherent or consistent policy on state questions. Second, the Junto remained a thoroughly secret and informal group. Such secrecy meant that little could be done to build a centrally controlled, statewide mass-party organization.

External relations. Finally, any strategic group's impact on differentiation is shaped by its relations with other groups. Accordingly, an analysis of the types and results of coalitional and conflictual relations, and a discussion of the general structural factors that condition these relations is necessary to understand the dynamics of master trends as well as uneven differentiation.

Two general points are pertinent to strategic groups' coalitions with other collectivities. First, the social structures in which strategic groups seek support set limits on the number and types of possible coalition partners. That is, the number, diversity, and nature of potential allies greatly affects strategic groups' ability to exert control over the course of institutional development. Generally, the more decentralized and diverse the social structure in a given subunit, the more advantageous the bargaining position of entrepreneurs, followers, and accommodationists. Obversely, the more the power and resources are concentrated in a small number of groups, the more likely it is that entrepreneurs, followers, and accommodationists will have to modify their institutional vision in a fashion acceptable to a prospective coalition partner.

The Regency operated in a social context characterized by a relatively pronounced egalitarianism, a relatively expansive constitutional structure that opened most local and state offices to virtually all adult white males, and a considerably fragmented pattern of stratification that dispersed power across several distinct elites and even gave some power to the middle and lower classes and various ethnic and religious groups. For this reason, the Regency was successful in allying itself with the burgeoning working class and with religious and ethnic out-groups. In forging these coalitions, the Regency nevertheless retained considerable autonomy and was able to realize its modern conception of party organization.

On the other hand, Virginia's Richmond Junto was confronted with a cultural, social, and constitutional context that concentrated power in the hands of a planter elite. In order to institutionalize its own restricted view of modern parties, the Junto allied itself with the dominant planter groups, which, in turn, compelled the Junto to moderate its already temperate view of party.

Unlike entrepreneurs, accommodationists, and followers, institutional conservatives are more likely to secure support in social contexts in which power is concentrated in relatively traditional groups. The Calhounites organized in a state that continued to emphasize deference to traditional elites, possessed a restrictive constitutional opportunity structure that limited mass access to local and state offices, and exhibited a pattern of economic and social stratification that concentrated power in the merchant-planter elite. All these factors worked to the advantage of

Calhounites, who were closely allied with the interests of powerful South Carolinians.

The second condition affecting coalitional activity is critical to institution building: control over the distribution of pertinent material resources. Beyond that, the nature of resources and the criteria for their distribution vary. Entrepreneurs and followers tend to employ quite specialized material resources (e.g., political office) and to use relatively specialized criteria (e.g., demonstrated loyalty to the organization) for distributing those resources. Institutional conservatives, on the other hand, tend to employ somewhat more diffuse material resources (e.g., political office, but also access to exclusive status groups) and to use more general criteria (e.g., performance, but also "character" and "connections") for their distribution. Finally, accommodationists employ several types of material resources and use both specialized and general criteria for their distribution. However, the central dynamic is movement toward greater specialization in both the content and distribution of resources.

Even if strategic groups are successful in constructing powerful coalitions, they invariably encounter opposition from other collectivities. Such conflict can have several consequences. It can result in defeat of strategic groups and their project. Alternatively, even when strategic groups are relatively successful they may not thoroughly dominate the opposition, so the outcome of differentiation can be a composite of diverse and even contradictory elements.

Study of mass-party development in the antebellum United States suggests that when conflict between groups assumes a competitive form, with clearly defined winners and losers, there is a tendency toward convergence and eventual institutionalization of the initially victorious group's project. The tendency is the same whether entrepreneurs, and their followers, or conservatives emerge as decisive winners. In either case, opponents, seeking a path to victory, often adopt the very organizational and normative framework they initially opposed. Thus when entrepreneurs and followers are clearly successful, competition tends to promote greater differentiation. However, when conservatives are clearly successful, competition tends to inhibit differentiation.

Political change in antebellum New York provides a dramatic example of how competition can promote differentiation. The first attempts to build mass-party organizations, to open up political office to categories of men previously excluded, and, generally, to create a more inclusive polity were undertaken by the Regency. The incipient Whig leadership, assuming the role of institutional conservatives, vigorously opposed these organizational and normative innovations, and sought to mobilize a large constituency in defense of traditional, deferential patterns. However, adherence to conventional patterns of authority and repudiation of populist egalitarianism were largely responsible for the Whigs' inability to compete effectively against the Democrats for political office. By 1834, important elements of the Whig leadership decided not merely to adopt but to improve the innovations introduced by Democrats. The electoral campaign of that year marks the genuine institutionalization of mass political parties in New York and the near publically, unquestionable ascendance of an egalitarian style of political leadership. In this case, it is clear that the opponents, who initially emerged to combat the Democrats' structural and normative innovations and to defend traditional arrangements, served, in the end, as agents of institutionalization. Thus countermobilization actually promoted the institutionalization of more differentiated political structures.

It is true, of course, that differentiation via competition may hide a continuing disaffection about innovative structural arrangements. That dissatisfaction may emerge at a later date to fuel movements aimed at either dedifferentiation or higher levels of differentiation. In New York, for example, the opposition group did not fully embrace the structural innovations championed by the Regency, and several opposition leaders continued to harbor a profound ambivalence about the value of mass parties. That ambivalence persisted throughout the antebellum period and became an important impetus to civil service reform, with its vigorous assault on party and its movement toward a new level of structural differentiation.

In South Carolina, institutional conservatives established the terms of political conflict, and their political success compelled their opponents to adopt a similar organizational and normative framework. Thus following the lead of the powerful Calhoun faction, opposition groups also publically eschewed party, developed temporary and personalistic factions that dissipated after the resolution of a given issue, and avowed commitment to the traditional patterns of leadership that presumably distinguished the South from the rest of the nation. In short, the Calhounities' notable political success inhibited their opponents from proposing radical innovations. The overall effect of competition in antebellum South Carolina was to impede the growth of differentiated political institutions.

When accommodationists are confronted with competition, there is usually considerable movement toward more specialized and differentiated structures. In the short run, competitors are ineluctably drawn to structures that promote progress toward clearly defined goals, and more specialized structures often provide a competitive advantage. However, accommodationists' lingering commitments to traditional institutions and values often inhibit movement to the highest levels of differentiation.

The ambiguous effects of competition on accommodationists are illustrated by political change and continuity in Jacksonian Virginia. On the one hand, the leading opponents of the Junto were drawn primarily from the gentry. That opposition envisioned society as an organic order, one whose true interests could be determined only by its "natural leaders," and assumed that hierarchy and deference to the upper classes were necessary components of a well-ordered society. On the other hand, however, the emergence of sustained competition between partisan groups served as an important stimulus for greater structural differentiation. By 1834, Junto opponents were able to secure a majority of seats in the state legislature and were organizing at the national level to oppose the election of the Junto's choice for President. The opposition's political success forced the Junto and its allies to become better organized. Between 1834 and 1839, both groups elaborated their organizations, increased their discipline, altered their campaign techniques, broadened the nature of their appeal, and moved toward relatively more differentiated political institutions.

Nevertheless, the Junto and its opponents were unwilling to relinquish completely the older traditions; conventional patterns of leadership retained a vitality that prevented the full differentiation of modern political structures.

CONCLUSION

Cognizance of uneven differentiation broadens the empirical scope and elaborates the explanatory scheme of differentiation theory. It is also significant because it has distinctive structural consequences. Two potential consequences of uneven differentiation are noteworthy.

First, structural differentiation typically produces a distinctive institutional substratum for the formation of relatively autonomous elites. However, examination of uneven differentiation suggests that the institutional interests and the prevailing orientations of elites vary across geographical subunits. Accordingly, cooperation between and coordination of these elites becomes difficult and interelite conflict more probable.

In this regard, it is interesting to note that political elites in South Carolina, the least politically differentiated state in the antebellum union, led the nullification movement in the early 1830s, led the secession movement in the early 1850s, and were a driving force behind the outbreak of the Civil War.

Second, even if the master trend of differentiation is clearly the dominant pattern of institutional change, the presence of less differentiated structures provides a refuge and haven for critical assessment of the master trend. Not enveloped by the new circle of interest and ideology associated with more differentiated structures, those inhabiting less differentiated structures may formulate critiques that prepare men's minds for new directions of change: either toward higher levels of differentiation or toward dedifferentiation.

Uneven differentiation is thus an important type of institutional change. The concept supplements study of the master trend identified by differentiation theory and gives that approach greater historical specificity. It also prompts refinement of differentiation theory's explanatory framework. Finally, it underscores the tensions and conflicts produced by structural differentiation.

NOTES

1. Differentiation has been used to describe social change at different levels. We adopt Alexander's (1978) distinction between cultural, structural, and psychological differentiation.

2. This strategy for generating a more comprehensive theory of social change has many parallels with the procedures outlined by Turner (1980) for constructing an integrated role theory.

3. Unfortunately, there is much terminological confusion. What we have termed unequal development has also been referred to as uneven differentiation and partial modernization. We prefer to employ the phrase "uneven differentiation" to designate the phenomenon described in the next paragraph of this chapter.

4. Lipset and Rokkan's (1967) analysis of cleavage structures represents a thoughtful and incisive, multidimensional analysis of tensions in modern social systems. Unlike materialist or idealist schemes, their theoretical framework gives equal analytic status to all subsystem conflicts.

5. The following analysis elaborates ideas presented in Colomy and Rhoades (1984).

6. The concept of prototyping was introduced into sociological discourse by Ralph Turner (1970), who developed it in the context of his interactionist role theory. Also see Colomy (1982b).

7. There are at least two other forms of prototyping. The first uses prototypes from other existing societies. The second employs what Parsons (1966, p. 95-108) calls "seedbed societies" as prototypes.

REFERENCES

Alexander, J. C. (1978). Formal and substantive voluntarism in the work of Talcott Parsons: A theoretical and ideological reinterpretation. *American Sociological Review, 43,* 177-198.

Alexander, J. C. (1980). Core solidarity, ethnic outgroup, and social differentiation: A multi-dimensional model of inclusion in modern societies. In J. Dofny & A. Akiwono (Eds.), *National and ethnic movements* (pp. 5-28). Beverly Hills, CA: Sage.

Alexander, J. C. (1981). The mass news media in systemic, historical and comparative perspective. In E. Katz & T. Szecsko (Eds.), *Mass media and social change* (pp. 17-52). Beverly Hills, CA: Sage.

Alexander, J. C. (1984). Three models of culture and society relations; toward an analysis of Watergate. *Sociological Theory, 2,* 290-314.

Alexander, J. C., & Colomy, P. (1984). Institutionalization and collective behavior: Points of contact between Eisenstadt's functionalism and symbolic interaction. In E. Cohen, M. Lissak, & U. Almagor (Eds.), *Tradition and modernity: Essays in honor of S. N. Eisenstadt.* Boulder, CO: Westview.

Alexander, J. C., & Colomy, P. (in press). Toward neofunctionlism: Eisenstadt's change theory and symbolic interaction. *Sociological Theory.*

Ammon, H. (1953). The Richmond Junto, 1800-1824. *Virginia Magazine, 61,* 395-413.

Banner, J. M. (1974). The problem of South Carolina. In S. Elkins & E. McKitrick (Eds.), *The Hofstader aegis: A memorial* (pp. 60-93). New York: Knopf.

Bellah, R. (1964). Religious evolution. *American Sociological Review, 29,* 358-374.

Benson, L. (1961). *The concept of Jacksonian democracy.* Princeton, NJ: Princeton University Press.

Blumer, H. (1939). Collective behavior. In A. M. Lee (Ed.), *Principles of sociology* (pp. 165-222). New York: Barnes & Noble.

Calhoun, J. C. (1853). *Disquisition of government.* New York: Peter Smith.

Capers, G. M. (1959). *Stephen A. Douglas: Defender of the union.* Boston: Little, Brown.

Chirot, D., & Hall, R. (1982). World system theory. *Annual Review of Sociology, 8,* 81-106.

Colomy, P. (1982a). *Stunted differentiation: A sociological examination of political elites in Virginia, 1720-1850.* Unpublished doctoral dissertation, Department of Sociology, University of California at Los Angeles.

Colomy, P. (1982b). *Proto-typing and role differentiation.* Paper presented at the annual meetings of the Pacific Sociological Association.

Colomy, P., & Rhoades, G. (1984). *Institutional entrepreneurs and institutional change.* Unpublished manuscript, University of Ohio at Akron.

Dent, L. (1974). *The Virginia democratic party, 1824-1847.* Unpublished doctoral dissertation, Louisiana State University.

DiMaggio, P., & Powell, W. (1983). The iron cage revisited: Institutional isomorphism and collective rationality in organizational fields. *American Sociological Review, 48,* 147-160.

Douglas, S. A. (1961). *Letters of Stephen A. Douglas.* (R. W. Johannsen, Ed.). Urbana: University of Illinois Press.

Eisenstadt, S. N. (1964). Social change, differentiation, and evolution. *American Sociological Review, 29,* 235-247.

Eisenstadt, S. N. (1965). *Essays on comparative institutions.* New York: John Wiley.

Eisenstadt, S. N. (1969). *The political system of empires.* New York: Free Press.

Eisenstadt, S. N. (1971). *Social Differentiation and stratification.* Glenview, IL: Scott, Foresman.

Eisenstadt, S. N. (1973). *Tradition, change and modernity.* New York: John Wiley.

Eisenstadt, S. N., & Curelaru, M. (1976). *The form of sociology: Paradigms and crises.* New York: John Wiley.

Formisano, R. P. (1974). Deferential-participant politics: The early republic's political culture, 1789-1840. *American political Science Review, 68,* 473-487.

Formisano, R. P. (1976). Toward a reorientation of Jacksonian politics: A review of the literature, 1959-1975. *Journal of American History, 63,* 42-65.

Fox, R. (1976. Medical evolution. In J. J. Loubser & R. C. Baum (Eds.), *Explorations in general theory in social science: Essays in honor of Talcott Parsons* (pp. 773-787). New York: Free Press.

Freehling, W. W. (1965). Spoilsmen and interests in the thought and career of John C. Calhoun. *Journal of American History, 52,* 25-42.

Geertz, C. (1973). The integrative revolution: Primordial sentiments and civil politics in the new states. In C. Geertz (Ed.), *The interpretation of cultures* (pp. 255-310). New York: Basic Books.

Goldman, P. M. (1970). Political rhetoric in the age of Jackson. *Tennessee Historical Quarterly, 29,* 360-371.

Granovetter, M. (1979). The idea of advancement in theories of social evolution and development. *American Journal of Sociology, 85,* 489-515.

Harrison, J. H. (1970). Oligarchs and democrats: The Richmond Junto. *Virginia Magazine, 78,* 184-198.

Hofstader, R. (1969). *The idea of a party system.* Berkeley: University of California Press.

Huntington, S. (1968). *Political order in changing societies.* New Haven, CT: Yale University Press.

Kass, A. (1965). *Politics in New York State, 1800-1830.* Syracuse: Syracuse University Press.

Keller, S. (1963). *Beyond the ruling class.* New York: Random House.

Lechner, F. (1984). *Fundamentalism and sociocultural revitalization: On the logic of dedifferentiation.* Unpublished manuscript, University of Pittsburgh.

Lenski, G. E. (1984). *Power and privilege: A theory of stratification (2nd ed.).* New York: McGraw-Hill.

Lipset, S., & Raab, E. (1970). *The politics of unreason.* New York: Harper & Row.

Lipset, S., & Rokkan, S. (1967). *Cleavage structures, party systems and voter alignments.* New York: Free Press.

Luhmann, N. (1982). *The differentiation of society.* New York: Columbia University Press.

McCormick, R. P. (1966). *The second American party system.* Chapel Hill: University of North Carolina Press.

Meyer, J. W., & Rowan, B. (1977). Institutionalized organizations: Formal structure as myth and ceremony. *American Journal of Sociology, 83,* 340-363.

Moore, W. (1979). *World modernization: The limits of convergence.* New York: Elsevier-North Holland.

Nisbet, R. (1969). *Social change and history.* New York: Basic Books.

Parsons, T. (1954). *Essays in sociological theory.* New York: Free Press.

Parsons, T. (1966). *Societies: Evolutionary and comparative perspectives.* New York: Free Press.

Parsons, T. (1971). *The system of modern societies.* Englewood Cliffs, NJ: Prentice-Hall.

Parsons, T., & Platt, G. (1973). *The American university.* Cambridge, MA: Harvard University Press.

Remini, R. V. (1958). The Albany regency. *New York History, 39,* 341-355.

Rueschemeyer, D. (1976). Partial modernization. In J. J. Loubser & R. C. Baum (Eds.), *Explorations in general theory in social science: Essays in honor of Talcott Parsons* (pp. 756-772). New York: Free Press.

Rueschemeyer, D. (1977). Structural differentiation, efficiency, and power. *American Journal of Sociology, 83,* 1-25.

Smelser, N. J. (1959). *Social change in the industrial revolution.* Chicago: University of Chicago Press.

Smelser, N. J. (1962). *The theory of collective behavior.* New York: Free Press.

Smelser, N. J. (1971). Stability, instability, and the analysis of political corruption. In B. Barber & A. Inkeles (Eds.), *Stability and change* (pp. 7-29). Boston: Little, Brown.

Smelser, N. J. (1974). Growth, structural change, and conflict in California public higher education, 1950-1970. In N. J. Smelser & G. Almond (Eds.), *Public higher education in California* (pp. 9-141). Berkeley: University of California Press.

Smith, A. (1973). *The concept of social change.* London: Routledge & Kegan Paul.

Turner, R. H. (1970). *Family interaction.* New York: John Wiley.

Turner, R. H. (1980). Strategy for developing an integrated role theory. *Humboldt Journal of Social Relations, 7,* 123-139.

Wallace, M. (1973). *Ideologies of party in the United States.* Unpublished doctoral dissertation, Columbia University.

Wiltse, C. M. (1949). *John C. Calhoun.* Indianapolis: Bobbs-Merrill.

Chapter 7

MODERNITY AND ITS DISCONTENTS

FRANK J. LECHNER
Emory University

AFTER PARSONS'S DEATH in 1979 a number of reinterpretations of his work have appeared that sidestep many of the old criticisms of "functionalist" theory and deal with the action-theoretical research program in a more dispassionate manner (Adriaansens, 1981; Alexander, 1984; Bourricaud, 1981; Brownstein, 1982; Habermas, 1981; Luhmann, 1982; Münch, 1982; Robertson, 1980; Savage, 1981; cf. special issues of *Sociological Inquiry* [51, 3/4] and *Sociological Analysis* [43, 4]). Ranging from sympathetic reconstructions and extensions of Parsons's approach to logical critiques and alternative proposals, these and other works have raised the level of debate about Parsons's legacy. They also set the stage for serious consideration of the potential contribution of action theory to the further development of sociological theory. Although fundamental criticisms of Parsons's own work have emerged, at least the old complaints about functionalism's equilibrium orientation, its neglect of conflict and change, and its conservative system-bias have largely been overcome. The question now becomes, If "neofunctionalism" is beset by similar problems as old functionalism allegedly was, will it thus be judged to be flawed and irrelevant from the point of view of sociological theory? By neofunctionalism I mean, for the purposes of this chapter, the systematic development of a multidimensional, voluntaristic theory of action and order that builds on the action-theoretical research program in a constructive but critical fashion. In order to examine if neofunctionalism in this general sense can make a fruitful contribution to sociological theory while avoiding the pitfalls outlined by more conventional critiques, I will suggest three general points based on relatively Parsonian presuppositions and using some of Parsons's conceptual tools. In a more substantive vein I will suggest and illustrate a typology of discontents in modernity and value-

AUTHOR'S NOTE: I am grateful to Jeffrey Alexander, Rainer Baum, and Richard Münch for helpful comments on an earlier version of this chapter.

157

oriented, antimodern responses to such discontents. The overall purpose of the exercise is not to "defend Parsons" but rather to draw on his work in a constructive, though revisionist, manner.

First, consider Parsons's starting point: the famous "problem of order." Although this problem arose in a particular intellectual tradition, and in Parsons's work centered on the voluntaristic transcendence of utilitarian dilemmas, in its general form it expresses a fundamental aspect of the human condition, namely, that humans suffer from biological understeering and thus have to construct meaningful order. Reduction of complexity, to use Luhmann's term, is necessary for all forms of life; for human beings, who lack "natural" self-steering in action, it must take the form of meaningful order. Different traditions in sociological theory can actually agree on that fundamental point. But reduction of complexity does not mean that the problem disappears or that it is somehow solved. For Parsons, in fact, the problem of order was never (or at least not most of the time) a matter of simply achieving equilibrium: He continued to be impressed with its persisting "problematicity" and ended up producing more "problems of order" than he started with. At the level of presuppositions as well as that of substantive theorizing, the ways in and degree to which order is problematic in different domains remain important items on the sociological agenda. More important, we may now go one step further: In the face of biological understeering and meaningless environments of action (cf. Parsons, 1978, 1979), any form of meaningful order must contain tension between "ordering" and "disordering" dimensions of action. In any sociocultural setting as well as in symbolic interaction, in institutions as well as in personal biographies, meaning is continually gained as well as lost, complexity continually reduced as well as produced. Meaningful order, in whatever human domain, is an inherently fragile accomplishment. I suggest, then, a slight modification in our thinking about order by emphasizing the persisting *tension* between "ordering" and "disordering" aspects. That very tension, I would argue, also needs to be part of the presuppositions of the kind of multidimensional theory advocated by Alexander (1981). From this point of view, order is not only problematic at the level of theoretical presuppositions, but also at the more philosophical-anthropological and the more specific-empirical levels of the scientific continuum. Such a more dramatic view of order—as a fragile accomplishment emerging out of the tension with continually disordering factors—is not only possible within but is, in fact, a requirement for a multidimensional, voluntaristic theory of order and action. And I suggest that it is precisely from a voluntaristic, "neofunctionalist" perspective that we can systematically analyze aspects of "disorder" and collective attempts to deal with these, in terms of theoretical generalizations at a level below that of general theoretical logic and presuppositions.[1]

Second, in order to start analyzing the multidimensionality of ordering itself, consider the somewhat less abstract case of "modernity," the theoretically defined phenomenon that all reflections on order and the like were supposed to illuminate in the first place. Although "modernization"—or at least modernization theory in the conventional sense—has been declared dead, there may still be a role for "modernity" as a theoretical category, referring to a set of aspects of the modern human condition. We do not need to assume the substantive convergence of especially the classical contributions to argue that much of sociological theory has been developed to show how modernity is possible. From Action Theory—a body of work that tried to build and improve on the classical accounts—we can derive not only a fairly systematic account of modernity but also a proposition that was left mostly implicit by Parsons. Very briefly, modernity can be viewed as the state of high-level differentiation (including interpenetration; cf. Münch, 1982) of action systems along four functional dimensions. Following Parsons (1971), the state of each dimension can be characterized further by evolutionary outcomes in each case (value-generalization, inclusion, etc.). But then we not only have an outline of modern order but also a basis for conceptualizing four functional sources of *disorder*.[2] In other words, we can, as it were, turn Parsons on his head by using his framework in a direction counter to the one he gave priority to. Precisely with his order-oriented concepts we can identify *discontents* in modernity, which should contribute to a more truly multidimensional, though perhaps less "sunny," model of modernity. But discontents only count as *discontents*; they can only relate to the above-mentioned more problematic analytical view of order and can only be analyzed systematically if we *also* argue from within a neofunctionalist, modified action-systemic framework.

Third, after briefly suggesting some discontents, I will outline one more way in which neofunctionalism may prove helpful. For it is precisely within this framework that we can conceptualize collective efforts to restore meaning, to reconstitute order, and to deal with discontents, albeit often in reductionist, unstable, and disequilibrating form. That follows from an additional proposition: Modernity as a specific form of meaningful order *also* systematically produces certain types of *syn-*

dromes, as modes of dealing with order and its discontents in modernity. In modernity, such "antimodern" movements are *to be expected.*[3] In other words, if we assume, as a presuppositional matter, that tension between ordering and disordering is inherent in all sociocultural order, and if modernity entails fundamental forms of disorganization, then radical modes of countering such disorganization and restoring meaningful order in all spheres must be part and parcel of the model of modernity as well. The general perspective on such matters is well-established in the "functionalist" tradition, especially in Durkheim's work on effervescence and Smelser's work on value-oriented movements. More specifically, generalizing Smelser to what Parsons called the general action level, I will suggest a classification of such syndromes. Theoretically, they can be seen as one-function reductionist attempts to restore "order" by dedifferentiation across levels; more concretely, they can be interpreted as "revitalization" movements. Treating ostensibly antimodern movements in terms of a relatively abstract, ideal-typical model should help clarify their thrust and implications. From a "functionalist" point of view such responses to fundamental sources of disorganization in modern sociocultural order are overly radical in their attempt to restore meaningful order across the board on the basis of a particular value-principle. But, as will appear below, in other respects they differ.

ON DISCONTENTS

Before presenting the classification of syndromes, let us take a brief look at some of the discontents predicted by Action Theory. Discontents can be derived systematically, again at the level of a theoretical model, if we simply use Parsons's terms naively (without evaluation or elaboration, by only spelling out implications). We only need to assume meaningful ordering of action in four spheres or subsystems (behavioral system, personality system, social system, cultural system) in addition to modernity as a state of high differentiation and specific evolutionary outcomes for each dimension (with a slight modification of Parsons's (1971) value-generalization, inclusion, individuation and adaptive upgrading theories).

Differentiation as such, to start with one of Parsons's major but controversial variables, suggests a general source of discontent. Without in any way supposing that "traditional societies" were somehow a seamless web (the point here is a theoretical, not a historical one), differentiation produces multiple sources of tension and raises the problem of the articulation of the spheres with each other. With various spheres or "subsystems" following their own "logic," complexity is reduced internally but produced externally. New degrees of freedom in action thus may entail new sources of anxiety. Short of legitimate and institutionalized "interpenetration" (Münch, 1982), relatively disorderly, tension-ridden configurations of subsystems are likely to occur. For many societies and individuals, then, differentiation can be expected to pose a problem. Order becomes more than a presuppositional concern.

Value-generalization, Parsons's evolutionary variable for the pattern-maintenance domain, implies that bounds of a tradition have been loosened, that commitment has become more abstract, and that greater reflexivity is required in interpreting and implementing values. Beliefs no longer "hold" but have to "be held" (Geertz, 1968). Insofar as taken for grantedness (*not* absence of change) is characteristic of a tradition, that suggests that the very coherence of the value-framework can be perceived as being at stake. Having become more autonomous, the value-framework can be seen as being more distant, more objective, and less directly meaningful. With more degrees of freedom at other levels of action, these may be felt to suffer from cultural understeering. Greater tolerance for different interpretations or deficits in implementation is required. Given relativization of old core values, new reflexivity, and problematic coherence and implementation, the very cybernetic role assigned to values in Parsons's scheme and the very "pattern" to be maintained can actually come to be at stake. The main source of compensation for biological understeering may thus itself come to be depleted.

Inclusion, the evolutionary variable for the integrative domain, suggests that the bounds of a community have been loosened, that solidarity is extended to "strangers," and that collective sentiment stretches beyond our "brothers." Insofar as (ideal-typically speaking) diffuse, ascriptive bonds are characteristic of a traditional community, that suggests that the very coherence of the societal community can be perceived to be at stake. Having become more autonomous, the solidarity-framework can be seen as more distant, impersonal, and less directly meaningful or binding. With more degrees of freedom in action a community can be perceived as suffering from normative understeering. Greater tolerance for diversity and generality in solidarity is required. Given relativization of old ties, distance to other aspects of action, and problematic coherence, the very integrative role assigned to solidarity in Parsons's scheme can actually come to be at stake.

Individuation—my translation of Parsons's "differentiation" for the personality level and closely related to his notion of institutionalized individualism (cf. Bourricaud, 1981)—suggests that the bounds of a biography have been loosened and that greater reflexivity is required in cathecting, interpreting, and implementing resources in the interest of personal identity. Insofar as personality as such was traditionally (again, ideal-typically speaking) to be taken as a given, this suggests that personal identity as such can be seen to be at stake. Having become more autonomous and the object of a "cult," the individual is left more to his or her own devices and his or her identity becomes something to be accomplished. With more degrees of freedom in terms of doing identity work, personality can be perceived as suffering from affective understeering. Greater tolerance for different value-interpretations and solidarity-contexts is required. Given relativization of a state of undifferentiated incorporation into society, problematic coherence, and reflexivity in identity work, the very goal-attainment via personality-organization as an aspect of meaningful order can come to be at stake.

"Adaptive upgrading," the rather broad term for evolutionary process in the adaptive domain, suggests that the limits of traditional adaptation to nature have been transcended, that world-mastery has increased and become more abstract and self-sustaining. Inso far as (ideal-typically) acceptance of natural constraints is characteristic of a "traditional" relation to nature, this suggests that, paradoxically, the very possibility of control can be seen to be at stake. Having become more autonomous, intelligent adaptation can be seen as itself out of control, distant from other spheres of action, and no longer oriented to the problems that are meaningful to solve in the first place. With more degrees of freedom for behavioral-system operation (in a very general sense), it may be perceived as producing more problems than it solves, becoming controlled by its own products, and creating uncertainty by infinite learning. Generally, in modernity, greater tolerance for autonomous problem solving, openness to learning, and actual limits to adaptive capacity is required. Given relativization of "deeper" concerns, problematic maintenance of intelligent control, and the anxiety of potentially infinite learning, the very adaptation via behavioral-system operation as an aspect of meaningful order can come to be at stake.

REVITALIZATION SYNDROMES IN
ACTION-THEORETICAL PERSPECTIVE

From the "functionalist" tradition we can also derive a way of conceptualizing radical modes of reducing complexity, attempts to restore meaningful order in response to threatened understeering in the form of such discontents. Technically stated, the general point is that given radical understeering, overcomplexity, and meaninglessness in several dimensions, there will be movements at the highest "cybernetic" level to revitalize (from the movements' point of view) specific aspects of a value-pattern perceived to be underemphasized and to radically restore order by dedifferentiation from the highest level down. Without wishing to imply negative medical connotations, such theoretically defined, ideal-typically "oversteering" movements can be called "syndromes." The neofunctionalist (or better termed, "action-theoretical") rationale for such syndromes can be derived primarily from Durkheim and Smelser.

In Durkheim's *Elementary Forms* we have a general perspective on movements, meaning, and order. On the one hand, "religion" emerges in periods of intensification, transcendent phases of social life—when man becomes "different," fuses himself with society, and sacred representations emerge (Durkheim, 1960, pp. 293ff.). On the other hand, society itself is the object of the cult practiced in such periods of effervescence (p. 306). "Revitalization," to use a contemporary term, is the societal mode of self-transcendence. Once they achieve some homogeneity, which gives society a sense of itself, such movements come to symbolize the corresponding representations (p. 330). This line of reasoning applies to "society" as much as to "religion": Society cannot (re)create itself without at the same time creating the ideal (pp. 603-604). With perhaps an idealist bias (Alexander, 1982), Durkheim even suggests that society is in fact constituted by the idea it has of itself. The implication of his argument is that revitalization must be inherent—at least an inherent *capacity*—in all societies. Given his emphasis on the role of revitalization and on the problematic institutionalization of modernity, combined with his intense practical concern with the revitalization of modern French society, we may even infer the conclusion that modern societies may well require an even greater capacity for self-revision. The homogeneity in movements symbolizing the corresponding representations, the (re)creating of "society" (which can perhaps be translated more generally as "meaningful order") while (re)creating the ideal, revitalization being inherent in (especially modern) societies—all these elements apply directly to the syndromes to be described below. The point about self-revision as being more to be expected, even the norm, in modern societies can be amplified with the action-theoretical categories as used above. The general formula I have suggested elsewhere (cf. Lechner, 1985) is the following: Differentiation introduces tension; value-generalization legitimates the tension; one aspect of adaptive upgrading is dealing actively with such tensions, but that only increases the problematicity of normative order; hence no one form can be taken for granted; all must be subject to systematic revision and revitalization. Although Bellah (1964) may go just a little bit too far, life indeed becomes an "infinite revisability thing."

In Smelser (1962) we find a well-known model of movements that provides much that can serve for the conceptualization of syndromes. First, revitalization movements can be classified into Smelser's value-oriented movements (Smelser, 1962, p. 313; cf. Wallace, 1956). Theoretically speaking, such movements are uninstitutionalized attempts at restoring meaningful order on the basis of generalized belief by means of "vertical" action down the hierarchy of components of social structure. Although movements need not reach the value-oriented level (that depends in part on conditions of structural conduciveness), once a value-oriented movement is initiated (generally by upward escalation) other aspects of social order down from the value-level will be affected as well. The general model in Smelser is in fact rather Simmelian: conditions of strain providing the dynamic "life-forces," the conditions of conduciveness and generalized beliefs providing the controlling institutional and symbolic forms. The short-circuiting in all types of collective behavior that Smelser emphasizes is especially characteristic of those that are cybernetically highest.

Taking several features from Smelser's value-oriented movement, we can technically define revitalization syndromes as one-function reductionist attempts at diachronic self-steering via reconstruction of order and identity across levels of action. I only go beyond Smelser in four respects: I use the concept dedifferentiation rather than short-circuiting; revitalization syndromes I regard as inherent in modernity; relativizing the rather "medical" model of movements in Smelser (Marx & Holzner, 1975, 1977), I have substituted the more general concept of discontents for Smelser's "strain"; and I suggest that Smelser's treatment can be lifted to what Parsons would call the "general action level."

Given the basic sources of discontent outlined above, such a generalization of Smelser is contained in the main proposal of this chapter, namely, that on the basis of modified Action Theory, we can distinguish between four types of objectively possible revitalization syndromes according to the functional aspect that is given primacy and the resulting dedifferentiation across levels that results from this emphasis. Again relying largely on Parsons's own conceptual apparatus, the analytical description of the four types refers to the four subsystems of the so-called General Action System (Cultural System, Social System, Personality System, Behavioral System), and their respective A-G-I-L subdifferentiations (so that LI = constitutive culture, Li = moral culture, li = societal community, etc.).[4] The heuristic to be used is in part inspired by Münch's (1980, 1982) suggestion that it is possible to treat subsystems in various configurations other than interpenetration, such as configurations in which dynamizing subsystems dominate controlling ones and vice versa.

The first syndrome to be distinguished—and the main type of anti-modern response to problems of meaning in modern social order—is the one oriented to the discontents inherent in value-generalization and characterized by the dominance of "controlling" over "dynamizing" aspects of action in the form of dedifferentiation on the basis of L-primacy. That syndrome I have called "fundamentalist" (Lechner, in press). At each level the pattern-maintenance aspect comes to dominate all others. In this syndrome ultimate belief (LI) takes priority over all else, leading, at the cultural level, to ultimization of moral, expressive, and cognitive culture, and, secondarily, to the moralization of expressive and cognitive culture. Lower down the so-called cybernetic hierarchy, community, polity, and economy become moralized; legitimacy becomes ultimized as well; and stratification tends to become one-dimensional, with moral virtue as the only relevant ranking criterion. Tracing the fundamentalist pattern further through the Chinese-box structure of Parsons's General Action System, personality is moralized and "socialized" via an emphasis on collectively determined "ego ideals" and "superego"; learning is dogmatized; and common sense is socialized. A fundamentalist movement in this sense will be characterized by Bund-like solidarity (Schmalenbach, 1961), based on conscious commitment to absolute principles.

Empirical cases that can be interpreted in terms of this syndrome include Islamic fundamentalism (Akhavi, 1980; Esposito, 1980; Fischer, 1980; Kramer, 1980), the Chinese Cultural Revolution (Dittmer, 1974; Lee, 1978), and American fundamentalism (Hunter, 1983; Marsden, 1980; Liebman & Wuthnow, 1983). Although origins, context, and implications differ in each case, they have top-down dedifferentiation in common. A model incorporating such top-down dedifferentiation provides one example of the fruitfulness of neofunctionalism, in this case by showing in systematic terms the coherent, all-encompassing thrust of a fundamentalist-type movement. It allows us to trace more specifically the impact of dedifferentiation on the basis of absolute belief "down the line"—in the areas of stratification and authority as well as socialization and personality. Second, this type of model enables us to ask more specific questions about the preconditions and outcomes of fundamentalism. For example, for top-down dedifferentiation to be possible, generalized belief legitimating such dedifferentiation must be available; Shiite Islam and radical Maoism serve very well in this respect. The outcome of a fundamentalist-type movement depends on the availability of institutionalized buffers in the social context that prevent it from spreading down the action-systemic line; in this respect American fundamentalism is obviously more likely to be coopted than either Chinese or Islamic fundamentalism (cf. Lechner, in press).

A second objectively possible syndrome is characterized by dedifferentiation on the basis of I-primacy, in response to the discontents of inclusion (Lechner, 1984). Normative concern with diffuse, historic solidarity is the major concern that reverberates across levels, and even upward in the cybernetic hierarchy. This can be called the "Romantic" syndrome. Given primary concern with solidarity, the polity, economy, and sociocultural sphere will tend to become "socialized." Authority will be considered legitimate insofar as it expresses particular communal identity; stratification will be made to reflect the superior quality of the particular "chosen group" in comparison to others, hence producing a split system. At the cultural level, moral culture will come to dominate both higher, ultimate beliefs and expressive and cognitive culture. Similarly, efforts will be made to reintegrate personality into the social context; internalized obligations are given priority over other aspects of personality. Abstract learning or independent creativity will have to yield to established social knowledge and expectations, that is, to *common* sense. The form of solidarity emphasized in this syndrome is the presumed given historical community ("Gemeinschaft").

Major empirical cases that can be interpreted in terms of this syndrome are ethnic or national movements. Integrative primacy is clearly a major theme in the literature on ethnic movements—in all, regaining a sense of uniqueness, diffuse solidarity, historical community, and communal boundary-maintenance is the core concern (e.g., Connor, 1972, 1973; Smith, 1979, 1981; Said & Simmons, 1976). Whether the assumptions of a preexisting historical community and primordial ties are valid or not, the point is that such movements do, in fact, and must operate on such an assumption. Let me mention two examples of how integrative primacy in addition to dedifferentiation may be fruitful in interpreting the thrust of such movements. First, combining integrative primacy and Parsons's cybernetic hierarchy, in which "I" controls "G", at the social system level leads to the expectation that ethnic movements *should* strive for effective corporate organization grounded in a particular community and should resist objective political domination. Hence tension between "ethnie" and "state," resistance to a state-dominated "integrative revolution," and efforts to make communal and political organization congruent are *to be expected* (cf. Connor, 1972; Francis, 1976). I-G dedifferentiation is clearly at the core of such movements. Second, combining integrative primacy and the cybernetic hierarchy, in which "L" controls "I" at the social system level, leads to the expectation that the relation between ethnic groups/movements and cultural institutions (or what Parsons called the "fiduciary sphere") should be ambivalent in the sense that ethnic revitalization movements can be expected to appropriate cultural patterns "downward" to suit solidarity purposes while in fact having to face potential pressure from "transcendent" values and beliefs. Boundary-maintenance indeed turns out to be more important than common culture or cultural content as such; the relation of the cultural factor to the core concern is in fact variable, although the movement generally tries to incorporate it; and both the increasingly ideological character of ethnicity and neotraditionalism (both of which would shift the emphasis to the L-level) tend to undermine the movement (Barth, 1969; Parming & Cheung, 1980; Smith, 1979, 1981). Ethnic revitalization movements indeed do involve attempts at I-L dedifferentiation.

These first two syndromes have something in common: Both constitute an attempt to resolve the discontents of modernity by an "escape from freedom" into new, all-pervading constraint. The attempt to retreat to such traditionalist security bases and "reject" the pattern of modernity as such adds complexity to the lives of those who radically wished to reduce it and in fact makes them quintessentially modern. The remaining two syndromes, while still being reductionist and dedifferentiating, aim in a different direction by trying to "escape from constraint" in an attempt to resolve all problems by a kind of superemancipation. Here modern premises have been partially accepted (they are to be revitalized), but they are turned against the uncertain, alienating course modernity actually has taken, at least from the point of view of the actors involved.

More "modern" in appearance, these syndromes still count as antimodern by virtue of their dedifferentiating thrust and rejection of major features of the modern model.[5]

The third syndrome, oriented to the discontents inherent in individuation, is the one resulting from dedifferentiation on the basis of G-primacy. Because the emphasis is first of all on the quality and gratification of the individual (and on restoring the primacy of goal-attainment as a value-principle), it may be called the "expressive-therapeutic syndrome." Given the emphasis on regeneration of a sense of healthy personality (the main focus of "revitalization" in this case), ego ideals and internalized norms are to be adjusted to the demands of ego. Organized social life will be directed to serve personality, relativizing independent normative or value-concerns. Hence the "political" sphere must take priority over others, leading to the politicization of the economic, communal, and sociocultural spheres. Because there are neither shared values nor interests to be implemented, authority becomes arbitrary; because all societal ranking becomes irrelevant, stratification tends to become randomized. At the cultural level, constitutive, moral and cognitive culture will be made to serve aesthetic-expressive purposes; culture as such will be linked to the needs of personality. Self-awareness and individual experience become more important than formal knowledge or common sense. The forms of solidarity to serve best in this kind of syndrome are ideological primary groups (Marx & Holzner, 1975) at the private level and bureaucratic Gesellschaft-ties (to serve and protect the private sphere) at the public level.

Although I cannot elaborate on it here, it seems that much of the work on recent trends and movements in the United States can be analyzed along these lines. For example, Turner (1969) has argued that the primary theme of many modern movements has become "psychological"; the "expressive-therapeutic" syndrome can be seen as a way to analyze the thrust of such movements (e.g., the Health Movement, the self-help movement, EST, some new religious movements, and related aspects of countercultural phenomena, as a general movement in Blumer's sense). Robertson's (1978) notion of "ascetic mysticism" and Kavolis's (1970) description of the countercultural side of modern man seem to fit the syndrome; work by Rieff (1966), Sennett (1973), Lasch (1979), Martin (1981), and Tipton (1982) can be interpreted along expressive-therapeutic lines as well. Apart from displaying G-primacy, the expressive movement concerned with self-growth, personal identity, and ego-gratification has been accompanied by an emphasis on expressive aspects of culture to be used in personal identity construction and gratification, and an emphasis on bureaucratic mechanisms to develop a "welfare" state. As examples of the fruitfulness of using a functionalist approach, consider the following two examples. Insofar as romantic attempts are made to regain a sense of solidarity, this must lead to "destructive Gemeinschaft" (Sennett, 1973). In functional terms, G over I represents functional distortion/confusion; to strive for intimate integration on the basis of G-primacy *must* lead to *destructive* "Gemeinschaft." Strictly speaking, expressive-therapeutic solidarity is impossible—one reason why bureaucracy may serve well in this syndrome to fill the solidarity gap. Second, although the "movement" may become ideologized, in fact it cannot attain a shared sense of moral purpose or ultimate belief; hence the ideology necessarily remains fragile. In functional terms, "G" over "L" represents functional distortion/confusion; to strive for legitimacy in terms of shared values on the basis of G-primacy leaves all culture-construction as mere ideology, permanently undermined by more dynamizing factors (cf. Lasch, 1979, pp. 140-141, on the problematic nature of shared values and moral solidarity in this syndrome). Destructive Gemeinschaft and mere ideology should make ideological primary groups (Marx & Holzner, 1975, 1977) intense, but fragile and temporary. The narcissism involved in the syndrome in fact makes all judgments arbitrary—a personalistic relativism that also favors bureaucratization.

Finally, dedifferentiation on the basis of A-primacy, with "dynamizing" factors dominating "controlling" ones (cf. Münch, 1980), leads to what I call a "Promethean" syndrome. Adaptive primacy here refers to the restoration of full control over environments of action through emancipation of individual creativity. Given concern with regeneration of the "productive" capacity of action systems (and with restoring the primacy of adaptation as a value-principle) in the face of the discontents inherent in increased world-mastery and unrestrained learning, the problem-solving capacities of adaptive individuals are emphasized. Thus their behavioral-system aspect is considered more important than their personality aspect. At the level of personality, generalized energies dominate internalized norms and ego-ideals. At the social system level, itself dependent upon the productive-adaptive capacity of individuals, the economic sphere dominates the political, communal, and sociocultural ones, all of which are made to serve the forces and mode of production, as the latter are most directly relevant to restoration of societal world-mastery and societal emancipation. As part of the emancipatory project, societal and individual interests are considered determined by "economic" position and capacity. Authority will be legitimate insofar as it contributes to objective emancipation; stratification will be based on objective achievement only, hence becoming one-dimensional. At the cultural system level, objective-scientific knowledge—debunking forms of false consciousness and instrumental to restoring world-mastery—becomes a source of meaning, value, and aesthetic models as well; ultimate belief has to yield to positive knowledge; that is, "realistic" reasoning relativizes "soft" moral concerns. The form of solidarity most suited to this syndrome is the free association of productive individuals with shared objective interests.

Again, I cannot elaborate here. But the main empirical movements conforming to this syndrome are Marxist ones.[6] A-primacy appears in Marx's vision of emancipatory praxis as rooted in the creative capacities of human beings, in the reliance on man's essential nature as "worker," and in the Promethean and Enlightenment strands in Marx's thought and Marxism generally (see especially Kolakowski, 1978, pp. 408ff; Avineri, 1968; Dumont, 1977; McMurtry, 1978; Tucker, 1964). Materialism and the emphasis on man's relation to nature are not simply analytical or philosophical devices, but are logically part of an effort to restore world-mastery. At the social system level, again, the forces and mode of production play a special role in restoring societal control over its natural and social environments. Stratification, which reflects these basic forces, is simply instrumental in generating actors to participate in the emancipatory project and will eventually wither away as the free development of all guarantees equality. Existing authority must in the final analysis represent the interests of a particular, economically dominant class; in emancipatory praxis authority is only to be derived from objective contributions to revolutionary transformation and will similarly wither away. Short of revolution via Bund-like solidarity among workers acting on (finally) enlightened class consciousness and expressing their natural creativity, all solidarity and forms of consciousness must in the final analysis be false. The point is to make free association among men possible in which their essential nature as workers can be realized via revolutionary introduction of a nonexploitative economy. Culturally speaking, objective knowledge of the laws of history serves to unmask false consciousness and irrational moral concern; simply to follow them is more important than developing new, ultimate beliefs and defines collective responsibility clearly enough to make any other moral or ultimate convictions irrelevant.

Not only can much of Marxism thus be interpreted as a reductionist, syndrome-like way of dealing with modernity, but a neofunctionalist approach like the one proposed here can also interpret some of the recurring ambivalences and unintended consequences in actual Marxist praxis. For instance, combining adaptive primacy and Parsons's cybernetic hierarchy, in which "I" stands over "A," we would *expect* tension between the economic and the societal community spheres. Problems along the so-called A-I axis show up in the Marxist problem with the "national" question, the problem of achieving class solidarity on the basis of economic interests alone, the efforts to reorganize the community in terms of objective economic conditions alone, and the recurrence of nationalist and other sources of solidarity in ostensibly Marxist movements. Insofar as romantic concern with reintegrating individuals and reestablishing genuine solidarity (the third strand in Marx according to Kolakowski, but also relativized by him) persists, this syndrome must produce a form of destructive Gemeinschaft of its own—as I think it has. Combining adaptive primacy and Parsons's cybernetic hierarchy, in which "L" controls "A," we would also *expect* tensions between the economic and pattern-maintenance spheres. In Marxist theory and practice, problems along these lines are especially apparent in the problematic status of ideology—which in terms of the Promethean syndrome per se should be merely derivative but which in recent theory and socialist practice have become important to the point of dominating the very role of the productive capacity of individuals, the mode of production, and the natural solidarity of exploited classes. That the movement to end all ideology has had its greatest impact *as* ideology is an irony fully understandable in neofunctionalist terms.

CONCLUSIONS

In conclusion, let me indicate some of the general implications of the preceding discussion for neofunctionalism or revisionist Action Theory as a research program.

First, I have suggested that it is possible to fruitfully deal with discontents and syndromes in modernity from a revisionist action-theoretical point of view. With theoretical arguments and some empirical illustrations—leaving a more full-fledged empirical application for another context—I have tried to show that both the thrust of such syndromes and their instabilities can be analyzed systematically. Precisely from a multidimensional, voluntaristic point of view, various types of reductionism in action can be used as heuristic models at a level below that of presuppositions; instability and ambivalence appear at that level as well (cf. Alexander, 1982). Such concern with instability and disequilibrating reductionism might seem to betray an old-functionalist concern with order in the sense of system-equilibrium. However, it is here part of an effort to show some heuristic strengths in revisionist Action Theory.

Second, the analysis is also intended to contribute, as I said above, to a more multidimensional and more dramatic conception of order, namely, one in which aspects of "disorder" challenge "ordering" factors (in the old sense) and understeering, oversteering, and risky balancing acts are all to be taken into account. Moreover, the application of multidimensional presuppositions to the analysis of modernity leads to a richer conception of the latter. For if discontents and ostensibly anti-modern movements are, at least from an analytical point of view, inherent in modernity, then the very nature of modern sociocultural order is also determined by the thrust and direction of the dominant radical responses to the discontents it entails. In light of the preceding discussion, it can even be suggested that, in addition to the interpenetration of various subsystems as analyzed by Münch (1980, 1982), modernity is in part characterized by the interpenetration of and critical tension between different modes of dealing with order.

In addition, discontents and syndromes also provide a fruitful problem area in which a neofunctionalist, action-theoretical research program can be elaborated in two other directions. Third, the analysis of oversteering syndromes would also seem to require some analysis of the deflation of what Parsons called "general action media." This may give us some inductive clues for further development of the still rather underdeveloped general action media and thus may help us decide if this part of Parsons's legacy is sufficiently fruitful to be worth pursuing further. Finally, discontents and revitalization in modernity can hardly be analyzed only in terms of particular societal units. As a general point I would suggest that to analyze their sources and implications requires taking a trans-societal, world-system point of view. The issues dealt with here may well be an interesting site for the development of a voluntaristic world-system theory in order to complement current, more Marxist-oriented world-system theory and to integrate the classical sociological tradition into this emerging area of research. By addressing contemporary sociological concerns in these and other ways, in a critical and revisionist action-theoretical vein, the relevance of Parsons's legacy and the fruitfulness of a neofunctionalist research program can be more properly assessed.

NOTES

1. In fairness to Parsons it should be noted that he thought along such lines in at least four respects: (1) as mentioned above, he produced as well as "solved" problems of order; (2) from his analysis of National Socialism until the end of his life, he was concerned with "fundamentalist revolts" against rationalization and value-generalization, which also signaled his recognition of extreme and antimodern ways of coping with order in modernity, resembling some of the types of movements to be discussed below (cf. Baum & Lechner, 1981); (3) in his media-theory he was concerned with inflation and deflation, understeering and oversteering; (4) at the end of his life he was vitally concerned with aspects of the environment of action that were in principle meaningless, yet had to be dealt with in meaningful fashion, but also kept intruding as potentially disordering factors.

2. As a technical matter, note that this proposal is a simple one and does not consider cross-functional, especially axis-based, sources or the types of subsystem-dislocations suggested by Münch (1980, 1982).

3. This is, of course, a theoretical generalization, part of a relatively abstract "model" of modern sociocultural order; as such, it does not address significant empirical variations betweeen societies on this score.

4. Sources are Parsons, 1971; Gould, 1976; Lidz and Lidz, 1976; Baum and Lechner, 1981. See Robertson (1983) for another approach to reductionist modes of dealing with complexity.

5. It could be argued that all four types of movements are communal ones in view of the dedifferentiating, antimodern movement activity and the strong communally bound obligations necessary to activate any syndrome. However, I suggest that the more systematic neofunctionalist approach outlined here captures important differences between various forms of dedifferentiation, including the distinctive ambivalences, instabilities, and visions of communal solidarity in each case.

6. As Parsons (1979) has shown, there is at least a very important symbolic parallelism between Marxism and radical-utilitarian liberalism, the main difference being that the former is the collectivist variant and the latter the individualist one. This collectivist character is one reason why the empirical manifestations of Marxist Prometheanism are more readily interpretable as syndrome-like revitalization movements.

REFERENCES

Adriaansens, H.P.M. (1981). *Talcott Parsons and the conceptual dilemma.* London: Routledge & Kegan Paul.

Akhavi, S. (1980). *Religion and politics in contemporary Iran: Clergy-state relations in the Pahlavi Period.* Albany: State University of New York Press.

Alexander, J. C. (1981). *Theoretical logic in sociology, Vol. 1: Positivism, presuppositions, and current controversies.* Berkeley: University of California Press.

Alexander, J. C. (1982). *Theoretical logic in sociology, Vol. II: The antinomies of classical thought: Marx and Durkheim.* Berkeley: University of California Press.

Alexander, J. C. (1984). *Theoretical logic in sociology, Vol. IV: The modern reconstruction of classical thought: Talcott Parsons.* Berkeley: University of California Press.

Avineri, S. (1968). *The social and political thought of Karl Marx.* London: Cambridge University Press.

Barth, F. (1969). *Ethnic groups and boundaries: The social organization of cultural differences.* Boston: Little, Brown.

Baum, R. C., & Lechner, F. J. (1981). National socialism: Towards an action-theoretical interpretation. *Sociological Inquiry, 51*(3-4), 281-308.

Bellah, R. N. (1964). Religious evolution. *American Sociological Review, 24,* 358-374.

Bourricaud, F. (1981). *The sociology of Talcott Parsons.* Chicago: University of Chicago Press.

Brownstein, L. (1982). *Talcott Parsons' general action scheme: An investigation of fundamental principles.* Cambridge: MA: Schenkman.

Connor, W. (1972). Nation-building of nation-destroying? *World Politics, 24*(3), 319-355.

Connor, W. (1973). The politics of enthnonationalism. *Journal of International Affairs, 27*(1), 1-21.

Dittmer, L. (1974). *Liu Shao-chi'i and the Chinese cultural revolution: The politics of mass criticism.* Berkeley: University of California Press.

Dumont, L. (1977). *From Mandeville to Marx.* Chicago: University of Chicago Press.

Durkheim, E. (1960). *Les formes élémentaries de la vie religieuse: Le système totémique en Australie.* Paris: Presses Universitaires de France.

Espositio, J. L. (1980). *Islam and development: Religion and sociopolitical change.* Syracuse: Syracuse University Press.

Fischer, M.M.J. (1980). *Iran: From religious dispute to revolution.* Cambridge, MA: Harvard University Press.

Francis, E. K. (1976). *Interethnic relations: An essay in sociological theory.* New York: Elsevier-North Holland.

Geertz, C. (1968). *Islam observed: Religious development in Morocco and Indonesia.* Chicago: University of Chicago Press.

Gould, M. (1976). System analysis, macrosociology and the generalized media of social action. In J. J. Loubser & R. C. Baum (Eds.), *Explorations in general theory in social science: Essays in honor of Talcott Parsons* (pp. 470-506). New York: Free Press.

Habermas, J. (1981). *Theorie des kommunikativen Handelns* (2 vols.) Frankfurt am Main: Suhrkamp.

Hunter, J. D. (1983). *American evangelicalism: Conservative religion and the quandary of modernity.* New Brunswick, NJ: Rutgers University Press.

Kavolis, V. (1970). Post-modern man: Psychological responses to social trends. *Social Problems, 17,* 435-449.

Kolakowski, L. (1978). *Main currents of Marxism: Its origins, growth, and dissolution.* Oxford: Clarendon.

Kramer, M. (1980). Political Islam. *The Washington Papers* (Vol. 8, No. 73). Beverly Hills, CA: Sage.

Lasch, C. (1979). *Haven in a heartless world: The family besieged.* New York: Harper & Row.

Lechner, F. J. (1984). Ethnicity and revitalization in the modern world system. *Sociological Focus, 17*(3), 243-256.

Lechner, F. J. (1985). Fundamentalism and sociocultural revitalization in America: A sociological interpretation. *Sociological Analysis, 46*(3).

Lechner, F.J. (in press). Fundamentalism as a path away from differentiation. In J. C. Alexander & P. Colomy (Eds.), *Differentiation theory: Problems and prospects.* Berkeley: University of California Press.

Lee, H. Y. (1978). *The politics of the Chinese cultural revolution: A case study.* Berkeley: University of California Press.

Lidz, C. W., & Lidz, V. M. (1976). Piaget's psychology of intelligence and the theory of action. In J. J. Loubser & R. C. Baum (Eds.), *Explorations in general theory in social science: Essays in honor of Talcott Parsons* (pp. 195-239). New York: Free Press.

Liebman, R. C., & Wuthnow, R. (Eds.). (1983). *The new Christian right: Mobilization and legitimation.* New York: Aldine.

Luhmann, N. (1982). *The differentiation of society.* New York: Columbia University Press.

McMurtry, J. (1978). *The structure of Marx's world view.* Princeton, NJ: Princeton University Press.

Marsden, G. M. (1980). *Fundamentalism and American culture: The shaping of twentieth-century evangelicalism, 1870-1925.* New York: Oxford University Press.

Martin, B. (1981). *A sociology of contemporary cultural change.* New York: St. Martin's Press.

Marx, J., & Holzner, B. (1975). Ideological primary groups in contemporary movements. *Sociological Focus, 8*(4), 311-329.

Marx, J., & Holzner, B. (1977). The social construction of strain and ideological models of grievance in contemporary movements. *Pacific Sociological Review, 20*(3), 411-438.

Münch, R. (1980). Über Parsons zu Weber: Von der Theorie der Rationalisierung zur Theorie der Interpenetration. *Zeitschrift für Zoziologie, 9*(1), 18-53.

Münch, R. (1982). *Theorie des Handelns.* Frankfurt am Main: Suhrkamp.

Parming, T., & Cheung, L. M. (1980). Modernization and ethnicity. In J. Dofny & A. Akinowo (Eds.), *National and ethnic movements* (pp. 131-141). Beverly Hills, CA: Sage.

Parsons, T. (1971). *The system of modern societies.* Englewood Cliffs, NJ: Prentice-Hall.

Parsons, T. (1978). A paradigm of the human condition. In T. Parsons (Ed.), *Action theory and the human condition* (pp. 352-433). New York: Free Press.

Parsons, T. (1979). Religious and economic symbolism in the Western world. In H. M. Johnson (Ed.), *Religious change and continuity* (pp. 1-48). San Francisco: Jossey-Bass.

Rieff, P. (1966). *Triumph of the therapeutic: Uses of faith after Freud.* New York: Harper & Row.

Robertson, R. (1978). *Meaning and change: Explorations in the cultural sociology of modern societies.* New York: Oxford University Press.

Robertson, R. (1980). Aspects of identity and authority in sociological theory. In R. Robertson & B. Holzner (Eds.), *Identity and authority* (pp. 218-265). New York: St. Martin's Press.

Robertson, R. (1983). Religion, global complexity and the human condition. In *Absolute values and the creation of the new world* (pp. 182-212). New York: International Cultural Foundation.

Said, A. A., & Simmons, L. R. (1976). The ethnic factor in world politics. In A. A. Said & L. R. Simmons (Eds.), *Ethnicity in an international order* (pp. 15-47). New Brunswick, NJ: Transaction.

Savage, S. P. (1981). *The theories of Talcott Parsons: The social relations of action.* New York: St. Martin's.

Schmalenbach, H. (1961) The sociological category of communion. In T. Parsons et al. (Eds.), *Theories of society* (pp. 331-347). New York: Free Press.

Sennett, R. (1973). *The fall of public man: On the social psychology of capitalism.* New York: Vintage Books.

Smelser, N. (1962). *Theory of collective behavior.* New York: Free Press.

Smith, A. D. (1979). *Nationalism in the twentieth century.* New York: New York University Press.

Smith, A. D. (1981). *The ethnic revival.* Cambridge, MA: Cambridge University Press.

Tipton, S. M. (1982). *Getting saved from the sixties: Moral meaning in conversion and cultural change.* Berkeley: University of California Press.

Tucker, R. C. (1964). *Philosophy and myth in Karl Marx.* Cambridge, MA: Cambridge University Press.

Turner, R. H. (1969). The theme of contemporary social movements. *British Journal of Sociology, 20,* 589-599.

Wallace, A.F.C. (1956). Revitalization movements. *American Anthropologist, 58,* 264-281.

PART III

Politics and Responsibility

Chapter 8

TOTALITARIAN AND LIBERAL DEMOCRACY
Two Types of Modern Political Orders

JEFFREY PRAGER
University of California at Los Angeles

DEMOCRACY, since the nineteenth century, has increased in popularity. Today, there is probably no other political concept that is as consensually endorsed by members of the world community. As Reinhard Bendix (1980) in *Kings or People?* has made clear, the idea of the mandate of the people, perhaps first manifest in its modern expression in the sixteenth century, has replaced divine sanction as the basis upon which political regimes must legitimate their rule. Nearly all modern political systems today assert, and in different manners institutionalize, the claim that ultimate authority rests in the hands of the people; political elites serve popular will.

Yet celebrating this modern achievement in which mass and elite are equally bound by constitutional convention cannot illuminate the different ways in which the mandate of the people becomes institutionalized in the modern world. There are important reasons why a contemporary theory of democracy has been unable to fully come to terms with the chasm that separates "liberal" democracy, like those in Western Europe and the United States, and "totalitarian" democracy, like those political systems in the Soviet Union and the People's Republic of China. First, the classical tradition of modern social thought—such as the writings of Tocqueville, Marx, Weber, Durkheim, and T. H. Marshall—defined democracy in relation to its historical predecessors, like autocracy or plutocracy. Although rightly recognizing its fundamental break from previous political systems, these theorists defined this new political form as part and parcel of the break with the traditional Western past and the emergence of a modern system of social, political, and economic organization. It was the "modernity" of democracy that they were intent on explaining; although employing different explanatory devices, they all agreed upon democracy's revolutionary quality. Having appreciated the rise of the revolutionary ethos of popular authority, these theorists understood the institutional reorganization necessary to respond to popular will. Many even attended to the dangers posed for political order because of majority rule and the new demands imposed upon the leaders in the exercise of power. J. L. Talmon (1952), in the frontispiece of his *The Rise of Totalitarian Democracy*, reveals Tocqueville's prescience in appreciating the dangers of liberal democracy. Tocqueville writes,

> I think, then, that the species of oppression by which democratic nations are menaced is unlike anything that ever before existed in the world; our contemporaries will find no prototype of it in their memories. I seek in vain for an expression that will accurately convey the whole of the idea I have formed of it; the old words *despotism* and *tyranny* are inappropriate: the thing itself is new, and since I cannot name it, I must attempt to define it.

Democratic universalism paved the way for contemporary liberal democracies, but it also, as Tocqueville appreciated but could not explicate, created the conditions necessary for the rise of totalitarianism. Democratic legitimacy provides for the first time the possibility of popular participation in political oppression. "For it is quite conceivable," Hannah Arendt (1962, p. 299) writes, "and even within the realm of practical political possibilities, that one fine day a highly organized and mechanized humanity will conclude quite democratically—namely by majority decision—that for humanity as a whole it would be better to liquidate certain parts thereof." The classical formulations of the features of a democratic order are not to be faulted for failing to explicate democracy in its totalitarian expression; nonetheless, they are not sufficient to comprehend alternative democratic patterns.

This theoretical "failure" to anticipate totalitarianism explains, in part, why theorists of totalitarianism, like Arendt (1962), Neumann (1957), Friedrich and Brzezinski (1956), and others, emerge only ex-post facto to account for Nazism and Stalinism. "Modern totalitarian democracy," Talmon (1952, p. 6) writes, "is a dictatorship resting on popular enthusiasm and is thus completely different from absolute power wielded by a divine-right king, or by a usurping tyrant." Or, as Herbert Spiro (1968, p. 107) writes, "the crucial difference between earlier forms of absolutism, tyranny or dictatorship and contemporary totalitarianism is found in the totality of control achieved by the latter, previously unattainable, at least for large societies, without the instruments of modern technology." These accounts and others focus explicitly on the modernity of totalitarianism. Its uniquely modern accommodation to democratic legitimation is only implicitly addressed.

The problem of understanding modern expressions of democracy has been further compounded because of the ideological struggle between East and West. Institutional fusion is identified as the essence of totalitarian politics, in which the absence of free elections and a one-party system are taken as the central features of politics. "The real difference between democracy and dictatorship," Franz Neumann (1957, pp. 268-269) writes, "consists first in the boundlessness of political power of dictatorship in contrast with the voluntary restrictions which democracy imposes upon itself—that and nothing else is the meaning of the rule of the rights of man."

Yet it is a questionable presumption, first, that totalitarianism—either in a fascist or communist form—rejects the modernist commitment to the rights of man. Totalitarian rule only rejects the liberal rendering of those rights and depends upon a popular acceptance of an alternative understanding of the modern project. Further, political rule in the democratic age depends upon popular support; the boundlessness of power is not a sufficient explanation for the achievement of the consent of the governed in a totalitarian state. Terror and force may have originally helped to engineer assent, but once the latter has been obtained, it makes its own significant contribution to political order. Considering the endurance of communist regimes, even the attractiveness that totalitarian forms of rule hold for nations outside of the Western and Eastern blocs, it is not sufficient to distinguish between the "power-state" of totalitarianism and the consensual order of liberal democracy.

There is a third reason that has impeded our comprehension of the essential differences between these two major political responses to the modern world. Post-World War II scholarship on totalitarianism recognized the slippery definitional terrain upon which the concept was erected. Hannah Arendt's (1962) formulation, for example, of totalitarianism as a new form of government based upon ideology and terror raised more definitional problems than it resolved. Does totalitarianism not wrongly collapse fascism and communism into a single category, despite their obvious differences in genesis and objectives? Can National Socialism of Germany be rightly equated with Mussolini's fascism, with Franco's Spain, or with Salazar's Portugal? Is there not a distinction to be made between the terrorism of Stalin and post-Stalin political rule in the Soviet Union; what is the relation of these two periods to a concept of totalitarianism? When and where research on totalitarianism has flourished, the result has been largely to distinguish between types and degrees and, therefore, to call into question the usefulness of the concept itself (e.g., Nolte, 1966; Neumann, 1957). The historical case has replaced the search for the universal qualities of totalitarianism; the conviction that totalitarianism and liberal democracy represent qualitatively different forms of political rule has succumbed to the definitional problems that the totalitarian concept raises (cf. Linz, 1975).

The concept of totalitarian democracy offered here rests on a single presumption: Modern democratic order is a function not exclusively of the exercise of power, but also as a result of the establishment of certain patterns of legitimate authority suasive and meaningful to the population (see Parsons, 1960, pp. 170-198). There are contemporary commentators on totalitarianism who assert the contemporary absence of "legitimate" totalitarian societies, thereby denying the concept's analytic usefulness. Michael Walzer (1983), for example, offers in place of the concept of totalitarianism that of "failed totalitarianism." He argues that a vital totalitarian system depends upon an active political movement, a sense of motion and transformation that cannot (or has not) become routinized. "Russia today," Walzer (1983, p. 302) writes, "is a dictatorship resting on popular apathy, the hollow shell of a totalitarian regime." His point is that no totalitarian system has successfully become institutionalized; therefore, the essential distinction between it and other forms of authoritarianism is overdrawn. Walzer recognizes that the ideal of totalitarianism has motivated political actors in the past and continues to do so in the Third World; but because of the instability of these systems, totalitarianism as an ideal has "failed." Walzer (1983, p. 304) writes, "The result is one or another variety of authoritarian rule, dressed up to look 'total,' in which this or that aspect of communist or fascist ideology is haphazardly acted out."

In an analysis that complements Walzer's assessment of contemporary communist societies, Jean-François Lyotard (1984, p. 20) argues that totalitarianism is despotism mediated by its universalism and legitimation through myth. But current communist regimes hardly fit the mold, he argues, for "the people of those countries we call communist know what bureaucratic power is: the delegitimation of the legislator." For Lyotard, as for Walzer, totalitarianism knows no contemporary expression.

Yet empirical studies on the political culture of the Soviet Union have produced findings supportive of the proposition that the regime remains legitimate in the eyes of the population (see, for example, on the Soviet Union, Inkeles & Bauer, 1959; Bronfenbrenner, 1971; Lane, 1976; on China, see Solomon, 1972; Pye, 1970; Schurmann, 1968). Dissatisfaction with specific features of life or with particular policies do not imply, these studies all suggest, the absence of basic value compatibility between the rulers and the ruled. The presence of apathy and/or cynicism—even when widespread—is not, in short, sufficient to conclude an absence of support for the regime and for the values for which it putatively stands. Moreover, in the absence of more powerful evidence, it is a dubious assumption that the ruling ideology in totalitarian systems—self-consciously employed as a political weapon—fails substantially to integrate the population within the political order. When there is no countervailing or competing oppositional political movement within the nation (e.g., Solidarity), it is safe to assume that common political values—perhaps only the most general ones—become shared. The depth and extent of political legitimacy in any nation, of course, remains an empirical question; the difficulties of measuring it are no less difficult here than in liberal democratic societies. But the available evidence does not justify a qualitative distinction between legitimacy in liberal as compared to totalitarian democracies.

The purpose of this chapter is to reassert the value of the concept of totalitarianism and to offer an alternative way of understanding the essential differences between totalitarian and liberal political responses to modernity. The objective is to provide ideal-typical descriptions of the two forms of rule and to present both systems as coherent to the outside observer and as comprehensible to members living within these systems. Liberal and totalitarian democracies do not exhaust the forms of contemporary political systems (see Linz, 1975), but these two systems are the subject of this analysis.

I will suggest that different value commitments lie at the root of the differences between the two forms of rule, resulting in a fundamentally different relationship and different patterns of expectation between the rulers and the ruled. These differences redound upon all aspects of the political and social structure. Totalitarian and democratic democracy each represent a distinctively modern adaptation to the mandate of the people, a particular response to the emergence of a public sphere whose members view themselves as the ultimate authority in the political order. Figure 8.1 indicates the important elements that distinguish totalitarian from liberal democracy.

TABLE 8.1
Distinguishing Features of a Totalitarian Versus
a Liberal Democratic Political Order

	Totalitarian Democracy	Liberal Democracy
Public Values	Egalitarianism	Egalitarianism and Individualism
Public Norms	Constitutionalism/Proceduralism. Principles of allocation and distribution legitimated according to value of egalitarianism.	Constitutionalism/Proceduralism. Principles of allocation and distribution legitimated according to values of egalitarianism and individualism.
Political Organization	Centralized, autonomous, and national political authority. Differentiation of adjudicative, legislative, and bureaucratic functions from civil society. Party fused with the state. State protective of the public sector yet committed to restricting formal participation in it.	Centralized, autonomous, and national political authority. Differentiation of adjudicative, legislative, and bureaucratic functions from civil society. Differentiation of party system from state structures. State protective of the public sector and committed to its universalization.
Character of Solidary Integration Between the State and the Societal Community	Value and normative integration between political structures, elites, and the national community. Civil ties (public commitments) stronger (more general) than primordial ones. Integration achieved through the identification of state with a particularistic solidary group or through an abstract collectivist or "nationalist" ideology. Citizen willingness to subordinate self-interest to the interest of the state.	Value and normative integration between political structures, elites, and the national community. Civil ties (public commitments) stronger (more general) than primordial ones. No formal state recognition of traditional, premodern attachments and no formal embracing of an abstract, collectivist, or "nationalist" ideology. Citizens' self-interests promoted and encouraged by the state.

PUBLIC VALUES

T. H. Marshall (1965) and Reinhard Bendix (1967) have both pointed to the "revolutionary" quality of the idea of citizenship. It is perhaps the most important idea of the modern era and its emergence is dependent upon the development of a public sphere differentiated from civil society. Its development is predicated upon a conception of a realm of freedom, distinct from that of necessity, and an understanding of egalitarianism in which in the public realm, each member is formally the equal of another. Each is similarly entitled to the same voice and to the same degree of participation and influence. The simultaneous development of the public and the idea of citizenship encouraged the understanding of individuals (except for those legally excluded) as standing in direct relation to the political ruler, not mediated through a hierarchical authority structure to which individuals have no access. All members of the societal community are bound together through a system of reciprocal rights and obligations.

Equality is then a political accomplishment, accorded to all those legitimately deemed as members of the political community. As Arendt (1962, p. 301) has written, "equality, in contrast to all that is involved in mere existence, is not given us, but is the result of human organization insofar as it is guided by the principle of justice. We are not born equal; we become equal as members of a group on the strength of our decision to guarantee ourselves mutually equal rights." But if equality expresses an essentially political relationship, as Arendt suggests, then the meaning of equality is a function of political discourse and contest; the way in which egalitarianism is implemented—that is, the kind of human organization—is a function of the particular bargain struck, at any given time, between members of the political community, the legal order (standing in for earlier bargains), and the representatives of the state structure.

Egalitarianism is inextricably connected with the status of citizenship; irrespective of one's place in the private sphere, one is entitled to the same treatment and common protection by the state. As an ideal, citizenship promotes among members of the public an abstract conception of rights owed, responsibilities due, and, perhaps most important, a conception of justice in which, in its formulation, the rights and responsibilities of citizens within a social order provide the central organizing principle.

It is important to appreciate that rights, as entitlements of each member of the political community, derive from the emergence of an egalitarian sphere independent of state structures. Although in liberal democratic societies the conception of rights is deeply overlaid with an appreciation for the sacred individual, rights are not inherently connected to a conception of individualism. Civil rights, for example, are guaranteed in modern political communities not necessarily because of their individual inalienability; instead, they emerge to protect the community from the state. Equal membership in a political community itself promotes an elaborated conception of appropriate entitlements that protect the equality of the community—both from the inequality of the private sphere and from the power of the state. The incomplete realization of equality, or the dangers of a state apparatus usurping that territory of equality, can be, and often is, the stuff of contest in the pursuit of the good society.

Modern citizenship facilitates a modern morality, one that presumes the existence of a coherent social or moral order and casts moral action as political challenges to the state. The state is understood as the protector of the citizenry and as the agency that promotes the values of the national community. In modern political orders, when the regime is the recipient of popular legitimacy, the values embodied in the status of citizenship have come to define largely the character of collective political action within the nation. In these societies, political debate and challenges—at least at the core if not in their manifest expression—embrace a conception of rights owed and rights violated.

As T. H. Marshall (1965, p. 92) writes,

> Citizenship is a status bestowed on those who are full members of a community. All who possess the status are equal with respect to the rights and duties with which the status is endowed. There is no universal principle that determines what those rights and duties shall be, but societies in which citizenship is a developing institution create an image of an ideal citizenship against which achievement can be measured and towards which aspiration can be directed. The urge forward along the path thus plotted is an urge towards a fuller measure of equality, an enrichment in the stuff of which the state is made and an increase in the numbers of those on whom the status is bestowed.

With politics understood as a struggle over rights to which no sphere of society is immune, the striving for an ever more egalitarian order—the expansion of the realm of freedom and the retraction of the realm of necessity—is the central political project characteristic of all modern societies, totalitarian and liberal democratic alike. The formal equality of all citizens produces a universal concern for the substantive realization of egalitarianism throughout the community; flourishing in the public sector, egalitarianism emerges as the dominant value by which social relations throughout the society are evaluated. As Marshall (1965) notes, the definition of rights and the meaning of equality are not firmly cast in stone and vary between societies. Within societies, its meaning has usually expanded and broadened over time. Similarly, the degree and character of state intervention in protecting the egalitarian public and in promoting egalitarianism is never absolutely established. In most modern societies, it has increased over time as the conception of rights has expanded and those defined as entitled to protection has broadened.

There has been, in sum, a tendency toward the universalization of the value, with the modern political community, on behalf of its citizens, increasingly encroaching on other coterminous communities (e.g., the family, the economy, the religious group). There has been an expansion of the realm of freedom, in which the state has protected the citizen from the blind forces of inequality characteristic of those spheres of "necessity," that is, private society.

Totalitarianism, as a legitimate and enduring form of political rule, is exclusively committed to this egalitarian value. It is a political system whose objective is to "public-ize" the population, to extend the boundaries of the political community to all spheres of social life, and to alter continually the balance between public and private by expanding the former and retracting the latter. The universalization of the value of egalitarianism requires a strong state, standing as the ever-vigilant protector of the rights of its citizens, joined together with them to realize equality. But in this "battle" against inequalities in the private sphere, the state necessarily arrogates unto itself the power to egalitarianize the society; there is no other force capable of expanding the public realm. From the vantage of liberal democracies, it is this "total" encroachment on the private realm by the state—on behalf of its citizenry—that makes totalitarianism objectionable. Egalitarianism is the legitimating value licensing the state to act; but the process by which the meaning of equality is generated is not an open one. Divergences from the state's understanding of its purposes are interpreted as expressions emanating from "private" society and, naturally, are deemed retrograde. The process through which the value is given substance is neither deliberative nor contingent. Rather, the meaning of equality is privileged; the implementors are the interpreters (cf. Lyotard, 1984, p. 9).

Totalitarianism represents the extreme form of the modern project: By promoting political egalitarianism the objective is to rid society of all its premodern residues. The dangers are clear. As Hannah Arendt (1962, p. 301) captures it, "Whenever public life and its law of equality are completely victorious, whenever a civilization succeeds in eliminating or reducing to a minimum the dark background of difference, it will end in complete petrification and be punished, so to speak, for having forgotten that man is only the master, not the creator of the world." The totalitarian state, in pushing egalitarianism to the extreme, closes off the private sphere from influencing the course of political affairs; the "irrationalities" of private life should not compete with the "rational" state in determining the fate of the nation. Social relationships, ideally, in the totalitarian state are preeminently political creations. The values that putatively characterize the relationship between ruler and citizen take precedence; they are intended to inform all other relationships. In this way, blind prejudices of inequality lose significance in the face of the enlightened spirit of political equality.

Liberal democracy's value commitment to individualism transforms the nature of the political bond between rulers and ruled, and alters the meaning and importance of citizenship in the political community. The origins of the value-commitment within Western democracies derive most broadly, first, from the Protestant Reformation in which each person came to be seen as equally sacred in the eyes of God; second, from the "bourgeois" revolutions of the seventeenth and eighteenth centuries that were fueled by the imagery of the liberation of the individual both from the estate and from political servitude. Individualism, in short, is infused with a deep cultural resonance peculiar to the West; in this way, its status as an organizing principle in the construction of political orders is more precarious than egalitarianism. Whereas egalitarianism, in large measure, is supported by the institution of citizenship, individualism imbues that institution with a transcendent meaning, one powerfully conditioned by Western cultural understandings.

Liberal democracy, as a subtype of modern society, is unique in its embrace of the dignity and autonomy of the individual. And although, as Lukes (1973) establishes, individualism stands as a composite term for multiple, culturally, and nationally specific meanings, in every case the individual is perceived as distinct (standing separate) from the society in which he or she lives. The person is seen as inherently alienated from the social and political order. The individual, not the citizenry, possesses certain inalienable rights that always remain independent of the larger whole. Here, the interest of the individual is a private one, protected in its personal expression by the convention of political membership—that is, citizenship—and democratic political rule.

The centrality in Western social science and theory of the concept of "interest" in comprehending human behavior is not unrelated to the importance of individualism in Western political affairs. It reveals the fundamental conviction that individuals relate to their world in a self-centered or reflexive and rational-calculating manner (Hirschman, 1984, p. 2). Standing apart from the whole, the individual is viewed as always in tension with a social order impeding the realization of private interest. Indeed, much of Western thought can be understood as the initial effort to calibrate individual interests with collective organization, as in the social contract, the invisible hand, etc. and, later, in the nineteenth and twentieth centuries to complement that optimistic view with a competing understanding of the social world as inherently adversarial to individual emancipation (Hirschman, 1982). As Albert Hirschman (1982) has argued, the market was viewed in the eighteenth century as promoting a harmony of interests (doux commerce) between the individual and the collectivity, only to give way later to a conviction of the market's destructive social force.

Self-interest, of course, has not only been the currency of intellectual discourse. It has long pervaded popular self-understanding. Tocqueville (1969, p. 526) writes about nineteenth-century America: "The Americans . . . enjoy explaining almost every act of their lives on the principle of self-interest properly understood. It gives them pleasure to point out how an enlightened self-love continually bids them to help one another and disposes them freely to give part of their time and wealth for the good of the state." Self-interest rarely today enjoys such unabashed celebration, nor is it often identified as serving the public good; nevertheless, its centrality to popular thinking about political and social affairs remains.

Individualism in liberal democracies counterposes the concern for egalitarianism with a concern for individual freedom. Democracy is not antiegalitarian, but, as Tocqueville (1969, pp. 505-506) observed, the commitment to equality must be tempered in a democratic order so as not to infringe on the liberty of the individual. The aspiration to a more egalitarian social order—which Tocqueville (1969, p. 505) insists is a more powerful impulse in all modern political orders than that of freedom—often infringes upon the protection of the abstract individual. It is this tension between egalitarian aspirations and individualism that characterizes liberal democratic politics. From these two fundamental value-commitments, in conflict with one another, the character of a liberal democratic community is defined.

Egalitarianism, as previously described, denies the intrusion of private interests in public life. In its rejection of premodern particularities, it insists on universalism; moreover, it entrusts the authority of the state to determine acceptable criteria to promote the equality of the citizenry. Individualism, too, is emancipatory. In minimizing the constraints of collective structures on personal action, it seeks to expand the terrain of freedom. Yet in encouraging the expression of individual self-interest, distinctive from state or other collective interests, it does not necessarily sever the links between the individual and relevant "premodern" collectivities, such as the family or other status groups. Personal interest maximization stands as the realm of freedom; it is the state's responsibility to protect and expand that realm. Because the calculation of interest results in an often shifting perception of self-interest (or "uncertainty as to ends" [Lyotard, 1984, p. 11]), because it is a function of social deliberation, and, as a consequence, because it produces a fluid pattern of collective associations promoting those interests, the state must continually "read" the changing calculus and the shifting alliances. The ultimate authority of the state is constrained because of the indeterminacy of interest calculation and the need of the state to be responsive to changing demands.

Individualism necessarily impedes the egalitarian impulse; indeed, its presence in political life significantly alters the power relationship between the rulers and the ruled. It introduces a political dynamic—largely absent in totalitarian democracies—that is highly contestatory and adversarial. What emerges in the politics of liberal democracies are debates over definitions, meanings, and interpretations, ultimately concerning both the meaning of equality and the meaning of freedom (see, for example, Pole, 1978). Seen in this way, politics concerns the shifting boundaries of the public, or the expanding and retracting role of the state in the affairs of its citizenry (see, for example, Starr & Immergut, 1984; Rustin, 1984).

These same political issues are not absent in totalitarian democracies. Pluralism, individual rights, and the rights of nonprotected status groups—like national and religious groups—describe some political action here as well (Lane, 1976, p. 109). But, as David Lane (1976, p. 116) has argued with respect to the Soviet Union, rarely do these actions attract mass support. Instead, they are articulated by the intelligentsia, the one group that suffers most from a single-minded commitment to egalitarianism. Moreover, these struggles often take either the politically mild form of petitions or appeals to the government or the extreme form of a great refusal whereby, as Agnes Heller (1984) has characterized it, dissent itself becomes a vocation. Denied other vocations because of their dissent, the dissidents become isolated from the political community, single-mindedly opposing state policy (see also Gilbert, 1984). These political issues, in short, do not capture the peculiar political relationship between the rulers and the ruled in totalitarian democracies, despite the interest with which these struggles are viewed in liberal democracies. Rather, political contests in totalitarian democracies become expressed more generally through battles over allocation and distribution of social rewards. This topic will be treated in the next section.

Liberal democratic commitment to individualism necessarily requires a sharper distinction, when compared to totalitarian democracy, between the state apparatus and the political community. While entrusted to protect its citizenry from the inequalities of the private sphere, the state is restrained by the voluntarism of the individual and the pluralism of collective associations. Voluntarism and pluralism are not separate value-commitments; they derive directly from the belief in the sanctity of the individual. The "deliberative process" in the public sphere (Lyotard, 1984, p. 9)—in which discourse between individuals and individually composed collectivities (e.g., political parties) occurs—shapes the self-understanding of the political community as to the ultimate purposes of the nation and the necessary means of achieving them (see Prager, in press, Chap. 1). These understandings, in turn, redound on the actions of the state, molding its authority in line with public expectations. The belief in individual autonomy impedes the ability of the state to rid the society of those features that make men and women different or unequal.

Voluntarism and pluralism in liberal democracies ensure a different status for private particularisms, as compared with totalitarian democracy. Only in liberal democracies is the individual simultaneously protected against the private sphere while voluntarily being able to remain connected to it. Even in liberal democracy, of course, there are limits to the expression of individual self-interest, a function of its egalitarianism. The political community is not without constraints in its functioning. But the "consent of the governed" holds a radically different meaning in liberal democratic societies. It is not "the people" who legitimate political authority, whereby the people stand for a nondifferentiated collectivity. Rather, legitimacy is a function of individually given consent of its citizens (Lukes, 1973, p. 79). This fact profoundly affects the relationships of the state to those who tender or withhold support on the basis of state action.

PUBLIC NORMS

Citizenship, I have suggested, is at the heart of modern political orders. It ensures a political community differentiated from other spheres of social life; the state protects the citizenry, freeing them—in varying degrees—from private necessity. Yet if egalitarianism and/or individualism are the motivating values that undergird the institution of citizenship, the relationships that are formed in the political community are normatively specified and juridically codified in a constitutional document. The constitution serves to define the special features of community: for example,

Who belongs? What are the terms of membership? It specifies the relationship and responsibilities of the state to the citizenry and the duties of the citizen to the state. Further, it establishes the aims and purposes of the state, identified as the agency of the political community, entrusted to realize the values and purposes of the nation. The constitution, in short, defines the set of practices and actions of all members of the community and institutions within it that, if adhered to, best realize the ultimate values upon which the community is based.

Whereas values refer to a set of judgments held by members of the community of what ought to be, norms specify sets of practices and actions within various institutions in pursuance of those values (Parsons, 1959, pp. 8-9). Constitutionalism—the belief in the constitution as the ultimate authority regulating behavior and procedures in the political community—defines the normative basis of modern political orders. Normative integration through the constitution is a feature of both totalitarian and liberal democratic orders. In both political forms, citizenship entails an adherence to a certain set of values and enables debate over their meaning. For both kinds of democracies, citizenship also means an acceptance of the constitution as the ultimate authority concerning the proper specification in different institutions of those value-commitments.

The revolutionary feature of constitutionalism, distinguishing modern political orders from those that historically preceded it, is that the state is identified as bound by the same, not higher or different, standards of morality. The belief in the constitution means that the state is perceived normatively as well as instrumentally. The state, rather than standing outside some system of morality, is now much in the center of that system. It is held accountable according to standards set by the constitution. As Kelly (1979, p. 24) writes,

> Its purpose is not to fulfill instantly the wants and needs of its citizenry (however organized in tribes, "estates," groups, or parties) but rather best to express the values that are its own in a lawful way. . . . It implies that the state require the capacity for wisdom, arbitration, and authority . . . the task of state-building and state-maintenance is to act so as to approach these conditions. . . . A state's *dignity* is articulated through its agents and magistrates; its *legitimacy* is confirmed or consented to by its citizens, that is, all those who hold rights within it and receive its protection.

Seen in this way, the constitutional state is appraised less for its ultimate achievement, in the sense of value-outcomes when these standards of performance are internalized, and more for its actions in pursuit of these goals. Common membership in the political community enables an evaluation of the state institutions distinct from those occupying distinct governmental offices. It allows for the persistence of a commitment to the normative state—in Easton's (1965, pp. 190-211) terminology, the regime—while withholding support for the authorities in power. The constitutional state generates for its office-holders a degree of trust essential for rule. But should that trust be violated, should expectations held of state action not be sufficiently realized, support for the office-holders may be withdrawn long before support for the normative state is undermined. It may well be the case, for example, that the cynicism and apathy expressed in many totalitarian settings coexists with a deep and abiding support for the normative- and value-commitments upon which the political regime is based.

A further consequence of the normative state is that the political community, identifying the state as part of the same moral universe as others in the political community, holds more moderate expectations of the state. It is a feature of the modernity of the constitutional state that it is no longer seen as the embodiment of all evil or as the harbinger of millenial dreams; rather, the state becomes the object and protector of moderate politics. Although this may not accurately capture the rise of the totalitarian state—in its "revolutionary" phase—the institutionalization of totalitarian democracy requires the moderation of expectations concerning the state's accomplishments. Political challenges and demands on the state, although surely not disappearing, are expressed principally in the context of rights, duties, and obligations of the state vis-à-vis its citizenry. Only in the face of extreme intransigence by the ruling elite or extreme strains in the political community—whereby the state and sectors of the community do not effectively interact—do these normative conflicts, first perceived as constitutional and procedural in nature, become generalized into value-schisms. When consensus no longer obtains concerning fundamental value-orientations, both the existence of the state and the stability of the political community are jeopardized.

Normative politics typically revolve around the state's role in allocating and distributing social rewards through the existing institutional apparatus. The ability of the state to establish and, to a degree, to implement principles of distribution consistent with the expectations of the political community largely determines, at this normative level, whether or not legitimacy for the government is granted. And it is this domain in which the differences between totalitarian and liberal democracies most clearly manifest themselves.

In the case of the former, allocation and distribution of resources proceeds putatively with an eye toward eliminating the "dark background of difference" and ensuring the absolute egalitarianism of the political community. All decisions—allocation of housing, distribution of educational opportunities, availability of medical care, etc.—are defended in terms of the goal to equalize relations between the legitimate members of the political community. Whereby children of urban, educated minorities are denied entrance into the university in favor of the children of rural, uneducated parents, or whereby new housing is granted to those of "favored" and underrepresented occupations, for example, the criteria for award depends upon the perceived equality needs of the society as a whole. Inequalities between status groups become the object of policy, not the promotion of individual equity. This univocal commitment to egalitarianism promotes, on the one side, an ever-acute sense of status differentiation among members of the political community and an elaborate bureaucratic apparatus to implement egalitarian policies. The result is the encouraging of contestatory politics between groups, particularly among those nonfavored groups. Even among Jewish "refuseniks" in the Soviet Union, for example, who have been denied a vocation because of their requests for exit visas, opposition to the government often does not extend to a rejection of the system; indeed, battle is waged by appealing to the failure of the ruling elite to live up to the terms of the constitution (Gilbert, 1984).

On the other hand, this implementation of egalitarianism encourages individual jockeying, inserting self-interest and private need in the face of a politics principally concerned with collective inequities. The prominence of bribery and corruption, in light of this overriding collectivist concern, is not coincidental. It is ironic—surely an unintended consequence of state distributive policy—that the impulse to rid the nation of "premodern" collectivities and the objective to promote a full-scale assimilation into the "status-blind" political community promote the opposite effect. In totalitarian polities, "modern" politics of distribution and allocation often become experienced through "premodern," or traditional, categories. The value of egalitarianism is understood in terms of its consequence on preexisting collectivities, which, rather than disappearing, often gain in political strength. The effect is not only to make continually salient these collectivities vis-à-vis the state, but, in addition, to preserve the importance of these categories in relations among one another in the society.

In liberal democracies, interest politics assume a different form. Here, the norms of constitutionalism and proceduralism are not only oriented to the value of egalitarianism but to democratic individualism as well. Liberal democratic principles of allocation and distribution must be formulated both in reference to the egalitarian status of the political community and in relation to the value-commitment to the abstract individual who is entitled to benefits irrespective of group membership. Whereas legitimacy in the totalitarian state depends upon support for the specific mechanisms employed by the state to equalize social relations between collectivities, it is the universalism of the liberal democratic state that becomes the standard of evaluation. It is the equalization of opportunity for individuals that defines the limits of state intervention. But the implementation of equality for all individuals lends itself readily to political controversy also, ensuring that resource allocation is hardly a nonproblematic domain (for elaboration, see Apter, 1971).

Liberal democratic orders, like their totalitarian counterparts, do not eliminate the status group as a functioning basis of collective association in the egalitarian political community. In some liberal democratic orders, the degree of cohesion within ethnic, racial, or religious groupings remains strong, making national politics resemble, on the surface, status contests in totalitarian democratic orders. But the commitment to individualism and the power of the vocabulary of individual rights, duties, and obligations tend to ensure that the salient status groups are "modern" ones, like class or occupational groupings. Constitutional language becomes the vocabulary of political protest. Assuming the achievement of some satisfactory compromise between parties, politics both express conflict between sectors of the community and underscore that all members coexist within a single political culture. In contrast with totalitarian orders, premodern collectivities become more readily assimilated into the political community. Even for the "tough case" of Afro-Americans in the United States, it has been persuasively argued that class position today is more significant in defining the life chances of American blacks than it once was and that class issues more powerfully animate black politics (Wilson, 1980). Racial politics, nonetheless, in liberal democratic orders bear the closest resemblance to status politics in totalitarian societies; indeed, the current debate over affirmative action posits the limits of a principle of distribution according to individualistic criteria (Prager, 1982).

POLITICAL ORGANIZATION AND STRUCTURE

I have already indicated why a modern political system requires the state's autonomy from the political community. The egalitarian public sphere, standing apart from more particularistic groupings, demands a state apparatus aligned to no one sector of the community and serving, instead, "public interest." Similarly, the state, seeking to defend its autonomy from private usurpation, depends upon an active citizenry to limit private influence. This interdependent relationship between the public and the state has been instrumental in promoting differentiated functions within the state apparatus itself. The process by which power and authority has developed into institutionally distinct functions— legislative, adjudicative, and administrative—can be seen as similarly motivated by egalitarian value-commitments and procedural normative ones in which no one individual or his or her staff exercise inordinate power or authority. The consequence, developing over the long history of the modern state, has been the emergence of distinct normative procedures governing the conduct of branches of government.

Structural differentiation is not the only consequence of the egalitarianism of the political community. Differentiation of political functions has become, on its own, the sine qua non of modern political orders. There has emerged, as Harry Eckstein (1979, p. 11) has suggested in a somewhat different context, "the normativeness of forms." The size and complexity of the society and the inherent difficulties of politically administering to the population further promote such institutional specialization. Yet the role of the state in preserving an egalitarian public both provides a built-in incentive for differentiation and proscribes certain activities to ensure a diffusion of power and protection of the community.

Although totalitarian and liberal democratic political structures share this common differentiation of function, they differ with respect to the relation of the party system to the state apparatus. As will become clear, this difference derives most generally from the different value-commitments that guide the political system. The unequivocal egalitarianism of totalitarian democracy demands a party system fused with the state, whereas the tension between egalitarianism and individualism in liberal democracy requires a differentiated party system.

The logic of egalitarianism, as an exclusive orientation, promotes "democratic centralism" in party organization. The single-interest articulating party is a key part of the political system; party organization is critical to the functioning of the state. The party is organized to be the institutional "watchdog" on behalf of the population, monitoring the actions of the governmental bureaucracy. In addition, it supervises the functioning of the political organizations, like the soviets in the Soviet Union, which mobilize on a more local level the population on behalf of the state (see Lane, 1976, pp. 76-77). In an explicit organizational way, the party serves both as the representative of the people monitoring the state activities and as a representative of the state in monitoring more locally based political activity of the citizenry. It represents the expression of aggregate public interest, organized to ensure public sentiment's representation in the state. But, more powerfully, it represents an organized state interest in "educating" the political community. Hardly independent of the state, this single party in totalitarian democracy is largely responsible for determining and implementing state policy. Moreover, it serves as the "vanguard" of popular sentiment, directing more than being directed by collective sentiments; serving the political imperatives of the state rather than constraining the state on behalf of the political community (Lane, 1976, p. 78). The political party is not only closely wedded to the state, but its membership is also limited to a small segment of the population who have demonstrated their commitment to the objectives and purposes of the state. Typically, about 5 percent of the population are members of the ruling political party.

This feature of totalitarian democracies not only underscores the fact that egalitarianism alone as a value-commitment strengthens the institutions of state vis-à-vis the political community. Party membership itself is allocated according to the principle that those should be rewarded for their service to the state. But it also reveals a special relationship established between the state and the political community. In totalitarian democracies, the political community is mobilized ideologically (to be discussed in the following section) and organized hierarchically to promote active public support for state rule. Neither the value of egalitarianism nor the principles guiding political rewards promote the open and free expression of political views; indeed, there is no incentive and little opportunity to debate the most appropriate ways to achieve ultimate values. Political outcomes—while involving the population through these structures—are "overdetermined"; there is little "play" in public discourse. Rather, discourse is structured to endorse already existing policy plans established by the various arms of the state. "In each realm of life for each purpose," Juan Linz (1975, p. 192) writes, "there is only one possible channel for participation and the overall purpose and direction is set by one center which defines the legitimate goals of those organizations and ultimately controls them." When antagonisms between the state and community intensify, the state attempts to be responsive. Politics becomes a form of crises resolution. And the response issues from the top down.

Again, totalitarian democracies reveal a profound disjuncture between ultimate aims of the political system and the unintended consequences of state actions. Active intervention by the state in shaping political action contravenes the totalitarian objective of equalizing relations between members of the political community. This disparity between objectives and outcomes points to a critical strain in totalitarian politics; it becomes an important basis for political action and opposition. The exclusivist and hierarchical character of political organization does more than simply circumscribe the range of political possibilities that a vital political community might produce in pursuit of the good society. Even more profoundly, it hypostasizes inequalities between members of the community. It creates a new and relatively permanent class (that is, a group who occupies a particular favored relation to the state and who is dependent upon the state's endorsement) of political elites. Members of the elite, party members, and those in control of the local political organizations attain a new status, rewarded by their political superiors for their service to the state. A "new class" is born, buffering the political elite from popular will and ensuring the continued formal endorsement of state policy by the community.

The arm of the state from above, rather than the will of the people from below, generates the political leadership class. Participation is extended to the extent that it can be contained. And the new political class, deriving their authority from above, is also empowered from above. This ensures a division between the leaders and the led at all levels of the political order. The value of egalitarianism rewards the local "implementors"—i.e., political elites—and, in so doing, secures a class of people through all levels of the society subject to their leadership. The relationship is a patrimonial one; as the history of patrimonialism well attests, political initiatives tend to flow from the top downward, not vice versa. The aspiration for egalitarianism, then, promotes a more rigid cast of political inequalities between those in leadership positions and those who are not.

The dual commitment in liberal democracies to individualism and egalitarianism expressed, as I have already indicated, both in terms of political values and normative practices produces political organizations that differ from totalitarian democracies. Whereas the party system in totalitarian democracies is composed of a single party, is closed to all but a small sector of the population, and is accorded a privileged relationship to the administration of state, in liberal democracies the party system is a competitive one, is mass-based, and is differentiated from other political structures. The question is how does this difference in party organization and functioning relate to individualism? How does the competition between value-commitments in liberal democracies fashion a distinctive relation between party, state, and community?

In liberal democracies, there is the insistence that the individual is the principal political agent in the community, that each individual independently assesses his or her interests, and that no single interest—including state interest—is automatically privileged over another. Public policy is the product of different constellations of interests competing to shape understandings and define priorities. With this understanding of the individual as principal mover, liberal democracy depends upon a plurality of groups organized together voluntarily on the basis of common interests; from the cacophonous voice of political debate and discord the course of state action is determined. Collective associations, at least in the commitments of liberal democracy, are the life-blood of the democratic process. This inherent tension between an ability to redefine continually interest in terms of abstract democratic values and a reality that necessarily falls short of ideals constitutes the basis for political mobilization in liberal democracies.

The party system mediates between the formulation of public policy by state agency and the expression of individual interest in the political community. Ideally, it serves as a conduit between community and institution; it organizes and channels interest-politics; that is, it disciplines the political community and serves to ensure the accountability of policymakers and implementors to members of the community. The important feature of the differentiated party system is that it enables different aggregates of individuals to have access to political power and to influence public policy. Parties represent the capacity of the system to integrate a politically active, diverse, and heterogeneous population within the democratic political universe. The isolation of any group of collectively organized individuals denies the potential for political representation and influence and jeopardizes liberal democracy. Therefore the possibility is raised that political challenges will no longer revolve around particular authorities and policies but around the constitutional regime itself. On the other hand, a differentiated party system ensures that state interest does not become synonymous with public interest because the final arbiter of public policy is the individual, collectively organized within a party system.

Despite its celebration of the individual as citizen, individualism simultaneously allows the individual political actor to remain voluntarily connected to a particular traditional past, to identify interests and to generate social identities with respect to this past, and to participate politically with respect to these interests and identities. Political parties provide the vehicle to ensure that traditionalist commitments become expressed politically in a modern democratic context. They serve as central structural mechanisms that mediate between the solidary sphere of the national community and the political apparatus. As Parsons (1959, pp. 214-215) has argued, the political party stands as the means through which traditional solidary attachments become expressed within the framework of modern politics. There is evidence of a reasonably strong relationship between familial and other traditional identities—extending over time—and identification with specific political parties, suggesting that rational decision making is insufficient as an explanation to account for party loyalties (Sears, 1978, p. 124). A differentiated party system ensures that diverse solidary groups identify their interests in accordance with modern political forms. Because modern political parties in liberal democracies are composed of more than one solidary group—for example, religious, racial ethnic—they serve both as potent integrative forces in developing alliances between "conflicting" solidary groups and they promote the transformation of traditional attachments into more modern ones.

This distinctive feature of liberal democratic organization is further expressed in a special expectation of a universally active political community. The contrast with totalitarian democracy is striking, in which active participation in the political community is restricted to only those already sharing intensely in the aims and values of the state. The state is not committed to universalizing participation in political life; rather, as I have already described, it serves to reward those exceptional members who distinguish themselves for their commitment to the state. This practice reveals—totalitarian ideology notwithstanding—little commitment to the promotion of an active, critical citizenry capable of debating policy options or considering political alternatives. The "new man," in formation within totalitarianism, is the man of the community, but without politics. The aim of the state, in fact, is to limit participation;

only in doing so is the achievement of equality on behalf of all a possibility.

Liberal democracy, in contrast, necessarily is committed to the expansion of political participation; only through participation in the modern political institutions, like the party system, can the political system be assured that traditionalist attachments will not become rigidified into a politics challenging the regime. The quest for liberal democratic morality places particular demands on the "social character" of the citizenry (Lipset, 1963, Chap. 8). The belief in the autonomy and dignity of the individual assumes, further, his or her rational character. Liberal democracy, because it does not abolish tradition, depends on activity in the political community. Only in this way can the individual emerge as the central figure in democratic politics, standing over and against collectivities organized according to primordial or ascriptive categories. The vitality of the democratic political community, it is presumed, militates against the volatility of politics that stand outside the liberal democratic moral universe.

CHARACTER OF SOLIDARY INTEGRATION BETWEEN THE STATE AND MEMBERS OF THE POLITICAL COMMUNITY

I have described thus far the relationship between values, norms, and political institutions. These relationships, I have argued, are a function of particular political value-commitments that impinge upon all spheres of political life. Although I have suggested that the two forms of democracy that are being described possess a coherence that makes them intelligible to an outside observer, this section will examine how "meaningfulness" is produced within the system, ensuring the comprehensibility of the system to the members themselves. It is through law and ideology that the cement of solidarity is applied; through these mechanisms, members identify and lend support to their political system. In examining these dimensions of political life, we return again explicitly to the problem of legitimacy.

Neither liberal nor totalitarian democracies could function if members of the political community did not share in a perception of themselves as members of the same community, governed by the same laws and entitled to the same rights. In a broader sense, this shared identification represents some realm of common agreement concerning the ultimate aims and purposes—some transcendent meaning—of the nation and some agreement as to the rightful members of the political community. Integration depends on both the subordination of the individual to the legal order and a more or less universal acceptance of an ideology (standing above particularistic interests), which enables members of the community to view the political process as culturally comprehensible. As Geertz (1973, p. 218) argues, only in a truly traditional society—characterized by a homogeneity of thought and feeling—is a transcendent ideology a largely unnecessary appurtenance of social life. In such a society, men are uniformly guided by unconscious thoughts and feelings, possessing no imperative to subordinate personal interest to collective good. The two are simultaneously enhanced or suffer similarly. But in modern society, an integrative ideology that binds the mundane political world with the more sacred cultural concerns of various groups is essential to support modern political order. Geertz (1973, pp. 218-219) writes,

> The function of ideology is to make an autonomous politics possible by providing the authoritative concepts that render it meaningful, the suasive images by means of which it can be sensibly grasped . . . the differentiation of an autonomous polity implies the differentiation, too, of a separate and distinct cultural model of political action, for the older, unspecialized models are either too comprehensive or too concrete to provide the sort of guidance such a political system demands.

Both the creation of a modern legal order and the genesis of an integrative ideology capable of sustaining political life are connected to particular political cultural pasts and to specific "traditional" understandings of appropriate behavior. In that sense, each integrated political community possesses a distinctive "civil religion" (Bellah, 1970), a secular formulation of national principles and values that comes to assume sacred meaning, which justifies the nation's existence and purpose. In addition, each community develops its own legal order whose specifications of appropriate relations between political community members and the state and among the members themselves are derived both from civil religion and the legal traditions of the past. Yet despite the fact that no two civil religions or legal orders could be the same, there are features that markedly distinguish liberal from totalitarian democracies. The differences reveal the distinctive patterns of integration that typify the two political systems.

In totalitarian democracies, integration is achieved through the legitimating myth of community. The modern project of emancipation is not abandoned on behalf of community. The rights of man continue to motivate totalitarian democracies. Yet according to the myth, personal freedom can only be obtained collectively, and only when each individual is in a position to be similarly liberated. Through the achievement of the egalitarian community—one both harmonious and nonoppressive—the good society will be realized. Thus the totalitarian vision, when compared to liberal democracy's, elaborates an explicit and concrete image of a future society. The present is in service to the future.

But the vision is even more powerful. Not only does the myth offer a specific picture of the ideal community, but it connects the movement toward it with some immanent law of nature or law of history. The result is to remove policy—intended to promote community—from the realm of politics. Policy itself is defended as immanent and immune from contest. The implications that follow from this communitarian ideology are profound.

First, as we have already seen from a different vantage point, the state's authority is supreme; only the state can realize community. The creation of this new world or the recreation of one that putatively existed in the past is a collective project, incapable of being realized through unregulated individual activity. The result is that the public interest—that is, the movement toward the good society—is defined as the state's interest. Private interest, when it conflicts, is subordinate to the state's. Politics, the arena in which competing interests vie, are subordinated to the image of the politics-free community. In the state's suppression of the realm of politics, the present is intended to resemble the future.

Second, communitarianism, connected with a transhistorical law, enables an exclusivist conception of community. Rightful membership in the political community is subject to narrow definition. In its most extreme formulation, whole peoples may legitimately be excluded when, for example, the law of nature defines only a single people as the rightful heirs to the community. The concept of the egalitarian community easily coexists with, perhaps even depends upon, the active exclusion from that community of all those who do not belong. More typically, exclusion is a function of those who fail to embrace the communitarian vision or the politics-free present, for example, intellectuals and other cultural elites. Ironically, it is the commitment to individualism in liberal democracies that prevents the narrowing—or expulsion—of membership in the egalitarian political community, not, as the example of totalitarian democracies demonstrates, the commitment to egalitarianism per se. With an eye to the future of a harmonious community, all those who, according to one law or another, are deemed incompatible are expelled. Here, again, the present operates as if it were the future.

Finally, the attachment of the state to this end-purpose also subordinates the law to the vision of the "community in formation." Roberto Unger (1976, p. 231), in describing a central characteristic of revolutionary socialist society, writes that there "is the willingness to subject society and nature to ruthless and radical manipulation. But the willingness is coupled with the belief that thoroughgoing instrumentalism will hasten the advent of a situation in which the conflict among individual will, social order, and nature will have disappeared because whatever oppresses man in a society of nature will have been wiped out." The law is similarly vulnerable to the state's instrumentalism; "formal law is subordinate to the law of revolution" (Linz, 1975, p. 220). Yet totalitarian rule is not lawless. As Arendt (1962, p. 461) writes of totalitarian states, "[their] defiance of positive law claims to be a higher form of legitimacy which, since it is inspired by the sources themselves, can do away with petty legality. Totalitarian lawfulness pretends to have found a way to establish the rule of justice on earth—something which the legality of positive law admittedly could never attain."

The result is an integrated political community, united around the myth of community, in which individuals are connected to one another through their equally powerless and vulnerable relation to the state. It is a pattern of integration decisively different than that in liberal democracies. There well may develop a common animus to the political authorities who serve the state and, in so serving, are privileged. Beyond that, integration is patterned on a posture of sacrifice: sacrificing private interest to the state interest, sacrificing the present for the future. Legitimation in totalitarian democracies represents a form of self-denial. That it has been achieved is testimony either to the power of the ideological apparatus, the power of the vision, or perhaps both.

Liberal democracies, in contrast, celebrate politics and deny the possibility of a harmonious, conflict-free community. The realm of freedom is enhanced through political activity; the rights of man can be secured through individuals promoting their own interests and rights. Liberal democracies discover oppression only when groups of individuals insist on its presence, only when they organize politically and persuade others that its existence infringes on the free individual. The central

characteristic of liberal democracies is the absence of any specific concrete image of the good society or any particular idea of what the future
might look like. In its place, there is an ever-shifting, ever-changing
assessment of the relationship between this society and certain ideals
(e.g., egalitarianism, justice, and movements to better realize them).
Although there typically is a belief in progress—namely, that life today
is better than in the past and improvements are likely to continue—it
is not endemic to the political system. There is not the belief in a motor
force of history or nature propelling the nation forward in a determinate
direction. And in contrast with totalitarian democracies, there is no conception of an end point, an ideal world. This fundamental difference
derives, once again, from the individualism of liberal democracies. Viewing the person as the key political agent and the expansion of the individual's realm of freedom as the ultimate aim of liberal democracy,
there can be no conception of a community absent of contest and conflict. This perspective has several important implications.

First, the state must compete, like other agents in the political community, to assert state interest (i.e., public interest) over and against
private interest. There is a constant interplay between the two (with the
state gaining ground in the long run) and the outcome at any one
moment is never certain. Moreover, the state can never assume for itself
a purpose or a mission other than better realizing private interests, equalizing opportunity among private parties, and so forth. Measures designed
to equalize the political community are defended in terms of the creation
of a community in which all individuals are able to compete more equally
for social rewards. In this respect, the state is always subordinate to the
interests as defined by members of the political community. The state
is not powerless in attempting to influence perceptions of self-interest,
but its ability to mobilize the polity on its behalf is not foreordained.

Second, the legal order—the system of rules that governs behavior
and social practices—that normatively defines relations among social
members powerfully integrates the political community. Perceived as
standing above particular interests and, in most respects, as autonomous
from the legislature and bureaucracy, the law expresses, where the state
does not, the essential elements of the democratic "creed." Indeed, legal
principles like fairness, equity, and the law's method of discovering truth
through impersonal procedures of adjudication emerge as central to the
self-understanding of members of the community. And at the heart of
this understanding is appreciation of the fact that the legal system serves
to constrain state power and enhance that of individuals. Whereas

totalitarian democracies sacrifice law for "state" ideology, in liberal democracies the relation between the law and state interest is a contested one. On balance, it is safe to say that the legal order holds the edge; for it is law, not the state, that is viewed as the agency that protects and promotes personal freedom.

Finally, the centrality of political action to liberal democracies' self-definition promotes the appearance of a political community with little cohesion, sharing few of the same values or beliefs. The society is perceived often as overly contestatory, as too litigious, and as insufficiently concerned with the welfare of the community. It is a society of conflict, not of consensus. Political critiques—both from the right and the left— offer in its stead a conception of a cohesive community governed by the objective of substantive justice. Such a vision is offered as an alternative to the liberal, individualistic, atomized order. The law is often criticized for its proceduralism, sacrificing substantive justice in the interest of protecting the impersonal procedures upon which the legal order is built. These critiques of liberal democracy surely have merit. But more to the point is that the openness of the political process and the discursive freedom allowed in liberal democracies require, at all times, an acceptance of indeterminacy and ambiguity in social life. This uncertainty is often difficult to tolerate. The aspiration for community and the concern for substantive justice represent a reaction to this indeterminacy, much like the voice of individual protest in totalitarian orders is a reaction to the strength of the communitarian vision. In the case of liberal democracy, the impulse for community stands as an alternating current for a system committed both to the individual and to equality.

CONCLUSION

The aim of this chapter has been, first, to present the two political systems as comprehensible ones and to describe the various parts of each system and their relationship to one another. In capturing the coherence of the system (from the outside) by reference to public values, I have argued that both systems are capable of commanding support from the political community. Totalitarianism stands today as a legitimate form of rule, although not, from our perspective, a palatable one. Moreover, by demonstrating the centrality of value-commitments to all aspects of political organization, it should be apparent that liberal or totalitarian democracies are not on a single political continuum. When state power expands in liberal democracies, for example, the conclusion cannot be drawn that it is becoming more totalitarian. Similarly, directions toward "liberalization" of totalitarian democracies must be understood in their own terms. Each of the systems generates their own particular strains that are always in relation to the strains inherent in the value system and political organization. There is no danger, in short, that the two forms of modern democratic orders will converge and become indistinguishable.

In addition, I have presented an admittedly idealized rendering of the two forms of democratic rule. As such, no political community or nation-state today corresponds exactly to the traits that I have described. But in describing the way it is meaningful to members living within it, I have attempted to identify some of the bases that explain strain within the system. For example, liberal democracy is presented ideal-typically as an arena in which members of an egalitarian political community organize collectively on behalf of private interest. Such a rendering ignores the presence of hierarchy and its continuing impact on social and political relations. Nevertheless, in describing liberal democracy normatively it is now understandable why the illegitimacy of hierarchy becomes a central axis for political oppositional movements. The issues that motivate these political actors express the gap that exists between liberal democracy's ideal expression and its reality. Similarly, in totalitarianism, we witness opposition in terms of the system's failure to realize the community of free individuals, able to pursue their own interests freely and without conflict. Freedom is not a value external to totalitarian democracy but is part of its imagery. And the assertion of individual rights represents not the intrusion of a foreign frame of reference but a product of the perception by members of the community of promises failed or deferred.

The forms of support and opposition to a given political system, in the end, derive from the promises offered within that system and the generation of particular perceptions within that community of how the system has failed to deliver them. But the endurance of these systems rests on the willingness of the community members to accept the regime's objectives, to accept the inherent gap between real and ideal. In that sense, the destiny of liberal and totalitarian democracies similarly rests on the will of the people.

REFERENCES

Apter, D. (1971). Equity and allocation in industrial societies. In *Choice and the politics of allocation* (pp. 72-104). New Haven, CT: Yale University Press.

Arendt, H. (1962). *The origins of totalitarianism.* New York: Harcourt Brace Jovanovich.

Bellah, R. (1970). *Beyond belief.* New York: Harper & Row.

Bendix, R. (1967). *Nation building and citizenship.* Berkeley: University of California Press.

Bendix, R. (1980). *Kings or people? Power and the mandate to rule.* Berkeley: University of California Press.

Bronfenbrenner, U. (1971). *Two worlds of childhood.* London: Allen & Unwin.

Easton, D. (1965). *A systems analysis of political life.* New York: John Wiley.

Eckstein, H. (1979). On the "science" of the state. *Daedalus 108*(4), 1-20.

Friedrich, C., & Brzezinski, Z. K. (1956). *Totalitarian dictatorship and autocracy.* Cambridge, MA: Harvard University Press.

Geertz, C. (1973). Ideology as a cultural system. In *The interpretation of cultures* (pp. 193-233). New York: Basic Books.

Gilbert, M. (1984). *The Jews of hope: The plight of Soviet Jewry today.* London: Macmillan.

Heller, A. (1984). *Totalitarian rule: Totalitarian Society.* Paper presented at the Hannah Arendt Memorial Symposium in Political Philosophy, New School of Social Research, New York, NY.

Hirschman, A. O. (1982). Rival interpretations of market society: Civilizing, destructive, or feeble? *Journal of Economic Literature, 20,* 1463-1484.

Hirschman, A. O. (1984). *Interests.* Paper presented to the Social Science Research Seminar, Institute for Advanced Study, Princeton, NJ:

Inkeles, A., & Bauer, R. (1959). *The Soviet citizen.* Cambridge, MA: Harvard University Press.

Kelly, G. A. (1979). Who needs a theory of citizenship? *Daedalus, 108*(4), 21-36.

Lane, D. (1976). *The socialist industrial state: Towards a political sociology of state socialism.* Cambridge, MA: Harvard University Press.

Linz, J. (1975). Totalitarian and authoritarian regimes. In D. Greenstone & N. Polsby (Eds.), *Handbook of political science* (Vol. 3, pp. 175-411). Reading, MA: Addison-Wesley.

Lipset, S. M. (1963). *The first new nation.* New York: Basic Books.

Lukes, S. (1973). *Individualism.* Oxford: Basil Blackwell.

Lyotard, J. F. (1984). *Notes on legitimation.* Paper presented at the Hannah Arendt Memorial Symposium in Political Philosophy, New School of Social Research, New York, NY.

Marshall, T. H. (1965). *Class, Citizenship and Social Development.* Garden City, NY: Doubleday.

Neumann, F. (1957). *The democratic and the authoritarian state.* New York: Free Press.

Nolte, E. (1966). *Three faces of fascism.* New York: Holt, Rinehart & Winston.

Parsons, T. (1959). Durkheim's contribution to the theory of integration of social systems. In K. H. Wolff (Ed.), *In Emile Durkheim, 1858-1917: A collection of essays, with translations and a bibliography.* Columbus: Ohio State University Press.

Parsons, T. (1960). Authority, legitimation, and political action. In *Structure and process in modern societies.* New York: Free Press.

Pole, J. R. (1978). *The pursuit of equality in American history.* Berkeley: University of California Press.

Prager, J. (1982). Equal opportunity and affirmative action: The rise of new social understandings. In R. Simon & S. Spitzer (Eds.), *Research in law, deviance, and social control 4* (pp. 191-218). Greenwich, CT: JAI Press.

Prager, J. (in press). *Building democracy in Ireland: Political order and cultural integration in a newly independent nation.* New York: Cambridge University Press.

Pye, L. (1970). *The Spirit of Chinese Politics: A psychocultural study of the authority crisis in political development.* Cambridge, MA: MIT Press.

Rustin, M. (1984). Psychoanalysis and social justice. *Radical Science, 15,* 98-112.

Schurmann, F. (1968). *Ideology and organization in Communist China.* Berkeley: University of California Press.

Sears, D. O. (1975). Political Socialization. In D. Greenstone & N. Polsby (Eds.), *In Handbook of political science* (Vol. 2, pp. 93-154). Reading, MA; Addison-Wesley.

Solomon, R. (1972). *Mao's revolution and the Chinese political culture.* Berkeley: University of California Press.

Spiro, H. (1968). Totalitarianism. In *International encyclopedia of the social sciences* (Vol. 16, pp. 106-116). New York: Macmillan.

Starr, P., & Immergut, E. (in press). Health care and the boundaries of politics. In C. Maier (Ed.), *The changing boundaries of the political.* Cambridge: Cambridge University Press.

Talmon, J. L. (1952). *The rise of totalitarian democracy.* Boston, Beacon.

Tocqueville, A. (1969). *Democracy in America* [J. P. Mayer, Ed.]. Garden City, NY: Doubleday.

Unger, R. (1976). *Law in modern society.* New York: Free Press.

Walzer, M. (1983, Summer). On failed totalitarianism. *Dissent,* pp. 297-306.

Wilson, W. (1980). *The declining significance of race.* Chicago: University of Chicago Press.

Chapter 9

BEYOND PARSONS'S THEORY
OF THE PROFESSIONS

BERNARD BARBER

Columbia University

AS JEFFREY ALEXANDER (1983) has reminded us, "controversy within most of the principal empirical subfields of sociology has, at one point or another, focused on a particular set of 'Parsonian' propositions, whether or not such alleged configurations accurately represented Parsons's own thinking." This is certainly true for the sociology of the professions. For the first 45 years up until the recent publication of the outstanding Heinz and Laumann study of the "Chicago Bar" (1982), nearly all theoretical and empirical studies in the field have oriented themselves to Parsons's seminal article, "The Professions and Social Structure" (1939), and a variety of his subsequent writings on the professions. Parsons's analysis of professional norms, structures,and processes has been applied by many, rejected by others, and modified by still others. It has been the essential seedbed for the development of theory and research on the professions. My purpose in this chapter is to describe where we stand today and where we need to go in the future for the most effective understanding of the place of the professions in modern society.

It will first be useful to describe the several sources of Parsons's interest in and analysis of the professions, as these sources help us to see better the virtues and limitations of Parsons's work. A description of these sources will also put in perspective the various criticisms, warranted and unwarranted, that have been made of Parsons's work on the professions.

1. The centrality of theory. As with all his work, Parsons's basic interest in the professions was theoretical. Central to his theoretical program was to establish that normative or "non-rational" elements were as much an independent factor in human action as the rational and instrumental factors that the utilitarian tradition in Western thought had defined as exclusive of all others. Before taking up a full positive analysis of the place of the normative factors in human action and the social and cultural systems it continually created, Parsons needed, negatively, to show the theoretical and empirical limitations of the utilitarian theory. In addition to arguing this negative position in abstract, theoretical terms in *The Structure of Social Action* (1937), he sought to show it empirically in the case of the modern professions. Their behavior, he argued, could not be understood solely on instrumental grounds. Although the professions shared the essential characteristics of individualism, activism, and universalism with businessmen, they differed in one important respect, which could only be explained by the fact of normative difference. Whereas norms for businessmen prescribed self-interested behavior on the market, norms for professionals prescribed "other-oriented" (later to be called "collectivity-oriented") behavior. As Parsons further specified in a companion article published the following year (1940), the differences were matters of normative determination, not matters of different rational motivation.

Parsons (1939) offered, as a contribution to his positive theoretical program, the first account of his pattern-variable scheme, a generalized theoretical statement of a set of analytical variables for describing the variable normative elements in all action. This scheme was important for Parsons throughout his subsequent theoretical development.

2. Empirical evidence. The second source of Parsons's analysis of the professions was empirical evidence. In the early 1930s, Parsons spent some time walking the wards of distinguished teaching hospitals in Boston, observing the behavior of clinicians and occasional medical researchers. It was a time, of course, when the former were dominant in teaching hospitals. Parsons went on rounds and listened to the formal and informal talk among teachers and students. He felt that the evidence thus collected confirmed his view that professional behavior could not be understood apart from the institutionalized—that is, normatively structured—situation in which it was enacted. As an observer of businessmen's behavior and its guiding norms, as a close student of the economic literature, indeed, as one who had started out in the discipline of economics, and as a keen observer of the current American society, Parsons felt fully justified in asserting their determination by institutionalized self-orientation. I shall return later to some of the weaknesses in Parsons's approach to empirical data and the problem of measurement.

3. Parsons's values and ideological orientation. Parsons's own values and ideological orientation were another interrelated source of his analysis of the professions. Early on, and throughout his work, Parsons not only saw but preferred the central modern Western values of cognitive rationality, activism, collectivity orientation, universalism, and institutionalized individualism. Although he admired these values wherever he saw them in modern society, he thought they achieved their fullest realization in the professions and in the university. For Parsons, the professions were one of the *differentia specifica* of the modern Western world. He very much approved of their existence and their great influence.

4. *Personal factors.* Finally, intermingled with these other three sources was a personal one. Parsons's older brother, whom he admired greatly and who died prematurely, was a physician with all of the characteristics Parsons saw in the professions as a whole. Moreover, in the Harvard-Boston medical community of the 1930s, Parsons found several other exemplars of high professional performance and devoted service to their patients. This was before the great development of scientific medicine and the great strain it has put on the therapeutic aspect of medical performance. (Barber, Lally, Makarushka, & Sullivan, 1973). In his class lectures in the 1930s and later, Parsons often referred to his Boston medical colleagues by name and most admiringly.

From these several sources, then, Parsons constructed a theory of the professions that was, *in principle,* like his sociological theory in general, that is, a mixture of rational, instrumental elements, on the one hand, and value and normative elements, on the other. However, *in practice,* in Parsons's writings on the professions and in those of some of his students, this basic multidimensional theory was often not realized. Parsons's analysis of values was sometimes translated too directly into empirical propositions; he sometimes underplayed the interests that also existed for professionals; and he did not as often as was necessary submit his ideas to the rigorous discipline of systematic empirical research, his own or others'.

The failure to realize Parsons's multidimensional theory can be seen very clearly in the work of some of his students and in many of his critics. For example, the work of Renee Fox, Parsons's most distinguished student in the field of medical sociology, has been criticized for putting too great an emphasis on value elements and their fulfillment in the activities of medical researchers. She has too much stressed, it has been pointed out in reviews of her work, *Courage To Fail* (Fox & Swazey, 1974) the burdens of medical researchers, their courage to fail, rather than their self-interested motives to gain prestige for their research and rather than the burdens of the human subjects of that research. On the other hand, critics of Parsons like Eliot Freidson, as distinguished a medical sociologist as Fox but with quite different and more instrumentalist theoretical views, have gone to the other extreme and attributed most medical professionals' behavior to their interest in dominating their work situations. This involves dominating both those who assist the physicians, like nurses, and the patients they are treating (Freidson, 1970a, 1970b). The same instrumental bias, in its extreme form, can be found in the work of neo-Marxist critics of Parsons and his views on the professions such as Larson (1977). At least implicitly, there is much of this instrumentalist bias in the recently published and much admired book by Paul Starr (1982).

But none of this is necessary. It is possible to follow the multidimensional Parsonian path and to describe both instrumental and normative factors in an analysis of actual professional behavior. It is possible to see, as Parsons pointed out, not only personality, social-structural, and cultural elements in professional behavior but that each of these three aspects is variable. One-dimensional, overdetermined analysis will not do. With this in mind, I would like to consider a few topics in the sociology of the professions on which I myself have constructed theory, done research, or considered as methodological matters to show how Parsons's own work on the professions needs to be corrected. I shall consider the following four topics: authority, power, and responsibility; collegiality; uncertainty and risk; and measurement and empirical evidence. All of the corrections I recommend are not only consonant with but are actually *demanded* by Parsons's general sociological theory and its specific application to the professions.

AUTHORITY, POWER, AND RESPONSIBILITY

Parsons defined the professions as "those occupations that possessed and applied highly generalized knowledge." This knowledge was derived from highly systematic theoretical and empirical study of *nature,* as in the scientific and medical professions, from *rules and laws,* as in the legal profession, from *morality and problems of meaning,* as in the religious profession, or from *other cultural elements,* such as history, art, and literature, as in the academic profession. Acquiring this generalized knowledge and its associated work skills usually required extended specialized training, but extended training was not in itself enough to define a profession. Training to be an acrobat or a baseball pitcher might take a long time, but the knowledge involved was not generalized and systematized. Because the knowledge acquired by professionals was esoteric, Parsons added to his definition that control of professional behavior had to be self-controlled by the professionals themselves. Professionals, finally, were defined as other-oriented, that is, normatively required by themselves and their peers to put their clients' or the general public's interest before their own self-interest. This was a necessary element of social control over the great power of the professions. Various other discussions of the nature of the professions have added other characteristics to the definition, but these are not essential characteristics.

Parsons never specified just what he meant by generalized knowledge or how it was esoteric. As a result, critics have pointed to the fact that nonprofessional occupations—e.g., plumbers—may have some esoteric knowledge and concluded that they are therefore no different from professionals. Indeed, one sociologist has raised the provocative question of "The Professionalization of Everyone?" (Wilensky, 1964). Esoteric knowledge seems elitist to some radical egalitarians who criticize any special designation for the powerful and prestigious professions as Parsons defined them. An essential task for the sociology of the professions remains to specify not only what is meant by generalized knowledge but what is its esoteric character. Preferably such specification would be based minimally on some rough measures that include the essential notion of *"degrees of professionalization."* There are professionals and professionals in the real world. Some do indeed have generalized knowledge—for example, of the law—but others have mere cookbook knowledge of particular rules and statutes. Are both professionals? Are they professionals to the same degree? I think the public makes important distinctions of this kind, as occupational prestige studies provide evidence. Should not the theory of the professions be able to do the same? Moving in this direction, for example, Etzioni has edited a volume on the "semiprofessions," a coinage that describes these distinctions (1969).

Although Parsons correctly indicated that esoteric knowledge among professionals calls for some irreducible measure of self-control, he did not specify how much, the mechanisms of informal and formal self-control, or the relations of professional self-control to larger political and social controls. Parsons seemed to hold that professional self-control was entirely based on internalized norms acquired in effective professional socialization. He did not inquire into the relations between these internalized norms and the formal mechanisms of control that the professions and society had to set up to control standards of training, licensing, and the elimination of incompetence and deviance. Nor did he pay any attention to how effective these established informal and formal mechanisms of social control actually were. We know that the formal mechanisms are hardly effective and some of the informal mechanisms push aside problems rather than solve them (Barber et al., 1973; Barber, 1979; Freidson, 1970b). A satisfactory Parsonian theory of the professions will pay attention to all of these questions about self-control. In modern differentiated society, all specialized activities (such as business and the professions) have ramifying consequences, for good and ill, that vitally affect the larger society and are therefore activities to be controlled in part by the larger social and political processes. Specialists, and especially powerful specialists like professionals, may overreach their proper sphere of expertise and authority. Both of these— appropriate sphere of action and legitimate authority—need to be defined as interacting between the relevant specialists and the rest of society. Special activities cannot be left to the specialists alone. Society cannot grant absolute power to any specialist group, for power must always be exercised responsibly, that is, either directly or indirectly in the public interest. Parsons did not systematically study the actual performance responsibility of his admired professions. His critics have often been justified in pointing to professional social irresponsibility. For example, many critics said that the medical profession had too much power over setting the terms of payment for its services; the legal profession was serving only the well-to-do and the "nonethnic" (Auerbach, 1976); and medical researchers were using human subjects, especially poor ones, without getting their informed consent (Barber et al., 1973).

Because Parsons wanted to believe the professions were indeed other-oriented and because he did not systematically study their actual behavior or pay enough attention to the results of the empirical research of others who pointed out their defects, he did not see that clients were often treated instrumentally, for the greater financial gain of the professional, for his or her own convenience, or for his or her own greater prestige. When the public murmured their complaints against professionals or when critics complained of the substitution of "dominance" by the professionals over their clients for legitimate authority, Parsons did not inquire into either the facts of this alleged dominance or what its social and cultural sources might be. For example, especially from the 1940s on, medical researchers often had an acute dilemma, a set of possibly conflicting values, the value of scientific discovery, on the one hand, and the value of patient service, on the other. Often, as in research on human subjects before outside control was imposed by the National Institutes of Health in 1966, the science value prevailed over the patient service value. The sociology of the professions still has not done the intensive, systematic study of what happens in doctor-patient or professional-client interactions to see what is actually going on, how much instrumental behavior there is, how much normatively determined behavior there is, and what the different combinations of these two kinds of elements are in different situations. We do not know how much dominance and how much authority are operative in what kinds of professional-client interactions. Just as the empirical evidence for Parsons's assumption that authority prevails is slight, so is the evidence for the contrary assumption that everything is dominant.

COLLEGIALITY

The problem of collegiality is another aspect of the structures and processes of authority, responsibility, and control among professionals that is in need of proper theoretical specification and necessary empirical research. As a thorough liberal, democrat, and voluntarist, Parsons admired collegiality as a pattern of authority and control wherever it might exist. He described it not only as the pattern among professionals themselves but even, occasionally, between professionals and their clients. For example, although he was very clear about the existence of what he called "the competence gap" between professional and client, he felt that they were engaged in a common enterprise that was best carried forward by mutuality and collegiality. The empirical reality, however, is somewhat different from what Parsons saw as coming entirely from the norm of collegiality. For example, to refer again to the use of human subjects in biomedical research, physicians did not give their subjects the full information and obtain the informed consent that are essential to collegiality (Barber, 1979). Moreover, Parsons did not pay attention to the self-interests that professionals could advance against their clients through the mechanism of collegiality. For instance, it has been pointed out that every medical code of ethics since the eighteenth century has been primarily about professional etiquette—that is, how physicians should respect each other's interests—rather than about disinterested service to their patients (Berlant, 1975). Furthermore, collegiality among professionals has been an instrument of resistance against controls from the larger society. Collegiality, both formal and informal, has been used to oppose reforms proposed by nonprofessionals through the political process, very often successfully, as in the matter of so-called "socialized medicine." Finally, collegiality has often been used by professionals as an instrument of particularism and discrimination, as in the treatment of minority and ethnic group colleagues by those from the dominant ethnic groups. Heinz and Laumann, in their study of the Chicago Bar, see it as divided into two bars, two different sets of legal professionals, on the basis of ethnic origin and affiliation (1982). Like the bureaucratic pattern of organizational authority and control, the collegial pattern has its functions and dysfunctions. All the consequences of collegiality for all the affected groups are what need to be analyzed and studied by an adequate sociology of the professions. Norms and interests both are expressed in and result from the collegiality that Parsons admired.

UNCERTAINTY AND RISK

In opposition to the predominant positivism of his time, Parsons very early attached much importance to the elements of uncertainty, risk, chance, magic, and meaning in social action. He knew, of course, about Weber's concept of "die paradoxie der folgen." He often spoke of and referred to the economist Frank Knight's book, *Risk, Uncertainty, and Profit* (1967). He was very much impressed by Chester I. Barnard's discussion, both in course lectures at Harvard and in his book, *The Functions of The Executive* (1938), of the problem of uncertainty faced by the executives of large business organizations, the way in which they got both more credit and more blame for events over which they had only uncertain control. Finally, in his discussion of science, religion, and magic, he made a great deal of the anthropologist Bronislaw Malinowski's analysis and evidence on these matters in his work on the Trobriand Islanders (1922, 1935).

It is not surprising, given this general theoretical interest in the phenomenon of uncertainty in human action, that Parsons was among the first to see the importance of this perennial aspect of action in the situation of medical practice (see Parsons, 1951, pp. 449-450 & 466-469). Parsons pointed out that medicine was not all science, that there were elements of uncertainty that called for nonrational responses by both physicians and their patients. It was a brilliant insight, derived from theory as much as from actual observation. However, Parsons never pursued, systematically and intensively, the necessary empirical research into the specifics of where, when, how, and how much uncertainty there was in medical practice. As elsewhere in his work, Parsons opened our eyes to new worlds by his account of uncertainty, but he did not stay to describe those worlds in empirical detail.

Fortunately, Parsons's distinguished student in the field of medical sociology, Renée Fox, has made a great deal of the concept of uncertainty throughout her career. In her long account of her use of this concept (1980), she begins by saying, "Uncertainty has been central to my work in the sociology of medicine since its inception. The importance of uncertainty in modern medical practice as a theoretical concept, an empirical phenomenon, and a human experience was first impressed on me by my teacher, Talcott Parsons." As a graduate student, Fox did excellent empirical research on the behavior of physician-researchers and their patients on a ward of the Peter Bent Brigham Hospital in Boston, where the first radical adrenalectomies were being performed and where cortisone was first used as an adjuvant to the first kidney transplants. It was a very special situation in which, as Fox nicely puts it, "uncertainty and death were the only certainties." For this very special situation, uncertainty was indeed an essential element of the medical situation.

Unfortunately, in later work, Fox has tended not to ground the existence of uncertainty in specific empirical situations. She has tended to overgeneralize the special situation described in the book that resulted from her original research (1959). She and others have not specified the *kinds* and *degrees* and *consequences* and *sources* of uncertainty in medical practice. A great deal of medical practice has practically no uncertainty in it. The result has been that the concept of uncertainty has become not just a scientific account of specific medical situations but an ideological justification of a variety of medical practices. For example, doctors can justify their authoritarian patterns on the grounds of an alleged intense and endless uncertainty that they do not actually face in many situations. Doctors can be glorified beyond merit as having the courage to fail when relatively little courage was involved or, at least, it had to be empirically demonstrated. If, as Fox says, doctors are "specialists in uncertainty," then they need practically unlimited autonomy to face this hazardous situation. But their autonomy is often at the expense of the autonomy of others, both their subordinates and their patients. For example, in the work of Fox's student, Charles Bosk, uncertainty is again stressed in an overgeneralized form (1979). In his account of the training of surgical residents in a premier teaching hospital, domination of these trainees by the surgical professors is justified on the ground that the professors need complete autonomy to cope with the perennial uncertainty of their practice. The guiding norm of the resident training formulated by the surgeons to their students, Bosk reports, is one of "no surprises," that is, "do not get me into trouble with unexpected news or outcomes." The norm tells the resident to protect the surgeons and his or her absolute autonomy. This is surely a way of dealing with uncertainty that may not always be in the interests of the patients. In general, there is the tendency in the work of all three of these "Parsonians"—Parsons himself, Fox, and now Bosk—to pay more attention to the uncertainty for the physician than that for the patient. This bias is not necessary in a more adequate Parsonian medical sociology. Empirical research could specify the degrees of uncertainty for physicians, researchers, and patients in different diagnoses, prognoses, and procedures. Some of the necessary empirical information is probably already available for collection from existing medical records; other data could be researched. This empirical information about uncertainty in medical practice could be shared among all the interested parties, physicians, and patients alike, probably reducing feelings of uncertainty in many cases and also more nearly balancing autonomy values and interests between physicians and patients.

MEASUREMENT AND EMPIRICAL EVIDENCE

I have already referred several times to the fact that one of the reasons why Parsons did not comply with his own theoretical understanding of the relation between interests and values was his lack of sustained concern with systematic empirical research, either by himself or others. I should now like to make a more general statement about Parsons's understanding of the functions of measurement and empirical evidence in social science. It was in no way true, as many of Parsons's critics alleged, that he did not understand the relation between theory and fact, that he was a mere maker of conceptual categories. A notable example of this mistaken view can be found in C. Wright Mills' book, *The Sociological Imagination* (1959). Mills damns Parsons as the prime example in modern sociology of "Grand Theory—the associating and dissociating of concepts" (p. 26). In fact, Parsons had an excellent understanding, in principle, of how theory influenced fact and fact influenced theory. In practice, however, as I have already indicated many times, he often did not satisfactorily act upon this understanding. This defect became greater in his later work. Parsons himself was aware of this defect, but was unable effectively to overcome it. Like all geniuses, he had his limits. He spoke of himself as an "incurable theorist," and so he was, often cultivating theory without the disciplining effect of recourse to detailed empirical research.

Although he was generally and strikingly a person not quick to take offense or respond to even strong aggression, Parsons felt defensive enough about such criticism as Mills's that in his intellectual and moral autobiography, "On Building Social System Theory: A Personal History" (1970), he discussed his knowledge of and use of the relation between theory and fact at considerable length. In his excellent, recent, admiring exposition of the work of Parsons, the distinguished French sociologist, Francois Bourricaud, feels obliged to defend Parsons on this issue; so does the American sociologist, Harry M. Johnson, a devoted Parsons student who writes the Foreword to the English translation of Bourricaud's book, *The Sociology of Talcott Parsons* (1981).

Against the overpowering empiricism of the 1920s and 1930s in social science, Parsons early on asserted the importance of theory, of what he called, following L. J. Henderson's phrase, "conceptual schemes" (Barber, 1970; Conant, 1947). From his youthful study of Kant, Parsons had adopted, long before it was more widely accepted, the "constructivist" view of the functions of theory. But Parsons was no absolutist, as some more recent constructivists are, in his view of what is now called, more generally, "the social construction of reality." In a crucially important statement, he states the following:

> Strategically crucial as the theoretical element of science may be, it cannot stand alone. Theory is important precisely in its function of organizing existing knowledge of fact, and of guiding the investigator to new observations and to the uncovering of new and hitherto unknown relationships between facts. The continual interaction between theory and observation is therefore of the essence of science. (Parsons, 1948)

This continual interaction, Parsons knows, is not always well ordered in the short run. "In a given phase of a scientific endeavor one or another of these aspects (theory and fact) may be in the forefront, but all of them are essential to the total movement" (ibid.). In his intellectual autobiography Parsons shows his great knowledge and systematic understanding of this problem of fact and theory by referring to discussions on the matter by Kant, Weber, Whitehead, Schumpeter, Pareto, and Conant.

Further in his own defense on this issue of empirical research, in his autobiography Parsons referred to various efforts at empirical research: his observation of medical behavior in the 1930s and his collaboration in the 1950s with his colleagues, Samuel Stouffer and Florence Kluckhohn of the Harvard Department of Social Relations, on a survey research study of social mobility among high school boys in Boston. In the 1960s and 1970s, with a variety of colleagues, he participated in survey research on the American university, research that resulted in his book with Gerald Platt (1973). He might also have added a reference to his acquaintance, partly through reading and partly through collaboration with his specialist colleagues at Harvard, with a wide variety of empirical, historical, anthropological, and contemporary facts about many different societies. Parsons taught and wrote exceptionally interesting analyses, grounded in comparative empirical data, of the nature and origins of Nazism and Fascism (1954).

Moreover, as the examples I have given earlier in this chapter and others indicate, Parsons seems never to have had the disposition, and this was more and more true as his career developed, for being continuously and systematically influenced by the facts accumulated by intensive empirical research. He did not have the measurement problem or the factual validation concern "in his guts" the way he had the theory concern. But it is clear that there is no problem in principle, and there need be none in fact, with a fully Parsonian body of empirical research.

CONCLUSION: THE INTERACTION AND INTERDEPENDENCE OF INTERESTS AND VALUES

In social science there are currently at least two existing sets of presuppositional positions for the analysis of social behavior in general and the professions in particular. The first asserts that values and norms have an essential influence on behavior, always in interaction with rational, utilitarian, interested elements of course. The second asserts that only rationality (or irrationality), interest calculations, utilitarian concerns, and "strategies" determine behavior. This position is predominant in many of the now multiple versions of Marxism but is also prevalent in economics and in much of what is called "exchange theory" in sociology. Where norms, values, or institutional factors cannot be avoided by analysts taking this position, they tend to be constructed in an ad hoc, common-sense manner and epiphenomenal from interests.

Properly understood, despite Parsons's own lapses from this multi-dimensional position, Parsonian sociology takes the first stand. This is the stand on which social science must go forward. Interests and values are always interdependent in action. What social science needs is both much better measures than it now has of what is interest, value, or norm, and a great deal of empirical research on just what combinations of interests and values occur in which situations and what their sources and consequences are. The sociology of the professions, and social science in general, could well use this understanding for bringing together what now seem to be entirely disparate theories and bodies of knowledge. When brought together, the considerable body of knowledge that we currently have is an excellent base for still further progress in our attempt to enlarge our mastery of the social world.

REFERENCES

Alexander, J. (1983). *The modern reconstruction of classical thought: Talcott Parsons.* Berkeley: University of California Press.

Auerbach, J. S. (1976). *Unequal justice.* New York: Oxford University Press.

Barber, B. (Ed.). (1970). *L. J. Henderson on the social system.* Chicago: University of Chicago Press.

Barber, B. (1979). *Informed consent in medical therapy and research.* New Brunswick, NJ: Rutgers University Press.

Barber, B., Lally, J. J., Makarushka, J. L., & Sullivan, D. (1973). *Research on human subjects.* New York: Russell Sage Foundation.

Barnard, C. I. (1938). *The functions of the executive.* Cambridge, MA: Harvard University Press.

Berlant, J. L. (1975). *Profession and monopoly.* Berkeley: University of California Press.

Bosk, C. L. (1979). *Forgive and remember.* Chicago: University of Chicago Press.

Bourricaud, F. (1981). *The sociology of Talcott Parsons.* Chicago: University of Chicago Press.

Conant, J. B. (1947). *On understanding science.* New Haven, CT: Yale University Press.

Etzioni, A. (Ed.). (1969). *The semi-professions and their organization.* New York: Free Press.

Fox, R. C. (1959). *Experiment perilous.* New York: Free Press.

Fox, R. C. (1980). The evolution of medical uncertainty. *Milbank Memorial Fund Quarterly/Health and Society, 58*(1), 1-49.

Fox, R. C., & Swazey, J. P. (1974). *The courage to fail.* Chicago: University of Chicago Press.

Freidson, E. (1970a). *Professional dominance.* New York: Atherton.

Freidson, E. (1970b). *Profession of medicine.* New York: Dodd, Mead.

Heinz, J. P., & Laumann, E. O. (1982). *Chicago laywers.* New York: Russell Sage Foundation.

Knight, F. H. (1967). *Risk, uncertainty, and profit.* New York: Harper & Row. (Originally published 1929)

Larson, M. S. (1977). *The rise of professionalism.* Berkeley: University of California Press.

Malinowski, B. (1922). *Argonauts of the western pacific.* London: Routledge & Kegan Paul.

Malinowski, B. (1935). *Coral gardens and their magic.* New York: American Book.

Mills, C. W. (1959). *The sociological imagination.* New York: Oxford University Press.

Parsons, T. (1937). *The structure of social action.* New York: McGraw-Hill.

Parsons, T. (1939). The professions and social structure. *Social Forces, 17*(4).

Parsons, T. (1940). The motivation of economic activities. *Canadian Journal of Economics and Political Science.*

Parsons, T. (1948). *Social science: A basic national resource.* Unpublished report prepared for the Social Science Research Council.

Parsons, T. (1951). *The social system.* New York: Free Press.

Parsons, T. (1954). *Essays in sociological theory.* New York: Free Press.

Parsons, T. (1970). On building social system theory: A personal history. *Daedalus, 99*(4), 826-881.

Parsons, T., & Platt, G. M. (1973). *The American university.* Cambridge, MA: Harvard University Press.

Starr, P. (1982). *The social transformation of American medicine.* Cambridge, MA: Harvard University Press.

Wilensky, H. (1964). The professionalization of everyone? *American Journal of Sociology, 70,* 136-158.

DIFFERENTIATION, CONSENSUS, AND CONFLICT

Some Comments on Smelser, Colomy, Lechner, and Barber

RICHARD MÜNCH
University of Dusseldorf

ALL FOUR CHAPTERS under discussion pass beyond the confines of older functionalist theory and, in so doing, open up the theory to insights stemming from the application of other paradigms. It seems to me that a period in which a divide fell between functionalism and integration on one side and conflict theory and domination on the other has now been superseded.

The chapters by Neil J. Smelser, Paul Colomy, and Bernard Barber combine theoretical assumptions of earlier functionalism with assumptions of conflict theory. Frank J. Lechner is concerned with antagonisms inherent in the development of modern societies and the effects of the process of modernization that provoke movements against modernity. The central question stemming from these positive developments becomes whether a combination of functionalism and conflict theory will determine the future of sociological theory, whether this is in its present form an integrated paradigm, and whether it is indeed comprehensive enough. I will follow up this main question with its three subdivisions as I deal with several special questions regarding the different chapters.

NEIL J. SMELSER ON EDUCATIONAL DIFFERENTIATION

Neil J. Smelser demonstrates in his chapter how the explanation of the development of educational institutions becomes much more complicated and leaves room for far more different paths of development if we extend the functionalist theory of differentiation by combining it with the impact of group interest on the concrete historical processes of institutional change. This view leads to the explicit questioning of the assumption of a unidirectional and unidimensional process of structural differentiation. This is certainly an inevitable effect of introducing groups as corporate actors. The functional theory of differentiation addresses change in (social) systems as a process whereby systems adapt to an increasingly complex environment completely independent of the orientations of individual and collective actors. Those systems that become more differentiated will be better adapted to the environment and will survive in the long run. Conflict theory, as a contrary position, addresses the action of individuals and groups. The more we follow its path the more we approach historical explanations and the more we are required to become historians. The question then is whether anything remains to be done by the sociologist.

Smelser's treatment of educational change sheds light on the work that does indeed remain for the sociologist. The main point is that the differentiation of the educational system has to be conceived of as a complete process in which a new educational system is institutionalized. And here it becomes immediately evident that (as he demonstrates) the efficiency and adaptivity of the new system is not at all the only important criterion for its institutionalization. He adds the orientations and interests of groups and the process of compromising during group conflicts as further major factors that exert an influence upon the process of institutionalization. If we adopt an evolutionary perspective, and in this way a perspective that provides more generalizations than historical consideration, we may conceive of all factors Smelser reviews in referring to his earlier theory (Smelser, 1963) as selective criteria for the survival of educational patterns: their *conformity* to existing traditions, their *consistency* with general values, their *directedness* toward the goals of competing groups with more or less power, and their *adaptivity* to changing situations and increasing demands for qualification. In this way we can make use of Smelser's questioning of earlier assumptions regarding the consistency of value systems, the strategy of group conflict, the nature of decision making, and the efficiency of new institutions.

What we need is an integrated theory that specifies exactly the character of the effects exerted by these factors on the selection of educational patterns. In my view—with some radicalization of its objective logic—a Parsonian Action Theory can provide such a framework, which has nevertheless to be filled by the contributions of more specific approaches as Smelser demonstrates with the example of conflict theory. In this perspective differentiation proceeds in different directions. In the case of education, we have to begin with its embeddedness in the family, that is, with its basis in communal life. Its criterion is the conformity to family norms. Differentiation means extension of education beyond and/or separation from family life in three directions because in Parsonian terms three different environments exert pressures on it: the state, the economy, and cultural discussion. It becomes a goal-oriented organization of the state, an adaptive and pluralistic enterprise and a cultural institution, organized and bureaucratized, pluralized and economized, universalized and intellectualized. These factors have a very different weight and character in different societies and push the process of educational differentiation in different directions. In Germany, for example, education is primarily a state-organized and intellectualized institution; in the United States it is much more an economic enterprise and a case for the local community, thus varying between the particularism of neighborhoods and the efficiency demands of the economy. In addition to this evolutionary perspective, we may consider educational change as a historical process, but in this instance using the whole action-theoretical framework, which means that not only the political bargaining process of strategic groups is concrete action, but also communal association of individuals and groups, economic calculations and intellectual justifications, and criticism of institutions (see Figures 10.1 and 10.2).

PAUL COLOMY ON THE
DEVELOPMENT OF POLITICAL PARTIES

The last remarks lead me to Paul Colomy's chapter. He begins with factional politics, which are characterized by a close connection of communal association and political decision making. The latter is an outcome of the orientations of the honoraries, the prestigious and leading families. Again we have to distinguish three directions of differentiation of party politics from communal life: the organization and bureaucratization of parties resulting from their directedness toward collective goals, their pluralization and economization resulting from their adaptation to mass participation, and their universalization and intellectualization resulting from their orientation to intellectual discussion. Uneven differentiation has an additional meaning here, not only its different completion in dif-

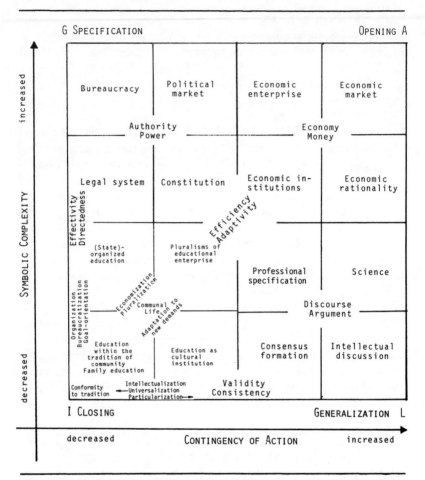

Figure 10.1 A Model of the Differentiation of Educational Institutions from Communal Ties

ferent regions of a society, but also its different development in different analytical dimensions.

Again German parties are more bureaucratized and intellectualized, whereas American parties are more bound to regional groups, situational movements, and the economic aspects of campaigning. The selective factors for the evolution of this system are its *conformity* to existing traditions, its *consistency* with general values, its *directedness* toward the goals of competing, more or less powerful groups, and its *adaptivity* to the economic calculations of voluntarily deciding voters.

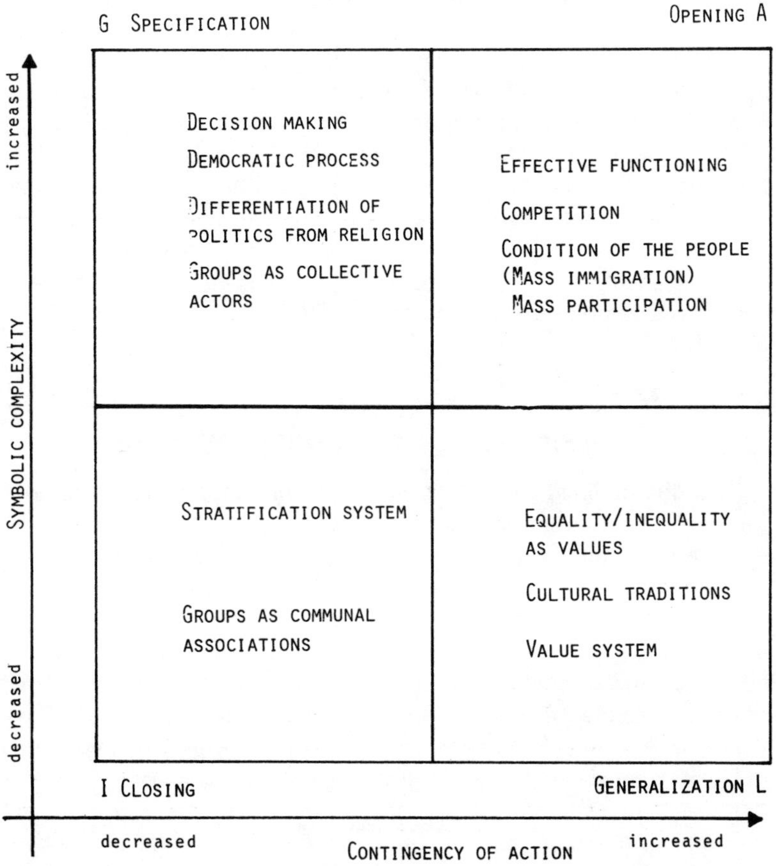

G SPECIFICATION   OPENING A

increased

| DECISION MAKING DEMOCRATIC PROCESS DIFFERENTIATION OF POLITICS FROM RELIGION GROUPS AS COLLECTIVE ACTORS | EFFECTIVE FUNCTIONING COMPETITION CONDITION OF THE PEOPLE (MASS IMMIGRATION) MASS PARTICIPATION |
| STRATIFICATION SYSTEM GROUPS AS COMMUNAL ASSOCIATIONS | EQUALITY/INEQUALITY AS VALUES CULTURAL TRADITIONS VALUE SYSTEM |

SYMBOLIC COMPLEXITY

decreased

I CLOSING   GENERALIZATION L

decreased   CONTINGENCY OF ACTION   increased

Figure 10.2 A Model of Smelser's Factors Explaining Educational Differentiation

If we turn from the systems process to the action of individuals and groups, again the compromising of conflicting groups is only one of several forms of interaction. Colomy takes, for example, communal cleavage structures, mass participation as allowed by constitutional rights, and the value of equality as major structural features furthering the process of differentiation that is more or less realized by strategic group action. However, we may also take group relations and the distribution of their power as structural features and contrast them with the action of voters who calculate economically, intellectuals who present and discuss arguments, and group members who associate together. What is structure and what is action are questions of our perspective. Strategic group action and bargaining are not the only possible forms of interaction. But this inclination toward identifying interaction with bargaining and negotiation is a general inclination of American sociologists.

A last point here is that the outlined concept of differentiation does not lead to a conception of differentiation as the growing autonomy of subsystems that are no longer influenced by the product of other subsystems. The differentiation of party politics from communal ties opens up such politics to bureaucratic, economic, and intellectual steering. The same holds true for educational differentiation (see Figures 10.3 and 10.4).

FRANK LECHNER ON
REVITALIZATION SYNDROMES

With the outlined view of differentiation in mind, some suggestions for Frank J. Lechner's argumentation in his chapter that differentiation is not a smoothly on-going process but a process that is permanently accompanied by movements against differentiation, leading at least to partial dedifferentiation, may be appropriate, in addition to Smelser's and Colomy's chapters. As he argues, a differentiated society is a rather fragile, balanced system that is always in danger of being tipped out of balance by the primacy of one of its differentiated subsystems. If we conceive of an undifferentiated society as living in a state of constriction of life by community ties, we may characterize antimodern movements as forces of dedifferentiation and of a return to the order of community, tradition, and stable commitment to norms. From these antimodern movements, we may distinguish unidirectional modernist movements, which are characterized by a complete addiction to utilitarianism and hedonism, political actionism and power politics, or intellectual skepticism and nihilism. I think some of Lechner's syndromes belong to the first category, others to the second; sometimes concrete examples might be better located in the first category although he puts them in the second.

The core of antimodernist dedifferentiation is the romantic syndrome that fundamentalism is a blocking of rational argumentation—a feature of social-cultural discourse—by some primordial and unquestioned commitments. The opposite modernist cultural syndrome would be intellectual skepticism and nihilism. The antimodern movement in the adaptive dimension is a return to the ethics of brotherhood; this indeed

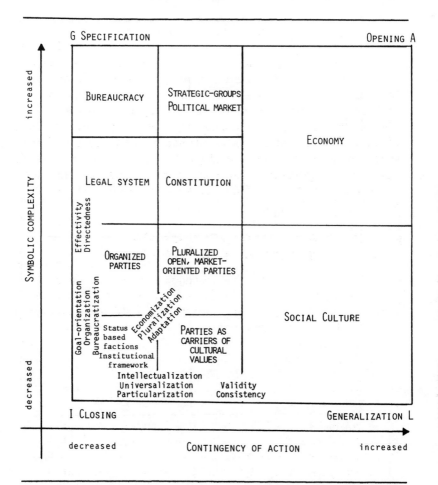

Figure 10.3 A Model of the Differentiation of Party Politics from Communal Ties

was a dream of Marxism and is the relevant aspect of Marx's approach in this context, rather than the economic bias of the theory. The true modernist tendency is unrestricted hedonism and utilitarianism as Weber (1920, p. 204) saw emerging in his vision at the end of the Protestant ethic study and Daniel Bell described in his *Cultural Contradictions of Capitalism* (1976). The expressive therapeutic movement is a return to the deep feeling present within an elective group, with its charismatic leaders exemplified by some religious sects. Decision making is reduced to the expressive commitment to a group and its leader. The modernist

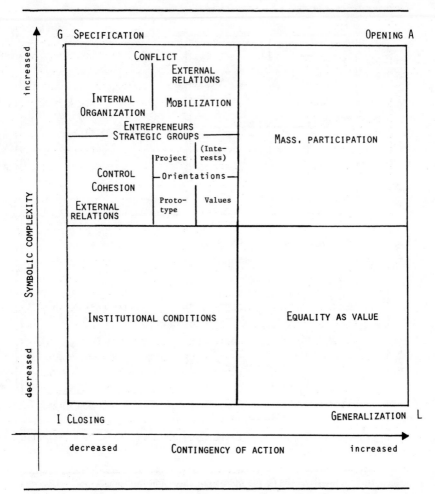

Figure 10.4 A Model of Colomy's Factors Explaining the Development of Political Parties

counterpart here is the unrestricted political actionism and power politics (Realpolitik) of dominating elites (see Figure 10.5).

BERNARD BARBER
ON PROFESSIONAL ACTION

Bernard Barber demonstrates at various points in his chapter where Parsons's theory of the professions failed and had to be completed by

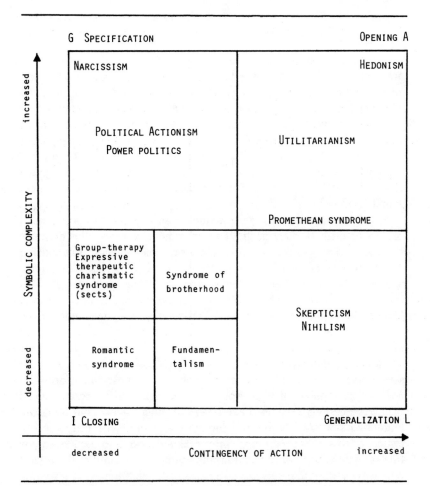

G Specification   Opening A

increased — Symbolic complexity — decreased

Narcissism	Hedonism
Political Actionism Power politics	Utilitarianism
	Promethean syndrome
Group-therapy Expressive therapeutic charismatic syndrome (sects)	Syndrome of brotherhood
	Skepticism Nihilism
Romantic syndrome	Fundamen-talism

I Closing   Generalization L

decreased   Contingency of action   increased

Figure 10.5   A Model of Modernist and Antimodernist Movements

the contributions of conflict theory (see also Barber 1978, 1980, 1983). In my view, Parsons's formulations in this field were insufficiently theoretically abstracted (Parsons, 1951, pp. 428-479, 1954, 1968a, 1978). Some of his writings gives the impression that he was providing a model for the concrete action of professionals. But this is a flagrant violation of his rule of analytical abstraction (Parsons, 1968b, pp. 3-42, 727-775).

A theory is not a *description* of facts, but instead allows its explanation; it is not empirical in the sense that it tells us how a concrete professional behaves; it explains how he or she will act *if* certain factors, and only these factors, guide his or her action; it contains *analytical* laws on the relationship between certain aspects of action defined analytically as sharply as possible. A hypothesis may postulate that the higher the cohesion of a professional group the higher the conformity of its members to its norms. Whether this norm conformity also means a commitment of the professional to society or to the client (which is not the same) depends upon the connection of the professional group with the other societal groups and upon the relationship of the professional to the client.

Parsons's model is only meaningful as an ideal type of a balanced professional-client relationship. The falsifying instance for this model is not the deviating professional, but the professional-client relationship that is in balance and helps the client in developing his individuality without following the path of Parsons's model. When Paul Starr (1982), for example, demonstrates in his book on the medical profession in the United States how professionals followed a pure power and interest politics, he has quite another object of explanation than Parsons had in his theory.

However, Parsonian Action Theory can be used in a much broader sense than Parsons's ideal type of a balanced professional-client relationship exemplifies. It is an irony that the defect in Parsons's model of the professions may not have been too much theory, but too little. Here we have to apply the full range of the action-theoretical architectonic, which allows much more empirical variation than the ideal type. Professional action varies according to the relative weight of the effects emanating from the various social subsystems; namely, communal association of individuals and groups, political decision making, and economic activity and social culture (the latter with its own subsystems of intellectual discussion, scientific investigation, consensus formation, and the professional specification of culture). Such action is therefore dominated to a greater or lesser extent by the commitment to the professional group and/or other societal groups, to culture and abstraction, to authoritative decision making, and to client interests and economic calculation.

Let me compare briefly German and American lawyers in terms of how their action is differently determined and directed along different paths by the enumerated factors (see Rueschemeyer, 1973). The professional orientation of the German lawyer under codified law is determined by a dominance of abstraction and authority. He or she is less dependent on client interests and on a societal community. His or her independence is based on ascribed elite status and authority and on the fusion of the professional group with the state. He or she interprets the general and statute law of the state. The American lawyer considers his or her activity much more as a business. He or she is first committed to the paying client and second to the societal community as far as it is the carrier of the common law that he or she interprets.

We may expect in the German case a professional code of ethics that stands *above* the citizen *and* the lawyer, and hence is a less economically motivated deviation from ethical norms. The professional group is less engaged in unconcealed interest politics because its status is unquestioned, is traditionally given, and is rooted in the principle of the Rechtsstaat (rule of law). The professional-client relationship is shaped by status-differentiation and authority. We may expect less commitment to the client. Highly abstract ethical commitment is accompanied by a low commitment to clients.

The American lawyer and the professional group gain their status from success in competition; status is based more on achievement and less on ascription. Their sole desire is to beat their opponents. This implies a commitment to client interests, interests that pay fairly well. The professional group has to secure its status on the market; thus the salience of interest politics is natural and the bar is much more internally differentiated in income and prestige than the German bar. Less highly abstract ethical commitment is accompanied by much greater commitment to client interests (see Figure 10.6).

CONCLUDING REMARKS

Let me conclude with a general remark. In my view the term "neofunctionalism" has connotations with which it need not be burdened any longer. I am thinking of connotations such as functionalist methods of explanation, stability bias, systems bias, neglect of the individual actor, and so on. I would prefer the use of the term "Action Theory" in a comprehensive sense, which is open for the contributions of all the different sociological approaches. And it is indeed true that further advances in sociological theory are only possible if we recognize the contributions of each of the different paradigms. Thus if we are first committed to the advancement of Action Theory, this does not exclude the idea that

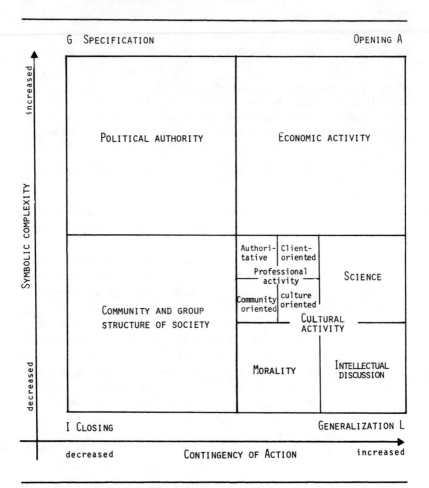

Figure 10.6 A Model of Professional Action

there is much to be learned from other paradigms (Münch, 1982, 1984).

REFERENCES

Barber, B. (1978). Control and responsibility in the powerful professions. *Political Science Quarterly, 93,* 599-615.

Barber, B. (1980). *Informed consent in medical therapy and research.* New Brunswick, NJ: Rutgers University Press.

Barber, B. (1983). *The logic and limits of trust.* New Brunswick, NJ: Rutgers University Press.

Bell, D. (1976). *The cultural contradictions of capitalism.* New York: Basic Books.

Münch, R. (1982). *Theorie des Handelns: Zur Rekonstruktion der Beiträge von Talcott Parsons, Emile Durkheim und Max Weber.* Frankfurt: Suhrkamp.

Münch, R. (1984). *Die Struktur der Moderne: Grundmuster und differentielle Gestaltung des institutionellen Aufbaus der modernen Gesellschaften.* Frankfurt: Suhrkamp.

Parsons, T. (1951). *The social system.* New York: Free Press.

Parsons, T. (1954). The professions and social structure. In T. Parsons (Ed.), *Essays in sociological theory* (pp. 34-49). New York: Free Press.

Parsons, T. (1968a). Professions. In D. L. Sills (Ed.), *International encyclopedia of the social sciences* (Vol. 12, pp. 536-547). New York: Macmillan.

Parsons, T. (1968b). *The structure of social action.* New York: Free Press (originally published 1937).

Parsons, T. (1978). Research with human subjects and the "Professional Complex." In T. Parsons (Ed.), *Action theory and the human condition* (pp. 35-65). New York: Free Press.

Rueschemeyer, D. (1973). *Lawyers and their society.* Cambridge, MA: Harvard University Press.

Smelser, N. (1963). *Theory of collective behavior.* New York: Free Press.

Starr, P. (1982). *The social transformation of American medicine.* New York: Basic Books.

Weber, M. (1920). *Gessammelte Aufsätze zur Religionssoziologie* (Vol. 1). Tübingen: Mohr Siebeck.

ABOUT THE CONTRIBUTORS
AND EDITOR

JEFFREY C. ALEXANDER is Professor of Sociology at UCLA. He is the author of the multivolume work, *Theoretical Logic in Sociology, Twenty Lectures: Sociological Theory Since World War II* and *Structure and Meaning: Essays in Sociological Theory.* He is past Chair of the Theory Section of the American Sociological Association and currently is a Fellow at The Institute for Advanced Study at Princeton, where he is working on a study of the Watergate crisis and American culture.

BERNARD BARBER is Professor of Sociology on the Barnard College and graduate faculties of Columbia University. His latest book (in press) is *Effective Social Science: Relations Between Empirical Social Research and Social Policy.*

PAUL COLOMY is Assistant Professor of Sociology at the University of Akron. He received his Ph.D. from the University of California at Los Angeles in 1982 and has published articles in the areas of sociological theory, social change, and social psychology. He is currently completing a book on the changes and continuities of antebellum political leadership.

S. N. EISENSTADT is Professor of Sociology at the University of Jerusalem, where he has been a faculty member since 1946. He has served as a Visiting Professor at numerous universities, including Harvard, MIT, Chicago, Michigan, Oslo, Zurich, and Vienna. He was a Fellow of the Center of Advanced Studies in Behavioral Sciences and the Netherlands Institute of Advanced Studies. He is a member of the Israeli Academy of Sciences and Humanities, Foreign Honorary Fellow of the American Academy of Arts and Sciences, Foreign Member of the American Philosophical Society, Foreign Associate of the National Academy of Sciences, and Honorary Fellow of the London School of Economics. His publications include *From Generation to Generation*

(Free Press, 1956); *The Political System of Empires* (Free Press, 1963); *Israeli Society* (Basic Books, 1968); *Tradition, Change and Modernity* (Basic Books, 1973); *The Form of Sociology*, with M. Curelaru (John Wiley, 1976); *Revolutions and the Transformation of Societies* (Free Press, 1978); and *Patrons, Clients and Friends*, with L. Roniger (Cambridge University Press, 1984); *The Transformation of Israeli Society* (Weidenfeld & Nicholson, in press); and *Society, Culture and Urbanization*, with A. Schachar (Sage Publications, in press).

MARK GOULD teaches sociology at Haverford College. His first book, *Revolution in the Development of Capitalism*, is forthcoming (University of California Press). His current work focuses on the tendential development of contemporary capitalism as it impinges upon organized workers in the Northeastern United States.

FRANK J. LECHNER is currently Assistant Professor in the Department of Sociology at Emory University. He received his Ph.D. in sociology from the University of Pittsburgh in 1985. He has published several articles on sociological theory, fundamentalism, ethnicity, and world system theory. His current research focuses on sociological theory and the cultural aspects of global change.

RICHARD MÜNCH was born in West Germany in 1945. He studied at Heidelberg University from 1965 to 1970, was Assistant Professor at Augsburg University from 1970 to 1974 and Associate Professor at Cologne University from 1974 to 1976. He has been Professor of Sociology at Düsseldorf University since 1977. His main interests are in sociological theory and in historical comparative sociology. He recently published *Theorie des Handelns* (1982) and *Die Struktur der Moderne* (1984). Forthcoming is *Die Entwicklung der Moderne* (1986).

JEFFREY PRAGER is currently a member of the School of Social Science, Institute for Advanced Study, Princeton, New Jersey, and is also an Associate Professor in the Department of Sociology at UCLA. He received his Ph.D. in 1978 from the University of California at Berkeley and has published articles on classical social theory, contemporary race relations, and political sociology. His book, *Building Democracy in Ireland: Political Order and Cultural Integration in a Newly Independent Nation*, is forthcoming from Cambridge University Press.

He is also Research Clinical Associate at the Southern California Psychoanalytic Institute.

INO ROSSI is currently Professor of Sociology and Anthropology at St. John's University. He received his Ph.D. in sociology and anthropology from the New School for Social Research in 1969 and has edited a number of volumes in cultural anthropology and social theory, his latest book being *From The Sociology of Symbols to the Sociology of Signs* (1983). He is currently working in the area of technological innovation.

DAVID SCIULLI is Visiting Assistant Professor of Sociology at Georgetown University. He completed his Ph.D. in 1983 (Columbia University). He is currently applying the notion of societal constitutionalism to contemporary Brazil and to corporate crime in the United States.

NEIL J. SMELSER is Professor of Sociology at the University of California at Berkeley, where he has taught for nearly three decades. He has published in the areas of social theory, economic sociology, collective behavior and social movements, social psychology, and the sociology of education. His current work involves a comparative study of the development of primary education in the United Kingdom and the United States in the nineteenth century.